STRANGERS
in the
HOUSE

RAJA SHEHADEH is the author of the highly praised memoir *Palestinian Walks*, which won the Orwell Prize in 2008. He also wrote the enormously acclaimed *When the Bulbul Stopped Singing*, which was made into a stage play. He is a Palestinian lawyer and writer who lives in Ramallah. He is a founder of the pioneering, non-partisan human rights organisation Al-Haq, an affiliate of the International Commission of Jurists, and the author of several books about international law, human rights and the Middle East.

Also by Raja Shehadeh

When the Bulbul Stopped Singing
Palestinian Walks

STRANGERS
in the
HOUSE

RAJA SHEHADEH

P

PROFILE BOOKS

This edition published in 2009

First published in Great Britain in 2002 by
Profile Books Ltd
3A Exmouth House
Pine Street
London ECIR OJH
www.profilebooks.com

First printed in America in 2002 by
Steerforth Press

1 3 5 7 9 10 8 6 4 2

Printed and bound in Great Britain by
CPI Bookmarque Ltd, Croydon, Surrey

A CIP catalogue record for this book is available from the British Library.

ISBN 978 1 84668 250 6

Mixed Sources
Product group from well-managed
forests and other controlled sources
www.fsc.org Cert no. TT-COC-002227
© 1996 Forest Stewardship Council

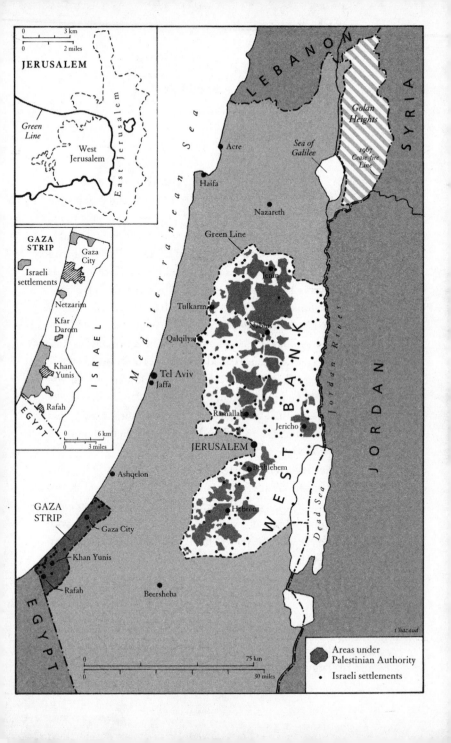

FOREWORD

In 1978 I met a Palestinian lawyer, Aziz Shehadeh, who was a fellow at Harvard University's Center for International Affairs that year. It was a time when Palestinian and other Arab leaders refused to accept the existence of Israel. Shehadeh had a different view. He believed that the West Bank and Gaza, then under Israeli military rule, should become a Palestinian state and live in peace alongside Israel. Aziz was a brave man: braver than I understood at the time. Back home in Ramallah, in the West Bank, Palestinian radio broadcasting from Damascus called him a traitor who wanted to "surrender and sell our birthright." He was threatened with death. Aziz told his son Raja that he understood why he was being attacked: He was challenging the accepted wisdom of Arab leaders, which was that there could be no compromise with Israel. Under that empty policy, Palestinians had lost much in 1948 and more in 1967, and they would continue losing if their leaders stuck to the fantasy of making Israel disappear.

Raja Shehadah is his father's son in the realism and humanity of his view on the conflict with Israel. But he is a very different person: more worldly, more Western, less gripped by the traditions of Arab culture and family life. The differences led to tension with his father. This book is the story of the relationship between son and father, a difficult, often painful relationship, with understanding cut short by the father's brutal and still unsolved murder.

It is not a political book. As Raja explained, "I wanted to tell a personal story, to celebrate life rather than settle scores or vent anger." Yet in a hundred different ways it is political. Even in exploring the heartache he experienced in yearning for a father who would "pay more attention to my needs as a young man growing up under difficult circumstances," he shatters the stereotype many Americans have of Palestinians. Hath not a Palestinian senses, affections, passions?

The Israeli occupation of his homeland is only the backdrop for the events Raja Shehadeh describes — not, say, the subject of a critical broadside. But no one can read his book without coming to understand the lawlessness, the vindictiveness that were practiced in the name of military necessity. They were simply a part of life's daily humiliations.

Raja Shehadeh founded a human rights group, Al Haq, that monitored legal conditions under the occupation. It was careful in its research and respected for its fealty to law; it was affiliated with the International Commission of Jurists. But Israeli military officers treated it with suspicion and contempt, taking its field workers into detention, harassing Shehadeh and even invading his father's law office and ransacking it. Then they imposed a huge fine on the Shehadeh firm for not paying a value added tax that Israel had just imposed on the occupied territories. Al Haq took the view that it was illegal for the occupiers to introduce a new tax, and no one was paying it. The Israeli authorities selected the Shehadeh law firm for exemplary punishment, no doubt, because of Raja's role in Al Haq.

All this comes into Raja's story only as a point of conflict with his father. Aziz was afraid that Raja's work with Al Haq made him vulnerable to violent attack. He wanted Raja to practice law in the old way, without challenging the occupation authorities. Not that Aziz lacked the courage to stand by principle. He not only took real risks by calling for compromise with Israel. Years before, he had agreed to be the defense lawyer for the men charged with the assassination of King Abdullah of Jordan; that made him suspect with the royal family that ruled the West Bank as well as Jordan until 1967.

The book gives us an insight into a characteristic that most Palestinians share: the sense of loss. The Shehadeh family had lived in Jaffa, the old Arab city adjoining Tel Aviv. From his earliest childhood Raja heard about the wonders of that former life: the strolls on the beach, the nightlife. "There were daily reminders of that cataclysmic fall from grace." That was in 1948, when the family fled to what had been its summer house in Ramallah.

But Aziz Shehadeh did not spend his life looking longingly at the past, and neither has his son. Too many Palestinians did, at least until at Oslo in 1993 the PLO agreed to mutual recognition with Israel. "We spent those years," Shehadeh writes of his people, "lamenting, whining, complaining, bemoaning the lost country." And meanwhile losing more, bit by bit.

It is the continuing loss of the Palestinian homeland that makes the most painful reading in this book. Years ago I took a long, arduous walk with Raja through a beautiful wadi, a valley untouched by development. Now it has been destroyed by Jewish settlements and the bypass roads that connect them to Israel. The story is the same in much of the West Bank. The occupiers' bulldozers have carved up the hills that gave the West Bank what visitors thought of as its biblical appearance.

When I have visited the West Bank over the years, it was the physical impact of the occupation that struck me the hardest — the rows of identical houses in the settlements, the bulldozing of olive groves. Shehadeh captures that as well as anyone I have read. "Most of these hills had never been smitten by the curse of machines. They had remained more or less unchanged since the time of the Prophets." But now it has changed. "The earth was turned over, sliced and cut and reconstructed. The terracing disappeared, and in its place wide expanses of flat land were created on which ready-made houses would be perched. . . ."

For a time Raja Shehadeh played a part in the efforts to reach agreement with Israel. At one stage of the endless negotiations he was legal advisor to the Palestinian delegation. But over the years, seeing his land smitten and finding no redeeming vision among political leaders, he has given up all participation in political life and even in human rights work. He practices law and cultivates his garden: his metaphoric garden. Which is to say that he writes.

But he has not lost his understanding that there are human beings on both sides of the conflict. In the spring of 2001, when I spoke with him by telephone about doing this introduction, the second Intifada was raging. It was not safe for Raja to take the familiar road to Jerusalem. His comment was: "The sad thing is the inhumanity on both sides. Too many people have been killed and wounded. It is heartbreaking."

Anthony Lewis

CHRONOLOGY

1878–1904 The first wave of Jewish settlers immigrate to Palestine from Europe under the banner of Zionism. The Zionist movement considers Palestine uninhabited, despite the fact that in 1881 almost half a million Arabs live there, forming more than 90 percent of the population. These were mainly Moslems, with a substantial Christian minority. There was a significant local Jewish population composed mainly of religious Jews. Other communities include Greeks, Armenians, and more.

1899–1902 Arab–Jewish tension following large Jewish land purchases in the Tiberias region.

November 2, 1917 The Balfour Declaration issued by the British government states: "His Majesty's Government view with favour the establishment in Palestine of a national home for the Jewish people. . . ."

December 9, 1917 Four centuries of Ottoman rule over Palestine end as Ottoman forces retreat and Allied forces under the command of General Edmund Allenby enter Jerusalem.

July 24, 1922 The council of the League of Nations places the British government as the mandatory for Palestine. Article Two of the terms of the mandate states that "the mandatory shall be responsible for placing the country under such political, administrative and economic conditions as will secure the establishment of the Jewish national home, as laid down in the preamble . . . and also for safeguarding the civil and religious rights of all the inhabitants of Palestine, irrespective of race and religion." The mandate witnesses rising tensions between Arabs and Jews, leading to the 1936–1939 Arab Revolt.

November 29, 1947 The United Nations General Assembly passes Resolution 181 recommending the partition of Palestine into two states — one Jewish and one Arab — and the internationalization of Jerusalem.

1948 War breaks out in Palestine. On May 14 Jaffa, located in the Arab part of Palestine according to the UN partition scheme, falls to the Jewish forces. Within a few weeks the total population of Jaffa falls to three thousand, out of an original Arab population of seventy thousand.

May 14, 1948 The Israeli state is established. The 1948 war breaks out on May 15. More than eight hundred thousand Arab Palestinian inhabitants are uprooted and dispersed. One hundred fifty thousand Arabs remain in Israel.

September 1948 The Lausanne peace talks fail mainly due to Israel's refusal to repatriate the Palestinian refugees.

December 11, 1948 United Nations General Assembly Resolution 194, Article Eleven, "resolves that the refugees wishing to return to their homes and live at peace with their neighbors should be permitted to do so at the earliest practical date, and that compensation should be paid for the property of those choosing not to return. . . ."

1949 Armistice agreements among Israel and Lebanon, Jordan, and Syria are signed; Israel holds about 80 percent of the total territories of Palestine; the eastern mountain area (the "West Bank") is under Jordanian rule; the "Gaza Strip" is under Egyptian occupation.

1950 The West Bank, including East Jerusalem, is annexed to the Hashemite kingdom of Jordan under King Abdullah.

July 1951 King Abdullah is assassinated in Jerusalem.

May 28, 1964 The Palestine Liberation Organization is established in Jerusalem.

1967 Following Israel's victory in the June war, the entire territory of the former Palestine mandate comes under Israeli control, as do the

Egyptian Sinai and the Syrian Golan Heights. East Jerusalem is annexed to Israel; the rest of the occupied territories (West Bank and Gaza) are put under military administration.

November 22, 1967 United Nations Security Council Resolution 242 calls for the "withdrawal of Israeli armed forces from territories occupied in the recent conflict . . . [and the] right [of every state in the area] to live in peace within secure and recognized boundaries free from threats of acts of force."

September 1968 The Israeli government approves Kiryat Arba, the first Jewish settlement to be established in the West Bank.

January 1973 The Palestine National Congress in Cairo approves the formation of the Palestine National Front as a PLO-guided framework for resistance to occupation.

November 27, 1973 The Algiers Arab Summit passes a resolution recognizing the PLO as the sole representative of the Palestinian people.

April 13, 1976 a pro-PLO slate wins municipal elections in the West Bank.

August 1977 U.S. Secretary of State Cyrus Vance meets with West Bank public figures; Israel continues efforts to find suitable West Bank representatives as "alternative leadership" to bypass the PLO.

September 1977 Agriculture Minister Ariel Sharon unveils the settlement plan "A Vision of Israel at Century's End."

September 17, 1978 The Camp David Accords are signed: Israel recognizes the legitimate rights of the Palestinians and commits to granting them "full autonomy" after a transitional period of five years. The number of Jewish settlers in the Gaza Strip is five hundred (0.1 percent of the population), and in the West Bank seventy-eight hundred (1 percent of the population). Establishment of more settlements is not halted.

1979 Law in the Service of Man (later renamed Al Haq) is established as the first human rights organization in the Palestinian territories.

Other nongovernmental and grassroots organizations dealing with issues of health, labor, and women are also established during this period.

1981 An Israeli civilian administrator of the West Bank is appointed by the military government after the Civil Administration is established by Military Order 947 in order to separate the civilian administration of Palestinians from that of Jewish settlers living in the occupied territories.

June 6, 1982 Israel invades Lebanon. The PLO is forced out of Lebanon.

1984 Jewish settlements in the West Bank and Gaza Strip have increased to about eighty thousand settlers.

August 4, 1985 The Israeli cabinet approves the policies of the "iron fist," whose architect is Defense Minister Yitzhak Rabin. Deportation, administrative and preventive detention, and other "administrative" punishments are imposed on the Palestinian population.

December 9, 1987 A general popular uprising, the Intifada, breaks out. A unified leadership of the revolt is formed inside the territories. Its directives are ratified by the outside PLO.

January 15, 1991 In the wake of Iraqui invasion of Kuwait, Allied forces led by the United States wage the Gulf War against Iraq. The West Bank and Gaza Strip are sealed to the outside world, and lengthy curfews are imposed.

October 30, 1991 The Middle East Peace Conference is convened in Madrid, cosponsored by the United States and the Soviet Union.

1993 A demographic Jewish majority is declared in Arab East Jerusalem.

September 13, 1993 The Declaration of Principles is signed between Israel and the PLO.

September 28, 1995 The Interim Agreement on the West Bank and the Gaza Strip is signed between Israel and the PLO, giving limited local autonomy over parts of the West Bank and Gaza Strip to the Palestinian Authority. Palestinian control excludes areas designated for Jewish settlement.

December 27, 1995 Israeli army re-deploys from Ramallah, handing over the town to the Palestinian Authority.

1996 The Jewish settlement population of the West Bank and Gaza Strip grows by 49 percent to 150,000, and the population in annexed East Jerusalem grows by 33 percent to almost 200,000 over the four-year period of the government of Yitzhak Rabin and Shimon Peres. Closures of the West Bank and Gaza Strip, demolition of Palestinian homes, and other administrative punishments continue unabated. Palestinian laborers are restricted from resuming work in Israel following a spate of suicide bombings inside Israel by Hamas Islamic activists.

September 2, 1996 A new road is opened between Jerusalem and the Etzion Bloc of West Bank settlements to bypass Palestinian towns. The twelve-kilometer route costs forty-three million u.s. dollars — the most expensive road project ever built by Israel.

1998 The approximate total number of Jewish settlers in the West Bank and Gaza Strip increases to 169,400.

September 2000 A second Palestinian Intifada breaks out.

February 2001 The number of Jewish settlements in the West Bank and Gaza reaches 205,000 and in East Jerusalem 180,000 living in two hundred settlements.

CHAPTER ONE

THE HOUSE WHERE my family lived, and in which I was born, was the summerhouse of my grandmother. Its proximity to the deep-set Ramallah hills could have made for a pleasant life except for the nagging feeling of being in the wrong place. I was always reminded that we were made for a better life — and that this better life had been left behind in Jaffa. Jaffa, I was told, was the bride of the sea, and Ramallah did not even have a sea. Jaffa was a pearl, a diamond-studded lantern rising from the water, and Ramallah was a drab, cold, backward village where nothing ever happened. Jaffa was affluence: a house with original oil paintings, and my grandfather's fully equipped Continental Hotel, which my grandmother always boasted had a restaurant with enough china and silver cutlery for two hundred guests. Jaffa was where my father had developed a comprehensive law library in his office in Nuzha Street; where there were courts, a busy nightlife, Dora, the excellent Jewish seamstress from Tel Aviv who made my mother's clothes, tasty pastries from Kapulski's, and orange groves. And above all these, Jaffa was the sea with the Abdo falafel stand right by the water, where my parents ordered sandwiches and strolled in the silver twilight on the golden sand in warm winter evenings with the waves of the sea gently rippling against the shore.

How I yearned throughout my childhood for these imagined pleasures! How I thought life would have been more resplendent and exciting had we still been there, across the horizon, in the beautiful city that I had only heard about and yearned to see.

This version of Jaffa that I grew up coveting was mainly my grandmother's. It was she who, after living for more than thirty years in Ramallah, remained *gareebeh,* a stranger. She was still the aristocrat from Jaffa, the daughter of the owner of the Nassar Hotel in the Street of the Kings in Haifa and the wife of Justice Saleem Shehadeh of Jaffa. Ramallah was but a village where she could never again have the kind of life to which she had been accustomed. Her eyes were always on the horizon, and through following her gaze I too learned to avoid seeing what was here and to fix my sight on the distant horizon. I saw Ramallah and its hills not for what they were but as the observation point from which to view what lay beyond, at the Jaffa I had never known. We would be walking home in the evening and she would stop me on the top of the hill before going down the street leading to our house: "Look," she would say. "Look at the lights on the horizon." And she would stand in reverent silence. I stood next to her, holding her soft warm hand, and held my breath as I tried to concentrate all my attention on the lit horizon, imagining what sort of place these lights illuminated. For a long time I was hostage to the memories, perceptions, and attitudes of others that I could not abandon. My sense of place was not mine. But I never thought I had the right to claim it. My elders knew better. I felt it was natural to defer to them on such matters.

In Ramallah we lived far away from the sea, but not so far as not to see it on clear days. Fold after fold of the cup-shaped hills rolled on to the sea. They were called partridge, duck, and swan, a whole herd of tumbling birds with their backs turned to us.

From our house I could follow the valley that meandered between the interlocking hills on both sides, making the land seem like a turbulent wavy sea that slowly dropped from where I stood all the way down to the horizon, folding and unfolding in a continuous stretch as far as the eye could see. Our house was the perfect observation point from which to watch the land to the west that I grew up hearing so much about.

The hills on both sides of the wadi were varied in texture. Some were rockier than others. Some were planted with olive and vine. This made them assume different hues at different times of the day. In the morning they had frank strong colors, white and brown and green. Midday the slowly moving clouds cast their shadows, creating different shades as they slid across the sky. Toward sunset the hills became rosy and luminous as the rays of the setting sun streaked the limestone boulders and rocks. But when the humidity from the sea wafted along from the west they became downy and covered with a velvet mysterious blue that blurred the vision. And when in autumn the weather became very humid we would wake up to find that the fog had filled up the spaces between the hills like a sea of white thick snow.

Unlike my grandmother, my father rarely spoke of Jaffa, at least not to us, his children. How did he feel when he stood angry and despondent among these same hills? Was he angry and despondent? Was he disdainful of the smell of the dung as he listened to the mooing of the hungry cows and the chatter of the refugees from Lifta, who came from their village in West Jerusalem and squatted in the large empty house across the street? He was handling an eviction case against them. His eyes invariably took a cursory scornful view of these Ramallah hills and would then focus on the distant horizon, the bluish line of the sea in the day and the glittering array of lights at night. Night after night he stood motionless, hardly breathing, seemingly captured by this grand vista and trying to imagine what went on over there, in the luminous world of Jaffa he had abandoned. Here was only brown thistle and stone, an arid land without hope or future. One part of him lived in the distance, in the lit horizon; the other lived in the cold, unwelcoming summerhouse of my grandmother across the street from the offensive smell of the cows of the Lifta refugees.

There was always a breeze coming from the hills. They were like a funnel through which the wind always blew. I would look at the hills next to our house for relief from the narrow confines of our close living quarters. To me they were the untamed wild, so close and yet so distant, a space of promise and mystery someday to be explored — yet for now but a funnel for the humid wind from my father's mythic Jaffa.

The house had two bedrooms for our family of six. Wind whistled through the pine trees in the garden. A constant gentle breeze in summer; in winter a strong humid wind that swept the needles off the majestic trees and added drama to the cold interior of our poorly insulated house. The incessant angry roar caused me to feel great insecurity and fear and increased my yearning with every ferocious wave for the mild and windless winters of the Jaffa of my parents.

Many of my parents' friends were leaving the city as early as December 1947. They were rich and either had houses elsewhere or were going to stay with relatives. They planned to stay away until the fighting stopped. My mother recalls walking up the streets and counting the number of empty houses that belonged to friends she used to visit. The population of the town was shrinking. Could we have made the wrong decision by staying, my father wondered.

They had a two-year-old daughter and my mother was pregnant with her second child. They continually asked themselves whether they would be left without food for the children and whether they would be safe.

Then, a truck carrying a load of oranges managed to elude the checkpoints and make its way into the center of the town. It was driven by members of the Stern Gang, the extremist Jewish group, who left the booby-trapped truck to explode, causing indiscriminate damage and scores of casualties.

This incident caused a new wave of departures from the city, but my parents were determined to stay. On April 22, 1948, the port city of Haifa fell to the Jewish forces, and many of my mother's relatives were forced to leave for Lebanon. It was becoming clear that Jaffa would be next. On April 26 the Irgun mortars began shelling Jaffa to cut the Manshieh quarter, not far from where my parents lived, from the main city. With daily shelling of the city, life became unbearable. The Arab forces were disorganized and ineffective, and the British seemed to step aside and allow the Jewish forces a free hand. My parents felt unprotected.

My parents are first cousins. Both their fathers had left Ramallah as young men and never returned. My paternal grandfather owned a weekly newspaper and a printing press in Jerusalem, where my father was raised. My maternal grandfather was a district court judge in Jaffa, where my mother was born. My father opened a law office in Jaffa in 1936, married my mother in 1945, and settled there. My maternal grandfather built a summerhouse in Ramallah, where he brought his family to escape the hot and humid summers of Jaffa. He deposited them there and went on his annual vacation to Austria. A question that will never be answered is whether my parents would have left Jaffa had my maternal grandfather not owned this house in Ramallah. Its presence at such close proximity to Jaffa provided them with a tempting alternative. Moving to it in April would save them from the hardship and danger of the skirmishes that were disrupting life in Jaffa. Once the situation became calmer they would move back. They thought they were leaving for two weeks. For a long time I wondered why they had fixed on a two-week absence until I realized that in my father's calculations the worst that could happen was the implementation of the UN plan for the partition of Palestine into a Jewish and an Arab state; if this happened, Jaffa was slated to be on the Arab side. The British were due to leave in mid-May. He left at the end of April, two weeks before what he thought was to be the decisive date. But the Palestinian population had rejected the UN plan, and the Jewish one had its eye on a larger territory — which they were able to secure through the war that ensued. The two weeks stretched into forever.

On May 14, three weeks after my parents left Jaffa, the establishment of the Israeli state was declared over an area of land larger than that reserved for the Jews by the UN. Jaffa was included. My father could not return. But if my father blamed himself for having left, these feelings receded with the events of the evening of July 17.

"It was a windless, warm evening," I later heard my father relay to friends. "We were able to sit out on the porch late into the night. It was already eleven when we finally turned in. Two hours

later, I was awakened by knocking on the door. When I opened the
door I found my close friend Dr. Bishara standing there, looking
very haggard and exhausted. He had refused to leave Jaffa with us
and instead had moved to Lydda to continue serving patients. I was
shocked to see him standing there so late at night. I will never forget
how he looked. He was so changed that he was like a stranger to
me. His face seemed longer than usual, with two lines down the
middle of each cheek. He was pale and withdrawn. His lips were
black and thin and his mouth was parched. But what stood out
most of all was the look in his brown eyes. The dark circles around
them were common enough after several sleepless nights, but Dr.
Bishara's pupils had an inward gaze. His eyes were not wilting
from lack of sleep. Opaque, they held a deeply pained, bewildered
expression of dread and emptiness, a vulnerable emptiness. Usually
filled with warmth and humanity, they had a look of revulsion. He
was unable to communicate the horror he had witnessed.

"Much as I wanted to know what had happened, I asked no
questions. I gently helped the doctor to the living room couch. The
yet-untold horrors he had experienced perturbed me. When we got
up the next morning we found that thousands of refugees who had
walked all the way from Lydda and Ramle were pouring into
Ramallah, each with a story of the misery and hardship they
encountered in the course of their forced march from the coastal
cities to the hill town of Ramallah."

That first winter brought one of the worst snowstorms
Ramallah had ever had. My father said that the snow seemed to
bring the hills across the valley closer to our house. The hills wore
single lumps of snow over their large humped backs and looked
like huge igloos. Down toward the west the snow was punctuated
by swerving dark brown lines along the terraces, dotted all the way
with green olive trees. Farther on along the horizon the hills
remained uncovered, shimmering with their usual range of blue
colors: a symphony in blue.

Thirty thousand refugees had poured into Ramallah, and most

of them had to take shelter in tents provided by relief organizations. Comparatively speaking, my father's circumstances were less desperate. At least he had a roof over his head, although it belonged to his mother-in-law. But what began as a temporary stay in Ramallah became a permanent one. Three years later I was born in that same summerhouse across the hills from Jaffa.

CHAPTER TWO

IT NEVER SEEMED possible to heat the summerhouse, not even during winters milder than that first one in exile. The cold and clammy wind seemed to find its way to my bed and dampen it, chilling me to the bone. Every night my mother wrapped me in thick blankets and put me down like a mummy under more heavy quilts warmed by a hot-water bottle. But still I was cold. The only warm place in the house was around the woodstove where in the evening the whole family gathered, toasting ourselves and placing the peels of Jericho oranges to burn and sweeten the air with an audible fizz and a sharp citrus smell. Even my grandmother admitted that these Jericho oranges tasted more tart than those from Jaffa.

But I did not like oranges. I did not like food altogether. Throughout my childhood I persistently tried to starve myself.

"Eat," my mother would plead, holding a spoon close to my face. She would be so close I could see the sweat in the pores of her skin. Kind but perplexed brown eyes beneath a wide brow looked into mine, asking: "Why? Why don't you want to eat?" *I don't know.* I want to make my mother happy, but I can't eat. I scrutinize her face, her high cheekbones, her thin nose, and her full lips. "But you must eat." I look at her fingers holding the spoon to my mouth and wonder how her thumbnail became slit in the middle. "For my sake, just this spoon." But I clench my teeth and refuse to allow food to pass my lips.

My mother, Wedad, used all kinds of tactics to distract me. The most successful was to tell me dramatic stories, which would enchant me to such a point that I would relax my jaws. As the tears welled in my eyes, my mother would slip the spoon between my teeth and sigh with relief at her temporary victory.

Sometimes she pretended that the spoon was a ship traveling through the sea of porridge she was trying to feed me. "Let's follow the ship sailing in the sea," she would say. She would pass the spoon around, causing a spiral of thick waves in the porridge. I thought of the hills outside, which I could see from the window across from where we sat on our small chairs. The hills were also like waves, folding and unfolding, and their color in winter was like the color of the porridge. The olive trees were like the granules in the porridge, thick and coarse. The ship completed its course at the center of the plate. Then it flew up. My mother rounded her lips and blew at the hot porridge to cool it. My mouth was the harbor where the ship had to dock. Thus I swallowed one shipload after another after they had completed their voyage through our hills and into my mouth.

I grew up weak and vulnerable and was confined to the house. My mother was overprotective. As for my father, he was critical of the excessive pampering I received. He refused or was unable to accept that a simpler way of dealing with my stubborn determination to starve myself could not be found. He tried gentle persuasion and then severe physical punishment. He even tried withholding food so that I would come asking for it. When none of these tactics proved effective, my father dragged me to the doctor and insisted that there must be a pharmaceutical cure for my condition. But my stubbornness knew no bounds. The only thing that seemed to work was storytelling. It was fortunate that my mother had a rich imagination.

I have often wondered if my eating disorder was related to my excessive need for attention. Perhaps it was my body's reaction to the pain and deprivation my family felt during those early years after 1948. What I am sure of is that my life then was shaped by the contrast between the meagerness of life in Ramallah and the opulence of life in the city across the hills. There were daily reminders of that cataclysmic fall from grace, and I could count on my grandmother always to point them out. One was the son of Issa passing by our house pushing a cart with a few objects for sale: an old bottle, a tin can, a few articles of clothing, and an old kerosene stove called a Primus.

"Look at him," my grandmother would say. "He was the son of a rich landowner and now he has nothing except this Primus. The poor man."

And later in the day the Salman brothers would pass by, peddling buttons, thread, and needles. They had been the proud owners of a prosperous women's clothing store in one of the most prestigious streets of Jaffa.

All these people, according to my grandmother, had been neighbors. The Toubasis had lived right next to us, the Issas were only one house away, and Salman — why, he lived as close to our house as that tree over there. She would make these declarations from her stately green wicker chair on the open veranda where the wind blew. "Ah," she would gasp, "the refreshing wind from Jaffa."

Much as I tried to envisage what Jaffa must have looked like, my imagination failed me. I wondered how so many people could live in such close proximity. I pictured my grandmother's house at the center of a strategic whirl of houses, with Grandma imperiously presiding over circles of the smaller homes of the families who now were scattered throughout Ramallah. In Jaffa she had only to open one of the many windows of her mansion to call these neighbors. They quickly responded and came over to have morning coffee with her.

Now my grandmother was no longer strategically situated. The only neighbor she could call from her window was her adversary in a dispute over the border between her garden and that of my aunt. In the disputed area my aunt had planted a passionflower climber, which then spread its leaves over the wire fence between the two plots. My grandmother insisted that my aunt had had no right to plant this climber, and I grew up thinking the worst of passionflowers. I modified my views only when I learned much later of the outstanding medicinal value of these flowers: they are known to relieve tension and lower blood pressure. How much in need they were then! But the two protagonists were not searching for a pacifier. Their battle over the two-meter area of land mirrored the other, real war with the Israelis. Through it the two women expressed the depth of emotions that could not be vented on their common enemy.

For years the two families fought a border war. The two generals were of course my grandmother and aunt, shouting their battle cries from the windows of their adjoining houses. Naturally I sided with Grandma, whose case I thought was just, but my aunt too had her strong points. She was very fond of me. I would be lifted over the temporary wire fence and handed over to her. "Come to me. Come to your aunt," she would say as she welcomed me into her big arms and soft large bosom. She dipped a biscuit in her coffee cup and put it in my mouth. When she was not angry, my aunt was a loving woman. It was my grandmother who seemed to bring out the worst in her.

My grandmother not only fought with my aunt, she also did not get along with my father. Whereas she was perfectly content to sit in her green wicker chair, smiling her winner's smile, happy to be herself, my father lived always for the next big event. He could not relax, was always propelled by a seemingly inexhaustible measure of nervous energy. He sought refuge from his dreary surroundings in work. There could not have been two more different temperaments. The biggest tragedy was that fate had brought them to live under the same roof.

How they fought! Their shouting matches always seemed to end on the same note: Grandma admonishing Father for his failure to bring back her furniture from Jaffa when she had given him her car and sent him back for this very purpose.

"You wasted a great opportunity," she would declare. "You could have brought back all my furniture. Instead you returned carrying the porcelain Buddha."

My father would not defend himself. He was too good a lawyer to do this. Instead he would go on the offensive: "It was your fault that you lost everything. You missed the best opportunity. You had an offer on the hotel before it all started and you refused it. 'Over my dead body,' you said. Didn't you? You have only yourself to blame."

I grew up hearing the description of my father's last visit to Jaffa, and it has left an indelible impression on me. My father's entire holdings were in and around Jaffa, the products of his own hard work. His father had left him nothing. How difficult it must have been to bid all this farewell. The image of my father, his every step echoing in the empty streets of the deserted city, still haunts me.

He had gone back, as Grandma never ceased to remind him, in her car. He was to rent a truck and fill it with their furniture. My father himself never described this last trip in full — I heard bits and pieces from him and from my mother and grandmother.

My father found the city more deserted than he had expected. He told us how he had lingered at the locked gate of the sumptuous house of the Dajanis, which he had always admired. He gripped the pickets and peered for a long time at the garden inside. He had always aspired to own such a garden and was saddened by the sweet peas, full of pods and beginning to droop. The proud garden was trying its best to hold its own, to cover up for the neglect of its owners, who were not there to water or prune or weed. It occurred to him how welcoming a garden can be, as if it were saying: I care, I have made all this appealing for you. I offer you this mix of colors — the flat red of the zinnias, the velvet purple of the snapdragons, and the bright yellow of the alyssum — just for your pleasure. But when it is abandoned and is seen from behind a closed grille, a garden appears stranded: an oddity in midlife prepared with the expectation of continuity and leisure, not flight and abandonment. Why did the Dajanis plant the garden if they were leaving? How could they stand to be away and leave behind such glory?

He moved on to the marketplace, empty except for a few shops that had somehow remained open. He walked passed Hinn's, his barbershop, and found it closed. The courthouse was closed, as were the clinics, the nurseries, the cafés, the cinema. The place was deserted, prepared to be captured. What have we done, he wondered. How could we have all left?

He climbed the steps to his own house and opened the door. It was dark and stuffy inside. His wife had closed all the windows and shutters and draped the new furniture with white sheets. It was strange to be alone in this empty house, moving from room to room without the usual sounds of his family. He could not stop thinking about what this house meant to him. It represented years of very hard work. It was the first house he had established. Until he had married he had lived at the Continental Hotel, which was owned by his uncle, my mother's father. But after twelve years as a successful lawyer in Jaffa he had been able to establish himself, marry, and furnish this attractive home, where he would finally live a happy settled life with his young wife and two-year-old daughter. Images came to him of his wife in her pink satin dressing gown, moving elegantly from room to room, peering at him with her Greta Garbo look. Had he come to bid all this farewell?

What should I take back with me? he asked himself. *Nothing. Nothing at all.* He was resolute: *I want it to stay as is, covered and preserved during our short absence so that when we return we will undrape the furniture, air the place, and resume our happy life.* At this point his eye rested on the porcelain statue of Buddha. It was the only object that had been left uncovered. It stood on a wooden ledge in one corner, presiding benevolently over the scene below. He came close and saw the calm squinting eyes, the mocking smile, the fat round belly with the aquamarine belly button. It comforted him to look at it. Perhaps this would be the best thing to take, he thought. He placed it under his arm and walked out.

This porcelain statue of Buddha has remained in my family's house ever since. We have taken it to every house we have moved to and kept it prominently displayed. And it has remained on its wooden base exuding a calm presence in the midst of the many disorders and tragedies that have befallen us. How furious my grandmother was when she saw that he had returned without a truck full of her expensive furniture.

"I lend you my car and this is all you bring? I told you I wanted my china tea set back. Did you forget? And my silver cutlery, you forgot this too?"

"What did you bring with you?" my father said in his defense. "Only a sack of lemons from your tree in the backyard." He could not count on her sympathy.

The only person who bid Jaffa a proper farewell was my grandfather, Saleem. How often I heard the description of the way he lingered by the gate of their house as they were leaving, seemingly lost in reflection.

"What are you doing?" my mother asked him.

"Bidding this house farewell," he answered.

"But why?"

"Because we shall never return," he said with a finality that left no room for doubt.

"How wise he was, how perceptive," my mother would say. I always wondered what he knew that the others did not, why he left his family and went to settle alone in Beirut. Perhaps that silent moment when he stood by the gate taking a last look at his house was the only moment of closure. Everyone was rushing about, thinking of trivial matters, and there was my grandfather with his self-absorbed, distinguished look, his thick round spectacles and pipe, taking the time to bid farewell to his house in Jaffa and to the life he had enjoyed in it. He alone seemed to have had the resilience to refuse to be led by the voices around him calling this a two-week departure. In his quiet, self-assured, almost mystical silence, he seemed able to experience the final flight from the city, which he insisted they were seeing for the last time.

But it was more than Jaffa that he was seeing for the last time. He spent two years away from his wife, in fulfillment of one of his lifelong wishes to spend time away from her. One day as he sat to have his lunch in a street café in Beirut he collapsed. His head fell on the table and when the waiter turned to find out where the sudden thump had come from, he found my grandfather already dead.

CHAPTER THREE

THE DEATH OF my grandfather meant that my grandmother, Julia, became part of my father's household. He called her *mart ammi*, wife of my uncle. Although their enforced cohabitation ended in 1953 when my parents were able to move to the downstairs apartment, Grandma always lived in close proximity and spent most of her time at our house. Despite her difficult circumstances she managed until the end to live on her own terms, always looking down on those around her. Was she not a Jaffa woman and the daughter of the owner of the prominent Nassar Hotel? Whatever my father did he remained in her eyes a Ramallah boy, even though the time he spent in Ramallah was not a day more than her time in the village.

The only picture of my grandmother's family that survived the Nakbeh — the term used by Palestinians to describe the events of 1948; literally, the catastrophe — shows my great-grandfather looking stern and stolid. His wife, Katbeh, sits on the other side, flanked by their four children: two daughters and two sons. The daughters wear dresses with low waists, which must have been fashionable at the time. They seem slim, sensuous, beautiful. This picture stood on the table in the front hallway of my grandmother's house. The table always had a clean, well-pressed cloth placed diagonally, with a long, dark red glass vase full of flowers, mainly roses picked from the garden downstairs. Behind this table was a wicker couch covered with a brown, furry woolen cloth imprinted with the picture of a large tiger. It had the same comforting smell as the rest of my grandmother's house, which was full of precious little corners. In one there was a shelf with ivory statuettes brought by her uncle, a colonel in the British army in Sudan in World War I; in another a stool with covers that she had embroidered. She loved bright colors: red, green, yellow. And she served the best tea.

I often gazed at the picture, trying to make out what sort of a man my great-grandfather had been. He must have been sure of his ways, but he did not seem to be the source of my grandmother's flair. Nor, perhaps, her bravery. It is no wonder, then, that it was she who saved their hotel from being expropriated by the British when they first came to Palestine. The story goes that it was Julia who confronted the British officer who came in and wanted to requisition their place. When everyone else seemed to cower with fright, Julia addressed him in perfect English: "Sir, you cannot take this hotel. It is where we live." In telling the story my grandmother always said that she came down the stairs and confronted him in the lobby. I imagined wide, slightly curved stairs, Julia standing tall in her elegant dress with the low waist, and the officer being taken by her charm, self-confidence and strong resonant voice. But I never knew whether the Nassar Hotel actually had a staircase. By the time we were able to visit Haifa, the place had been demolished. All we saw was the rubble.

My grandmother had a talent for creating atmosphere with the little that she was left with in Ramallah; she had an eye for beauty. She was also a good cook and knew how to present food. And she was impatient with sloppiness in matters that she cared about. She had her way of doing things, and those who didn't know better were looked down upon.

For many years I was sent to sleep upstairs with Grandma so that she would not sleep alone. We had a strong relationship. Unlike my mother she did not treat me as a delicate object; she did not worry that at any minute my weak body would collapse and end my precarious existence. While she seemed to enjoy having me around, she didn't go out of her way for me. She was the only person around me who was not tense, and her moments of repose remain in my mind as cherished memories of suspended time.

It took me many years to realize the powerful effect the Nassar side of the family had on me. They were aristocratic, elitist, and less intellectual. They suffered from a stifling sense of entitlement, which made them unable to adjust to changing times. The Shehadeh side had only what they'd been able to achieve. When this was lost they started rebuilding, with no feeling that they were entitled to more than what they could make. The aristocratic confidence of my grandmother meant that she was able to use the public bus to visit her friends in Jerusalem when she could not afford any other form of transport, but only on her own terms. When I accompanied her, I was instructed to keep my hands off the back of the seat in front of us because it was contaminated by the touch of the locals. She frowned and complained about the spitting. Even when she rode the bus with everyone else she remained imperious and distinguished.

Had Julia been born in a different age she might have been a successful businesswoman. But in her day it was impolite to ask what kind of work a person did: this implied that they did not have enough money to live on. There was no value to work. She never worked for money. Money was a dirty commodity. It was necessary to wash your hands every time you touched it. She had no grasp of the practical world of economics, but did believe that you held on to what you had. This may have been why she refused to sell when her husband informed her, just a year before their forced exile from Jaffa, that there was a buyer for the hotel.

"This hotel shall remain for our children and our grandchildren," she declared. And when Julia spoke she could not be contradicted. As a result, a year later it was all lost; she fell from being a rich woman to one of very limited means. The only property left was the summerhouse, which she was now providing to my father and his family as a home.

And yet, despite it all, my grandmother was not one for self-pity. She had wit and a sense of humor. Whenever she saw my sister sucking her thumb, she would say: "On duty again?" She behaved as though she were still the wife of an affluent and influential man who held high office in the government. Her face glowed with confidence and strength. She had beautiful large brown eyes, healthy red cheeks, and a slit between her upper front teeth. She had a strong physique and took great care of herself, but she could not come to terms with old age. When she was in her late sixties, she took one look at a passport photograph taken of her and proceeded to scold the photographer: "What sort of picture is this? You should be ashamed of yourself taking such a picture. What nerve. But it seems you have no shame. No shame." He looked at her wanting to say the obvious, but she would not allow him.

She always invoked the good old days of Jaffa. Even when she became afflicted with hypertension, she compared the pressure in her ears to those familiar sounds of Jaffa: "I feel I am sitting by the seashore and hearing the waves breaking and ebbing, breaking and ebbing."

With all the overwhelming changes that were brought on by the war of 1948, nothing changed my grandmother's routine. It was sacred, carried out punctiliously as if it served the greatest of purposes, as if the life of the family, if not the world, depended on it. She would get up in the morning, have her full breakfast, do a little housework, dress, and go for a visit to one of her friends from Jaffa. Then she would come back, have lunch, take a nap, get dressed again, and go out for another visit. It was doubtful whether her life had changed in any fundamental way. In Jaffa she had visited twice a day, and she maintained this routine religiously in Ramallah, visiting many of the same people. The only difference was that due to my father's failure to rescue the tea set from the lost city, she could not now serve them tea with her bone china. She brought this up so often that I began to wonder which loss was worse — Jaffa, or tea in her own cups.

"The tea tastes different," she would say, "when drunk from superior cups."

My grandmother always spoke her mind. She was not an emotional person. Her first comment upon hearing the news of my birth while she was away in Beirut was: "This is no time for having children."

And she may have been right. A few days after my birth the country was shaken by the murder of King Abdullah of Jordan while he was praying at the Al Aqsa mosque in Jerusalem. The king had been appointed ruler over the West Bank, which until May 14, 1948, had been under the British mandate government. The East and West Banks of the River Jordan were merged in 1950 to form the Hashemite kingdom of Jordan. Palestinians were suspected of the king's murder. This was the first major challenge to the hegemony of Jordan over the part of Palestine that was not included within the newly formed Jewish state.

My father was hired by the families of three of the accused to defend them in the murder case. This was the first opportunity he had had since losing his practice in Jaffa to recover his status as one of the foremost lawyers in the country. But the Hashemite regime did not appreciate his willingness to defend those accused of murdering the king. From that time his allegiance to the Jordanian regime was considered suspect.

Perhaps he should have realized that in a country where the legal system was not developed, there would be a price to pay for the passionate way in which he applied himself to the defense of his clients. He should have left politics, as his Uncle Saleem had advised, two years earlier. But as a refugee who had never been compensated for the loss of his property, he couldn't heed this advice.

In 1950 he decided to run in the Jordanian parliamentary elections. He had already served as secretary of the Refugee Conference and was sent to Lausanne as part of a four-man delegation to negotiate the return of the Palestinian refugees with the Israeli delegation. Nothing had come of these negotiations: the refugees could not return; nor were they compensated for their losses. My father now hoped to work with the Jordanian political establishment. These were the first elections to take place after the creation of the new enlarged kingdom. In his campaign, my father promised to expose whoever attempted to deceive the Palestinian people.

At first it appeared that he had won a resounding victory — but then he was declared the loser by a large margin. It was common knowledge that the authorities had rigged the election, and demonstrations against the government broke out in Ramallah. That night our house was surrounded by the Bedouin soldiers of the Jordanian regime. My father was not at home at the time; my sisters and I were alone with our mother. What I remember of this experience has merged with what I later heard from my mother: the heavy thumping of boots and raucous voices all around the house, the terror of being surrounded by strange people who banged with all their might on the metal shutters of our ground-floor house. I also remember seeing dark eyes peering through the slits of the louvers. My mother paced nervously across the living room, not daring to get close to any of the windows, and shouted: "I will never open the door. You can bang as long as you like. You cannot persuade me to open the door for you. Go back to where you came from." Then she moved toward the black telephone in the corner, hunched her body over the receiver, and whispered to the man at the central exchange to give her Dr. Jubran, a friend of the family whom my father had been visiting at the time. She asked for my father and when she got him whispered: "Aziz, the soldiers are surrounding the house. Stay away. Don't come back."

A few minutes later we could hear the soldiers picking up their rifles and marching away. One last farewell bang by a frustrated soldier and then all was quiet. Mother fell into a confused, uneasy silence. The man at the central exchange must have immediately informed the army of the whereabouts of my father, and they had gone to pick him up there.

My father was put on a truck and taken to the prison in a cement structure known as a Tegart building, named for the British architect who designed it. But his incarceration did not last long. After his release a few days later, he left for London on another big case concerning blocked accounts. After the 1948 war the Israeli government had seized the Barclays Bank accounts of Palestinians who had left the newly declared Israeli state. My father argued the case successfully, and the funds were returned to their Palestinian owners. But he also took the opportunity to give testimony before the British Parliament regarding the activities of the British commander of the Jordanian army, Glub Pasha, accusing him of forging the ballot papers. This proved too much for the Jordanian regime, which saw my father as a dangerous challenger to the status quo. A warrant for his arrest was issued for the crime of conducting negotiations with the Israeli enemy. When he learned of this he decided not to return home.

Instead he traveled to Rome and stayed with his friend, the artist Ismael Shamout. This was a confusing time in my father's life. Everything he had done with full conviction had been misconstrued. It was the only time in his life that he seriously considered emigrating to the United States. My mother had an American passport because her father had studied in the United States and served in the U.S. Army during World War I. The necessary visa was obtained, but at the last moment my mother could not imagine leaving her mother alone in Ramallah. She wrote that she could not agree to emigrate. Once again my father's life was determined by his mother-in-law.

He sought a pardon from the Jordanian authorities. Through the efforts of influential friends a meeting was arranged with the young King Hussein, who was visiting Italy. The king assured my father that there would soon be important developments in Jordan, and that Glub Pasha would be removed. He promised my father amnesty if he should return.

Father eventually did return to Ramallah, bringing back with him large glossy books with reproductions of the paintings of Raphael, Titian, and Andrea del Sarto. I used to stare for hours at these pictures, entranced by the colors: rose red, sapphire blue, saffron orange, raven black. They had strange religious figures with exposed breasts and pure smooth skin unlike anything I had ever seen in local churches. Raphael's Madonna wore a robe of pure sapphire blue with perfect folds, as peaceful as the expression of repose on Mary's face. In Andrea del Sarto's painting of the Assumption, Mary seemed to float in the sky wearing a robe of deep blue that took my breath away. Then there were Titian's portraits: men clad in velvet brown robes of mysterious depth and texture, with eyes I was often too frightened to look into. There was so much naked flesh, deep color, and captured motion; so much mystery and beauty. And they had been brought from Italy, the only objects in our house that came from Europe. These reproductions of famous paintings, kept on a large shelf in a small damp room facing the western hills, came to represent Europe to me. I would come back to stare at them over and over again, always filled with a sense of pride that my father had been in the land of these strange and beautiful paintings.

During his stay in Italy my father's friend asked him to pose for him. Years later Ismael Shamout came to visit us in Ramallah carrying a large oil painting of Father. When I examined the portrait, I was surprised at the lack of despair in Father's expression. I had always believed that these must have been extremely depressing times for him, but apparently this was not so. My father boasted that he never allowed despondency to bring him down. He never stopped fighting. "But I was disappointed," he later told me. "The blocked-accounts case was the only Palestinian success at wrenching anything from Israel's clutches. And my reward was to be called traitor. I knew why; I was challenging the accepted wisdom among Arab leaders: Let Israel take all. Soon we will take all of Israel.

"I always wondered," he would continue, "did the Arabs really believe what they were declaring? Did Arab politicians not have enough sense to realize that Israel was there to stay?" He suspected they did. But it was convenient to have an object for the anger of the Palestinians, perhaps even of all the Arabs. It was convenient to keep Israel at the level of the abstract rather than bring it down to the level of a mere enemy with whom one can find ways to battle, extract concessions, and possibly even coexist. Let Israel be the subject of fiery speeches in which the people's rage could be articulated and released — they would be distracted from dealing with all that was wrong at home.

My father refused to go along with this abstraction of the enemy. He insisted on poking pins into the body of the monster — only to discover that like any monster it had its weak points. We needed to learn how to fight. Contrary to what he had believed, his activities had been more subversive than he had realized at the time. He was tampering with a carefully nurtured official illusion.

My father soon realized that the Palestinian losses were going to be even greater than he had anticipated. It was not only that the Palestinians were bereft of their material possessions, their homes, and their future; they were also to remain for many years the victims of an anger with which they were not allowed to come to terms. They were to remain confined by conflicting negative passions that tore them apart, reducing them to tiresome complainers, ineffective communicators determined to tell their tale of woe and suffering to whoever would listen.

CHAPTER FOUR

THE ONLY PICTURE that has survived of my father as a young boy is one of him with his sister and cousin. This cousin was particularly good looking. He had long auburn hair that curled around his neck and came down his chest. Unfortunately, he had a degenerative disease and died at a young age. Next to him my father looks very dark, with closely cropped hair and big black eyes that fill his face. He refused to sit like the others; before the picture was taken he circled around and stood behind his sister and cousin so that he would look taller. His mother had died when he was four, and he looks disheveled and unruly. What comes across is his resilience and strong presence, qualities that continued to distinguish him throughout his life. His life seemed to go from one catastrophe to another, but he persevered, standing firm. How unlike my grandmother Aziz was. A self-made man, he inherited nothing; nor did he get any help from his father. Instead, his father needed Aziz's help. At the time of the Nakbeh, he was still capable of hard work and was determined to get back his former place at the top of his profession. By 1956 he had succeeded in establishing himself as one of the top lawyers in Jordan. The standard of the courts in Jordan was much lower than what he had been used to under the regime of the British mandate in Palestine, but he adjusted. Then, in 1958, he was arrested again.

This time it was the coup in Iraq and the toppling of King Faisal ii, an uncle of the Jordanian monarch, by Abdul Karim Qassim. Fearful that the nationalists and antimonarchists in Jordan might carry out a coup against the Hashemite regime, a state of emergency was declared and large numbers were arrested. My father was among them.

Once again our house was surrounded by the dark-skinned raucous Bedouin soldiers who banged on our door and threatened to break in. I was old enough that time that I now remember this incident clearly: the short, gruff, armed men pounding with their fists on the closed metal shutters of our windows. They shook our wooden front door so hard I thought it would break and they would barge in and murder all of us. Throughout they were screaming for my father to come out but Mother wouldn't let him go. To this day I still shudder when I hear knocking on my door, even from a friendly caller.

My father was arrested, handcuffed, put on a truck with many of his friends, and taken to the Tegart prison on the outskirts of Ramallah. They were kept there for a week and then packed back onto trucks like sheep with iron chains on their ankles and driven away. My father said later that despite the behavior of the Bedouin soldiers, who seemed to him to have descended from another world, he was in good spirits. By now he knew the prison routine. They were driven along the rolling hills of the West Bank and down into the green valley of the Jordan. They crossed the river along a creaky bridge and went on to the eastern bank, up the high mountains of Moab, and into another landscape, dry and arid and flat, deep into the desert past the town of Maan to the desert camp, known as El Jaffer. There they were kept without arrest warrants. No charges were filed against any of them, for martial law had been imposed and they were considered administrative detainees to be kept for an unspecified time until the military government deemed it was safe for them to be released.

El Jaffer was not a prison in the ordinary sense. There were no walls. They lived in tents with open spaces, challenged to escape into the dry and desolate desert. There were no common criminals among them, only professionals: doctors, lawyers, engineers, accountants, teachers, and other activists from all walks of life. Except for women, it was a complete society. Each member of this microcosm tried as best he could to contribute to the general well-being of the new community. My father always spoke of this time with nostalgia. "We had a strong sense of togetherness," he would say. "And we had time, plenty of time, to discuss the future."

During the long hours of the cold nights, he could reflect more lucidly than ever, huddling with his fellow detainees around an open fire beneath the star-studded sky. This is what his life had come to. In the daytime, with the scorching sun, and at night in the cold sweeping winds that blew from every direction, he had time to think of the life he had left behind. What a frivolous life we Palestinians had been leading. Because of our skewed values, we were unprepared for the onslaught of the Zionist threat. And yet, though he was critical of the richer class in Jaffa and their useless ways, he had to admit that he was no better. Had he not spent years in Ramallah dedicated to similar material pursuits? Was it not all vanity? Something was profoundly wrong with our way of life. We had failed in Palestine to develop into the kind of society that could preserve what we had, and now we were failing once again.

Every night they discussed these issues until the small hours of the morning — communists, Ba'thists, socialists, and Arab nationalists, each with his own stock answers, to which my father listened with sympathy. Perhaps this was why, according to the reports received by the Jordanian authorities, his record showed him to be each one of these at different times. The truth was he did not adhere to any of these ideologies. He listened sympathetically, but a realistic streak made him reject the sterile ultimate solutions these ideologies seemed to offer. To him life was multifaceted and in flux. It could not be captured by any single solution. It required continual adaptation. The only constant during these days in the desert was the almost mystical belief he seemed to nurture in a vague ethical imperative that bid him to exercise his will, to always remain free, to do what he believed to be good, and, when confronted with a choice, never to choose to inflict evil on others. My father always had a strong sense of his mission in life, of his potential for doing good regardless of what others may think. That inner voice was strengthened in the desert, and as the years passed it became strong enough to silence all other voices and empower him with the determination and single-mindedness to go forward and relentlessly pursue the path he had laid for himself.

I was seven years old at the time of my father's second arrest. I understood little of what was happening, or why, but I clearly remember the care that my mother took in preparing the parcels prisoners were allowed to receive from their families. Inside a cloth sack my mother stuffed all kinds of items she thought my father would need, including some prohibited things such as razor blades, which she sewed into one of the linings. It must have given my father particular joy when he opened his parcel and discovered within every fold of the cloth new and much-needed articles of clothing, cleaning agents, toilet paper, toothpaste, and food, as much food as she could fit in. But it was difficult for me to adjust to my father's new role: that of political activist leaving behind a nervous wife, who now participated in subversive activity herself by sewing razor blades in the lining of his prison parcel. I had been brought up to think of my father as a respectable lawyer, not a prisoner who grew a thick beard because he was not allowed to shave. I was neither ashamed nor proud of my father. I didn't know how to understand what was happening, and no one tried to explain it to me. I just hoped that his imprisonment would end, so my mother would be less insecure and tense and we could all go back to our normal life at home.

Altogether the time my father spent in the desert jail was not long. He was released after one month due to the intervention of some of his influential clients.

When the order came, the prison camp commander told my father that he was free to leave.

"What do you mean, *leave*?" he asked.

"You can take your things and go. Your detention order has been canceled."

The commander announced this in a sardonic tone that was not without malice. He knew that even with the lifting of the detention

order my father would be detained. The piece of paper, the bureaucratic decision, was of no meaning in this camp in the depths of the
desert. He was no less confined by the physical conditions than he
had been free before the order was lifted by the refusal of his will to
be shackled.

So he waited until the doctor from Maan came to the camp for
his rounds to ask if he could have a ride back. My father rode with
him to Maan and then called his friend Ibrahim Nazzal, the owner
of the Philadelphia Hotel in Amman, to send him a car. He arrived
in Amman looking the part of the scruffy desert camper.

This was the last time my father was arrested. For a few years
he managed to stay away from politics and concentrate on his legal
practice. That same year my brother, Samer, was born. My father
seemed to enjoy his second male child, and as he grew my brother
looked up to him and rebelled against my mother's smothering
care in a way I never did. But then times had greatly changed.
Father was no longer arrested every few years by soldiers who surrounded our house at night. He was a successful, well-respected
lawyer with no formal political involvement.

In the early 1960s Ramallah was discovered by oil-rich Arabs and
became a summer resort town. Land was bought and villas built.
The Grand Hotel with its large garden of pine trees, established a
decade earlier on one of the highest hills of Ramallah, had full occu-
pancy throughout the summer months. Other garden restaurants
were established, and many of the Jaffa refugees were making up
for what they had lost: Salman now owned a number of stores
selling buttons, thread, and sewing kits; Issa opened up a successful
falafel sandwich shop. Jaffa was relegated to memory; life was lived
in Ramallah.

My father's time in Italy had left him with a love for Italian
opera. Every night he played Verdi and Puccini at high volume, to
my mother's consternation.

It was striking how many families in this small town dreamed of their sons and daughters becoming famous musicians playing Western music. The Tabris sent their daughter to study piano in Germany; the Sous sent their son and the Nassers their daughter to the Conservatoire in Paris for the same purpose. My father himself had high hopes for his eldest daughter, Siham, as a concert pianist. How did it come to be that in a town with little exposure to music and few chances for a proper musical training, ordinary families entertained such dreams for their children? It may have been over-compensation for what they had lost; a way of proving their worth and of distinguishing themselves from the society around them.

I was not one of those children. In fact my family felt fore-warned by the experience of two of their friends — a couple whose son became so attached to the piano that he neglected his regular schooling — that they refused to allow me to take piano lessons. But I knew what lay ahead for me. After high school I was going to attend the American University of Beirut. And there, in the city by the sea, I would live a life as close as I could get to the bachelor life my father had lived in Jaffa. Meanwhile, in Ramallah, I yearned to be old enough to go out in the evening to "the Casino" at the Grand Hotel. Every night as I lay in bed I could hear from the open-air dance floor beneath the pine trees the live band from Italy playing famous tunes.

Even as these changes were taking place in Ramallah my life was dominated by the lost world of Palestine. The elders held the keys to that lost world, the world that gave my life its meaning: their reminiscences, their evocative descriptions, and nothing else. It was within that lost world narrative that I placed myself, defined myself, and assessed where I stood in the world. To be a man was to be the way my father was in Jaffa. The good life was the nightlife of Tel Aviv.

We could not really have any of these things here, even with the Casino and the evenings out, because Ramallah was not Jaffa. There was no sea; it was just not the place. The place was over there, in that unreachable world of the imagination, the world that was evoked by the words of my elders as they yearned and described, reminisced, dreamed, and remembered.

Even though some two decades had passed since the Nakbeh, there was not the slightest indication that anyone was abandoning the dream. There was no waning in the certainty that return was inevitable. Life in Ramallah was the only life I knew, but even for me there was a sense of it being temporary. I viewed it as a pale reflection of the other life.

Because the dream was stronger than the reality and because all my knowledge of it derived from the elders, I had no reality of my own. My own life could not be validated unless confirmed by their gaze. I was hostage to a world too imperiled to be taken for granted. My insecurity arose from the apprehension that this dream world would be lost if I closed my ears. Life here in Ramallah was lived day to day but it was not inspiring. There was no conviction or pride in it. This was the temporary abode, and you do not dig in and create roots in what is temporary. It will do for now but it is just for now.

On warmer evenings my father's friends would come over and spend the twilight hours outside on the porch, eating and drinking. Among them was Saadeh Jallad, the head of the Ramallah police, a corpulent, gregarious man who kept a strong hold on the town, making it secure and almost entirely crime-free. He had a round face with a short neck and a contagious laugh. He would describe how he spoke to the delinquents and those apprehended for petty crimes. Then when all was said that could be said about the events of the day, talk would invariably turn to the times of the British mandate, when he had also served in the police. He would switch into an imitation of his British superior: "Sire," he would shout, standing to attention, holding in his flabby cheeks, and fixing his gaze.

"Ah those days when everything ran like clockwork," he would sigh. "The British knew how to organize a force. The Jews learned a lot from them. And we thought we could fight. I will never forget when Abdel Wahab, the Iraqi commander, was brought in to take over command of what was called the Jaffa Brigade. It was composed of the baker, the blacksmith, a farmer and the man who sold newspapers. They all stood in crooked line in their work clothes. They had come to volunteer their services for the protection of their town. The Iraqi was not prepared for this.

"'Where is the army you want me to command?' he asked.

"'This is it, sir,' we answered.

"'*Mako askar, mako junoud, ma yaseer*'— these are no soldiers, it cannot be — ,' he said with his Iraqi accent. 'This crowd made of the baker and the carpenter and the porter you call an army? You want this crowd to fight and win a war? Bring me a proper army to command. With this you will get nowhere.'

"He turned around and left, refusing to have anything to do with the disaster that he saw as imminent.

"I saw the man the other day in Amman. To this day, he still tells his story. And I am now in his position. I have poorly trained illiterates with no skills or intelligence for policemen. But I keep them under control. Sometimes I feel like a headmaster in a school for delinquents. Gone are those days of the mandate when we had to be in top shape and would get reprimanded if we left our shoes unshined."

Such talk of mandate times, of Jaffa, of life by the sea seemed to bring back memories, painful memories of loss and desire that reflected on their faces. They would sit around drinking arrack late into the night and nibbling at a *mezza* of *labneh*, a variety of pickles and fried kidneys deliciously cooked in olive oil with plenty of garlic. Despite the bitter edge of their yearning, their laughter filled the air as the glittering lights of Jaffa sparkled in the short but unreachable distance beyond the now-dark mass of rolling hills.

Whatever the disgruntled Jaffa refugees felt deep in their hearts, they shared it only with each other. None doubted the inevitability of war against Israel, and yet there had been no serious preparations for what everyone believed to be imminent. The

military drills that the government introduced in 1966 in all the
schools in the kingdom was no exception.

Although the school I attended was Quaker and taught non-
violence, it was forced to submit to the royal decree. As a result,
every day after school for one long and painful hour the male students from the top three classes assembled at the upper campus
below the pine trees on the rocky ground facing the hundred-year-
old stone building. In World War 1 during Ottoman rule, this
building with its big windows and red-tiled roof had served as a
hospital for the casualties.

We had to march in formation under the military command of
the uniformed Jordanian army *shaweesh,* officer, who demanded
total and blind obedience. The training mainly involved marching
instruction, standing at ease, and then standing at attention.
Saluting. Marching. Turning corners and saluting at the same time.
All very complicated maneuvers. Our *shaweesh* barked his precise
commands and our fifteen-year-old bodies were expected to respond
as though we had all merged into one single military formation that
would lose the war if it faltered, raised one knee a little higher than
the other, or failed to stamp its feet at exactly the same moment.

At the start of these drills one day, the heavily mustached young
officer with the authoritative voice stopped before me, calling me a
mere child who did not deserve to participate in important matters,
which were only for men. I wondered what I had done to deserve
this reprimand when the session had hardly begun. He continued
his barrage of insults, and I continued to stand at attention,
checking to see if my feet were close together and my hands were
properly clenched. I couldn't figure out what I was doing wrong. I
had chewing gum in my mouth, and the more the officer screamed
the more vigorously I chewed until finally the frightened boy
standing at attention next to me whispered: "Stop chewing!" It was
only then that I realized my crime.

This unexpected and severe reprimand convinced me to accept
an offer made earlier by a classmate with a Saudi Arabian passport.

He was exempt from these drills and offered to swap places with me. Thereafter whenever my name was called, Mahmoud answered. The Jordanian officer never noticed my absence. I began to regret my abdication only when it was rumored that at the end of the school year we would all be examined in the various movements we had been taught. My punishment for failing, I was told, would be exile for the entire summer vacation at a Jordanian army camp somewhere in the desert, where I would be placed entirely at the mercy of this commanding officer. But my fears came to nothing. Before the end of the school year war fever had reached such a pitch that school was suspended. We were sent home, forfeiting the opportunity to put into active military combat any of the marching skills we had been practicing for the past four months.

After the severity of winter, springtime in Ramallah was a sight to behold. The fields became briefly green, and the new grass beneath the olive trees offered a beautiful contrast to the silvery leaves of the ancient trees. The hills and valleys became fresh and clean — until the desert winds started to blow, bringing with them a thin layer of dust that covered everything. In 1967 there was a long spring when these Khamseen desert winds were delayed.

Throughout this spring we were riveted to the Egyptian radio, which broadcast military music and the patriotic speeches delivered by the popular Arab leader Gamal Abdel Nasser. The more we heard these speeches, the more his popularity rose and that of our own King Hussein fell. Why was he not going to fight Israel as well? What was the use, otherwise, of having such a large army? And why wasn't Syria going to join? We wanted all Arabs to fight Israel, and we were sure victory would be ours. I don't believe that we agonized over the fact that the Palestinians themselves were not to have any role in the military fight against Israel. We were spectators who stood on the side, cheered our hero in Egypt, and denounced every other Arab leader who was not following in his footsteps.

"Wala zaman ya silahi," went one of the favorite songs of the time: I swear it has been a long time and now I yearn for my weapons. We sang along with the Egyptian singer and felt as though after a long sleep life was once again stirring in our dead limbs. The suppressed anger at being driven out of our homes no longer festered and poisoned our lives. Now our Arab brethren were going to fight and wrest back what had been taken away from us. With the confirmation that seven Arab countries were to partic-ipate in the war, victory seemed probable. How could it possibly be otherwise? Did these Arab countries not surround Israel from every side? Was Syria not in the best possible strategic position on the Golan Heights, overlooking the fields of the Galilee down below? Were these Arab soldiers not convinced of the righteousness of their cause? Were they not all brave soldiers who for twenty years had been waiting for precisely this opportunity to go into battle and fight the Jewish aggressor?

But doubts rose just after the war was declared on June 4, 1967. The first to articulate them was Said Abu Zayyad, one of my father's old friends from Jaffa. He was a man with little education but a strong perceptive mind and the self-confidence to say what he thought. To me he will always remain the prophet of doom.

CHAPTER FIVE

I WILL NEVER forget the appearance of my father's old friend at our house on the first day of the war that was to liberate Palestine. Tall, lanky, and with a no-nonsense voice that sometimes quavered, he wanted my father to drive up with him to Masyoun, the highest neighborhood in Ramallah.

"There is something I want to show you," he told my father. "You must come," he insisted, his voice starting in the lower register and rising to falsetto, "I want to show you what is really taking place."

Father took me along. We drove in our white Mercedes to the very end of town and parked by the last house to the south of Ramallah.

I can still picture Said Abu Zayyad standing tall underneath the pine trees in this windswept place, my father, a much shorter man, standing attentively next to him. It was all a mystery to me. Why had this man brought us here at a time like this? What strange things could be happening at Masyoun? Was this where the battle-field would be? But I could not ask my father any of this. He seemed more distant than ever, totally enveloped in a troubled silence.

"It's a repeat of 1948," Said whispered to my father. "There will be no fighting. You hear these bombs crackling in the distance? This is the Israeli army firing to ensure that the way is clear. I have been observing the scene for several hours now. All the firing is from one side. And the sound of the bombing keeps getting closer. It is a matter of a few hours before they cross the border. Just like 1948, so much talk and no action, just bravado: We will show the enemy, the Arabs declare, but when the fighting starts they disappear. Listen, can't you hear the firing? It's all from their side. Nothing from ours. Nothing. No response. And even since we arrived, have you not been aware how it is approaching, from the west? Our own side is already across the bridge on the other side of the river. It's over. The war is already over."

Like my father, Said had lived in Jaffa, and like him he had been forced out in 1948 and came to settle in Ramallah. He was not an emotional man. He walked soberly with a heavy tread, seeing things as they were. My family has always said that he was the first to realize that the war was over and lost. He declared this as early as June 1948 when everyone else seemed to harbor hopes that the Arab armies would still wage a serious fight against the Jews and secure the return to Jaffa. He is credited with saying: "There is no real fighting. The Arab armies are retreating. We have been deluded. We have left our town and will never be able to return."

These words were never forgotten, becoming part of my family's narrative of these fateful events. Because of them, Said held a special place for all of us as the prophet of doom. And here he was again.

I looked at Said's thick eyelids and black drooping eyes; at his wheat-colored skin peppered with small black warts, his tall, lanky figure and thick hair, and heard him repeat in his quivering voice: "It is over, I tell you, the war is already over."

At Said's bidding my father and I continued to focus our gaze southwest, and as I did so I began to look beyond the points I had seen in the past. The hills stretched as far as the eye could see in a gentle but continuous declension. How undefiled and peaceful they looked. Not far from where we stood we could see a few of the Arab border villages that huddled in the otherwise empty hills. In the distance stood the strategic Nabi Samuel hill. It was the only forested area. Otherwise the hills were rocky, with olive trees planted between the rocks.

The farthest point I could see was a light, vibrant blue. This must have been a point beyond the border that, I assumed, was not far from where we stood. From our house the view of the other side was separated by a drop-off, not this continuous stretch of land. Usually I looked at night when the other side was lit up and the land between was an expanse of darkness. Now the sun was low in the sky but it had not set. There was no natural divide between the two sides, just low rolling hills, pastoral and attractive in a muted, ancient way. How odd that I had never looked at the other side from here. It looked so close, I wondered would it yet come within reach.

The sky overhead was laden with low cumulus clouds struggling with the sun. As it began to sink, the sun turned into a ball of crimson that thrust its fire across the sky and was reflected in the unevenly scattered clouds, setting them aflame. But my attention was distracted by another rumble of guns, which Said claimed sent sparks to the sky. When I looked up again the sun had gone and the clouds had turned gray, dark, and ominous.

My father broke away and began to pace in circles, kicking pebbles on the rocky ground with his feet, saying nothing. Then he looked up and said: "Twenty years ago you brought me to this very spot and told me to say farewell to my Jaffa. I did not want to believe you then and continued to hope for the day of our return. Shall I believe you now?"

Said remained silent as we listened to the enemy's guns moving toward us steadily and consistently.

Then my father asked: "What shall we do?"

"Nothing," Said said with as much finality as his quavery voice could muster. "What can we do?"

"Then let's go home," my father said.

As we were walking away, my father turned to Said and asked: "How long do you think it will take them to get here?"

"It's a matter of some six hours, no more," Said answered with complete confidence.

On our return home I heard my father doubting for the first time his decision not to move to Amman, as his friends had urged him to do. But he was not one to brood or waver, and when other friends stopped by on their way to Amman, he told them: "The worst mistake of my life was leaving Jaffa in 1948. I will not repeat my mistake. Whatever happens, I'm staying. I shall not be homeless again. My advice to you is not to leave."

Our friends did not take my father's advice, and though he pretended not to be shaken by these worrisome developments, I could feel his rising anxiety.

It was as though that visit to Masyoun had brought the war home to my father. Before, he had shown no interest in making practical arrangements for the war: now he became irritable and impatient as he searched for the best location for the family to take shelter once the Israeli bombs began to fall.

Suddenly he remembered our downstairs neighbor, Samaan, and he went to ask his advice. Samaan claimed to have fought in World War II, and my father deferred to him this most important decision.

Our neighbor had a habit of drinking, and it was impossible to know whether he was sober when he walked with my father and me around the house inspecting various locations.

My father was walking briskly with heavy determined strides and Samaan trudged behind trying to keep up. When we reached the field next to our house, he stopped across from the old fig tree that our cousin Nur guarded all summer. Nur was an eccentric spinster who had once been beautiful. Now she wore her frizzy uncombed brown hair in braids around her head. She had intense blue eyes and skin so wrinkled it reminded me of an overripe fig left unpicked on the tree long after its prime. Her voice was high pitched. She was as dry and prickly as the yellow thistles that lined her field all summer, adding extra protection against intruders.

Even with his haggard look, his pursed lips, and beady eyes, Samaan managed to speak with authority. He puffed his chest, pointed to the field around Nur's unapproachable fig tree, and said: "I have tested the soil underneath Nur's tree and found it to be the deepest in the area. Should a bomb fall here it will penetrate the earth and explode underground, causing no damage whatsoever. This, in my opinion, is the best place to take shelter."

My father thanked Samaan, and we felt we had adequately addressed the subject of where to take shelter.

The Jordanian army had not installed sirens to warn us about impending air raids, so we depended on our wits and sharp hearing. I remember well when the first raid started. We were seated around the lunch table in our exposed dining room having a dish of *mulukieh,* which had just come into season. The planes began to streak through the sky, and suddenly my mother stood up and declared that she had left the laundry on the clothesline on the roof. Perhaps she thought it would attract the attention of the planes overhead, or that once we took shelter underneath Nur's tree we would be unable to collect it. She insisted that the laundry be taken down immediately. So we all left our lunch and rushed up to the roof with her, leaving my father alone at the table, lost in his troubled thoughts.

That night we slept in our house even though there was no second floor to lessen the impact if we were hit. Before going to sleep I made sure that my slippers were close to the bed so that I could quickly get into them and not delay the others. I was the only one who thought it necessary to carry at all times a self-prepared first-aid kit, which I also placed near my slippers for quick retrieval.

Throughout the night we heard the sound of warplanes zooming overhead but no sound of nearby explosions. The Arab stations continued to broadcast that victory would be ours. Said's premonition could yet prove wrong, I thought.

We heard the first close shelling in the early hours of the morning. I was awakened by my father, who was moving us to a safer place. For the first time since the beginning of this war, I was terrified. We could feel the frequent thunder of the bombs shaking the earth — it was as though they were falling right outside our house.

"Come on. Hurry up!" my father urged us.

Sleepy and moving slowly my sisters and younger brother began to put on their dressing gowns and look for their slippers. I

quickly slipped into mine and picked up the first-aid kit. As I
waited for the others to come, I looked out the window and saw the
figure of our family doctor, Salem Ghanam, on the stairs of the
neighboring house. At first I thought he was preparing to leave his
exposed building. But he wasn't. He was watching the sparkles
from the planes lighting the night sky as if he were watching fire-
works. He was a lone figure, with ginger hair and a punctured
throat from which a malignant tumor had been removed two years
earlier. Usually a self-engrossed man, he was now tempting fate.
Perhaps he wished that a bomb from one of these planes would
strike him, ending his life of waiting for death.

The air was full of dust. Once we reached the street, the air raid
began. Several bombs shook the earth. I froze and Samer, my ten-
year-old brother, began to cry. My father was full of rage as he
directed us down the street toward Nur's tree. Could he really be
taking us there, I wondered. But then he moved farther down the
street toward the Jaber house, a solid, two-level structure where he
thought we would be safe in the basement. But we found the basement locked and had to retreat and cross the street again with the
deafening sound of the planes zooming overhead. We were the only
people in the street. As we hurried nervously toward our downstairs neighbors I caught a glance of the famous tree of Nur. I tried
to imagine the family sitting in the open field below the war-filled
sky, protected by branches, half covered with the first growth of
leaves and unripe figs, as though we were on a picnic, a rendezvous
with death.

My father was now leading us to the basement apartment of the
World War ii veteran. We knocked at Samaan's door but there was
no answer. We circled down to the garden calling, "Samaan,
Samaan." Then we heard a faint muted response coming from the
wall. We searched for its source and found Samaan, his obese wife,
and their three children in the opening of a well that was built into
the wall. They seemed uncomfortable and had no room for a
mouse. And yet Samaan piped weakly:

"Come in, join us, please, you are welcome."

So this was where he had planned to seek shelter when he had directed my father to the open field. Despite the tension of the moment, the absurdity of it all dawned on me. How could my father have been so naive as to seek advice from such a man? Perhaps my father was thinking the same. He seemed so out of his element that he wanted to go back up to the house.

"But you shouldn't," my mother said. "It's dangerous. Let's try the other neighbors."

My father, now in a very surly mood, begrudgingly consented. We all stood at a neighbor's door and began to knock.

First there was silence. Would they not open the door for us? Could they have thought we were the army? Had fear already stepped in? Then we heard the shuffle of feet and the whispering of consultation and a reluctant opening of the door.

As we waited for the many latches of the heavily decorated green metal door to be pulled open I looked around at the sandbags on their porch, the taped windows, and the pail of water. This was a textbook preparation. They had strictly followed instructions and done everything they had been told to do. The thought entered my mind that the radio had also advised against answering calls and accepting visitors. Perhaps during such times each was on his own. Every family would barricade itself, abandoning all hope of more general succor, and exist alone behind their securely fastened door with enough canned food to see them through.

They were a family of five. The husband, a stout burly man, once worked as an instructor at the United Nations Relief and Works Agency (UNRWA) vocational school. Since his retirement, he spent his time making metal stands for flowerpots. He spoke with a deep bass voice and was very protective of his wife. She was a comely woman with light skin, full lips, and big hazel eyes with a distant abstract look. She rarely left the house. They had three beautiful children still in their early teens. Around this time the previous year their eldest son had been run over by a car next to the house. He had gone out to play while his mother prepared his breakfast. When she went out to look for him she found his battered body on the sidewalk. She was so traumatized that she had remained silent ever since. Although they were neighbors they rarely visited and as far as I could tell rarely received others. Perhaps they resented this intrusion. Now that we needed them we knocked at their door, when in better times we never did.

We went in and sat in their living room. There was not much that we could speak about. We had nothing in common. Once inside it seemed to become very peaceful. We could hear no more air raids. Could it be all over?

My father was obviously feeling stifled. He continued to announce that he wanted to leave. But my mother held him back. Here was a model head of the family who in every way was poles apart from my father. This UNRWA veteran had confidently followed the radio instructions of the civil guard and felt secure. My father could not feel secure. He felt betrayed, abandoned, and angry, though at this point he kept a painful, deadly silence.

The next day was quiet; a clear, cool June day. The family assembled on my grandmother's balcony shaded by the pine trees. Soon one of my parents' younger relatives, Shafiq, a bold, well-built man with a reputation for bravery, came to join us. He had volunteered for the civil guard, which he was now deserting.

"We were given metal helmets and told to be alert to put out any fires. But we weren't given a fire truck or any equipment, not even a hose. How on earth were we supposed to put out fires, with our bare hands? I was in command of a unit of young men from town. They were so excited to volunteer. But when they realized the Israeli army may be entering Ramallah they grew pallid and their Adam's apples bulged out. They began to shiver and wanted to go home. Those who had given us the job were nowhere to be found. I gave my miserable troops permission to go home. I disbanded the unit. It's all useless. Let them go home and relax and be with their families."

My grandmother sarcastically declared: "We had so much hope in you. The commander of our civil guard unit runs away. For shame. For shame."

"Just following in the noble ways of our esteemed leaders," Shafiq responded.

"I hear the Israeli soldiers are already in Bab el Wad," my father said, changing the subject.

"If they are in Bab el Wad then they must be invading Jerusalem through Nabi Samuel, and Ramallah through Beit Surik and Biddu," Shafiq answered, confirming the worst.

I could only listen. I had never heard of Bab el Wad before. The door of the wadi. The door that opens the wadi allowing the soldiers to cross the plains and the hills and capture East Jerusalem and Ramallah. I wondered if it was the name of an actual place, but I did not ask. It was not the proper time for a lesson in geography. But doors were opening. Doors that had been closed for twenty years, and through them the enemy soldiers would enter. I tried to imagine the land behind the doors swelling up with soldiers. What would happen when they came?

Toward noon women from the border villages began to file through the street near our house. Carrying their belongings on their head, they looked bewildered and exhausted. We stopped them to ask where they were from. Some said from Biddu, others Emwas. "What happened," we asked, "why are you running away?"

"The Jews destroyed our houses and forced us out." But they could not answer the one question I wanted to ask. Where are the men? Could they have been killed by the Israelis?

That night, as soon as it became dark, we heard incessant shooting by soldiers who moved up and down our street. My father was very stern as he gathered us all, crowding us into one corner of our sitting room away from the windows. I had never heard so much shooting. It started from a distance and was getting closer and closer. The Israeli army had invaded Ramallah.

At home we were very silent. And very still. Who would open

the door when the soldiers thumped up the stairs and ordered us with gruff voices and heavy pounding of boots: "Open the door. Open the door!"

They might not wait. They might break the door open with their guns. Once inside they would point me out along with my father and take us to the wall and shoot us. They must have shot the men of the women from Biddu and Emwas. This was why after the women passed, my father became very gloomy and would not talk about what we had seen. Would I be spared as a child? Or would I be considered a man?

Then the wave of shooting began to recede. Soon it could be heard in the distance and then, to our relief, quiet fell over the town. Now we were allowed to disband to our rooms. But even then we spoke very little, and when we did we whispered our words. My father was particularly quiet. He had hardly said a word since noon.

I went to sleep and woke up late the next morning. My parents were standing in the morning sun, their gaze turned southward toward Jerusalem. My father said: "Jerusalem has fallen."

I felt the despair and dread in my father's voice. First it was Jaffa that they spoke of as fallen. Now it was Jerusalem.

The term *fallen* was uttered with gravity and finality. When a fruit ripens, it falls from the tree. Was Jerusalem like a ripe fruit that had fallen? A woman of disrepute is also referred to as a fallen women, but what does it mean for a city to fall?

I stood by our porch under a clear blue sky pondering these matters. The morning was still and quiet after the nerve-racking shooting of the night before. I could not see any evidence of the Israeli soldiers who had apparently captured our town.

"Not a single shot was fired back," my father said. "They occupied the town without any resistance from our side."

I wondered what it would mean to live in an occupied town under Jewish rule. Would we have to learn Hebrew? I had never met a Jew and had no way of telling, but I was filled with the dread of the unknown.

Suddenly we heard yelling in a strange tongue that I assumed was Hebrew. We looked in the direction of the noise and saw that soldiers were stationed all along the fence of the Grand Hotel. They were pointing their guns at us and ordering us back into our house. So this was how an occupier sounds, I thought.

After we entered the house, I noticed that my mother stayed close to my father. She would not leave him. Later I understood why. The night before he had gone back to his room, pulled out the revolver from his bedside drawer, and made ready to kill himself.

CHAPTER SIX

THE WAR BEGAN on a Monday and ended on Wednesday. On Thursday began a week that would be one of the most critical in my father's life. It is very telling about our relationship that I have no recollection of what happened during this time. What I write here is based on the account of one of the Israelis involved in the events in which my father played a pivotal role.

I had been brought up to think of Jews as monstrous and Israel as an artificial creation that was doomed to perish. I had just been through a war that I had expected would bring victory and the fulfillment of all our dreams. Instead it brought defeat and all the consequent fears. On a warm Thursday afternoon on June 9, just three days after the start of that war, two young Israeli army reservists accompanied by the Palestinian editor of an Arabic daily appeared at our door. Their appearance and manner violated everything I had been taught to expect of Jews. They spoke good English, they were polite, gentle, and civilized, and they asked to see my father. What was I to make of them? Were these the monsters I had expected in some disguise? Or was I to believe their politeness and conviviality? Father didn't explain but instead began a flurry of activities. He asked me to help him type a document he was preparing for the visitors. I was frightened by what all this might lead to — not that I did not trust my father, but I had listened to my mother's warnings about how rash and impetuous Father could be and how this got him into trouble. Would it be the same this time? But this would be big trouble. This time he was dealing with the hated Jews.

When I was writing this book, I spoke again to Dan Bavely, who told me that he and David Kimche had come to Ramallah to search for Saleem Odeh, the man responsible for the Ramallah transmission station. Saleem Odeh's house was next to the newly established army headquarters at the Grand Hotel. After they had finished their mission the Palestinian from Jerusalem who brought them had offered to take them to meet a man whom they would find very interesting.

"It was around five on a clear balmy June afternoon," Dan recalled. "I remember it so well. Every detail of it. Aziz was wearing a white shirt with a stiff starched collar and brown-striped trousers. He stood outside the balcony, a few steps from the sidewalk. It was as though Aziz was waiting for us that day with his peace plan, as though he was expecting us. He had it all worked out: a Palestinian state to be established side by side with Israel in all the newly occupied territories. We told him to write up the plan and went back the next day and collected the memorandum. Aziz was a most amazing man."

This must have been the document my father asked me to type. I remember his frustration at not being able to reach his secretary because of the curfew. I can also remember my ambivalence. Was I typing a document that would change the history of the region, or was I helping my father carry out a dangerous task that he would later regret? I had a portable manual typewriter, and my typing was not perfect. I do not remember if I had carbon paper at home, and we certainly had no photocopying facilities then. Could this be why I cannot find a copy of this memorandum? What remains is a document based on my father's memorandum that Dan and David wrote to present to their government.

My father listed the names of forty Palestinians from different parts of the occupied territories. He believed that these forty dignitaries should convene and declare the establishment of the provisional government of the state of Palestine. They would declare their willingness to sign a peace treaty with the state of Israel on the grounds of mutual recognition and the immediate cessation of all acts of hostility. Negotiations would then immediately begin to resolve all aspects of the Palestinian problem. This would silence the Arab states, who never saved us from the disasters that befell us. If this was the will of the largest concentration of Palestinians, what was left for others to say? We, the Palestinians, who lost our lands in 1948 and remained in this part of Palestine despite the misery and deprivation. We, who were now resolved to come to terms with our history and to determine our future life in peace and reconciliation with our bitterest enemy. What right would any of the Arab states have to denounce such an action taken by the Palestinians themselves?

The legal foundation for the initiative would be United Nations Resolution 181, which had called for the partition of Palestine into two states: one for the Arabs and another for the Jews. This was how my father thought the conflict between Palestinians and Israelis would end.

It was a simple plan, one that he had worked out in full and believed must be implemented immediately if it were to succeed. The two Israelis carried his proposal and wrote their own memorandum, which they presented to the Israeli coalition government headed by Levi Eshkol.

These were the facts and they show the kind of man father was: brave, original, single minded, forward looking, decisive. A man with a vision. Three days after the war was my father's most important time, one that he continued to speak of as the "missed opportunity" for the rest of his life.

I marvel now at the amazing speed with which my father was able to switch from thoughts of suicide to embarking on a political initiative that he believed would change the history of the region. But then this was the way of my father: sudden switches of emotion. The bouts of profound pessimism when they hit him never lasted very long. He was always able to pull himself up and start again. He was blessed with this ability, which helped him go through one embittering experience after another. His iron will left him only in his last year, the saddest year of his life, when he experienced a deep despair that he seemed unable to conquer.

But in 1967 he was 55 years old. While others were paralyzed with fear, he was clear headed. He saw this misfortune as a repeat of an earlier round. In 1948 he had abandoned his fate to the Arab armies and ended up on the other side of the border having lost everything, defeated and destitute. Once again he had counted on the Arab armies to fight his war in 1967, and again the result was defeat as well as the occupation of the rest of Palestine. Now was the time, he thought, for the Palestinians to take their fate in their own hands.

Those who did not want a Palestinian state, he believed, included the Arab countries. They wanted to keep the Palestinians in bondage and continue to have the threat of war as a justification for not making long-overdue political changes within their own countries. He knew the odds were not in favor of the Palestinians' action. He predicted that this defeat would be followed by stirred emotions and bravado. And then people would wait for the next round of war, which would decidedly be another futile war, because he now believed that war was not the way Palestinians would achieve their national aspirations.

He also believed that Israel must be concerned about the prospect of controlling the million Palestinians now under its jurisdiction. He did not think that there would be any meaningful resistance by the Palestinians in the West Bank, but Israeli apprehensions of possible civil disobedience — or worse, street fighting in the narrow lanes of the old Palestinian cities — could be used as a factor to persuade Israel to agree to the final political resolution he was now proposing. For all these reasons time was of the essence. It had to happen now if it were to happen at all.

He seemed to have found an answer that satisfied him and he did not look back. A decisive man, he hated hesitation. He was brave to the point of recklessness. He took no precautions. He published several articles in local and international journals stating that the only resolution to the Palestinian–Israeli conflict was through the peaceful establishment of a Palestinian state in the West Bank, the Gaza Strip, and East Jerusalem. He made himself available to journalists and gave interviews to the many who flocked to our house. But most important, he drafted the declaration for the establishment of the Palestinian state, which he circulated to other Palestinian leaders in the area and then presented to the Israeli leadership. He knew that if he could garner enough support for his ideas among both Palestinians and Israelis, history could be changed.

But the Israeli government leaders to whom the plan was presented didn't even respond. They just let it pass. They, and we, missed another opportunity for peace.

Dan wrote a book called *Missed Opportunities and Dreams*. Talking to Dan helped me see the events of that time in their proper historical perspective. I told him that I didn't believe my father was a politician, instead he was a visionary. A politician assesses events and takes what actions he thinks he can get away with. How could my father have possibly thought he could get away with this one?

Dan disagreed: "Aziz was a strategist. He was shrewd and meticulous and had thought of every angle: the legal, the political, the economic."

"But do you really believe it could have worked?" I asked.

"Yes," he said emphatically.

"And what about the PLO?"

"It was not until 1968 that the organization came into prominence, after the battle of Karameh. At the time your father made his proposal the PLO was not yet in the picture."

"And Jordan?"

"Jordan wanted the whole thing back. In Israel we had no interest in returning the territories to Jordan."

"Was East Jerusalem to be included in the Palestinian state?"

"Jerusalem was not a problem then. Everything that you hear now about Jerusalem and the way it is presented as a central issue that is among the most difficult to resolve did not feature then. Yes, Jerusalem was part of the deal."

I said, "You were willing to agree to a full Palestinian state."

"A full Palestinian state."

CHAPTER SEVEN

I DO NOT know if all wars mark a break in time so great that all other events come to be arranged around them. For me, however, this feeling was so strong that when I went back to visit places I had not seen since the start of the war less than a week earlier, I felt as though I had been gone for a very long time. By walking from my house to the center of town, a distance of a few hundred meters, I was returning to the past. Six days ago was another epoch. It was before the war, before the invasion, before the fall of Jerusalem.

I remember visiting the center of town after the curfew was lifted for one hour. There was something wild, distant, and strange about it. Broken branches from the pine trees that had lined the streets, strewn electric and telephone cables, and piles of paper bags flying in the wind cluttered the main commercial street. Zarou's pharmacy at the corner had the front glass broken, and Salman's button store with its green wood and old trinkets in the window looked barely familiar. The poster on the wooden signpost announcing the last film that had played at the Cinema Dunia was badly torn. *The Thief of Baghdad,* which I had seen before the war, seemed from another era. The Grand Hotel with its Casino, now the headquarters of the Israeli Command, was beyond reach. The villas of the rich Arabs from the Gulf States had been taken over by the army as absentee enemy property.

During this first excursion I learned that the town had suffered three casualties: Abu el Habaieb, the old bearded man with the grim expression who sold newspapers (my grandmother once fought with him over the delivery of a newspaper), and two orphan sisters from the Anglican Home. The home had received a direct hit because it was close to the transmission station, apparently the target of most of the bombs that fell on Ramallah.

Meeting friends in the street, I greeted them with exaggerated hugs. I held on to them for a long time, as though we had not seen each other for decades and never expected to see each other again. After we parted, I remembered that I had seen them only a week before. But instinctively I felt that those of us who stayed behind had become very close and needed to stay together. Those who left might be gone forever.

I had stopped at Zarou's pharmacy to buy pills for my grand-mother's hypertension when a dusty army jeep shrieked to a stop nearby and the soldiers got out. This was my first close-up view of Israeli regular soldiers. I remember that one of them was not much older than I was then. He wore close-fitting army fatigues and carried a long rifle. His shirt was unbuttoned halfway down his hairy chest, and around his neck he wore an ivory horn. He flung his legs from the back of the jeep to the ground with confidence, acting like a king who could force his will on all of us. I wondered where this young man came from and assumed from his tan that it must be Jaffa. When he was not enjoying the beach, I thought, this young man had trained as a soldier and fought a war against us and won. And what had I been doing? A few marching exercises. What did I do to defend my own? I only cheered and hoped for the best and when the fighting began ran in my slippers to the street, carrying my ridiculous first-aid kit and looking for a place to hide under-neath Nur's tree. I felt more ashamed than I had ever felt in my life. But worse for someone who had just turned sixteen, I felt my man-hood compromised. Is this what it means to be occupied?

I strolled pensively through the garbage in the street won-dering who would put the town back in order. Whose responsibility was it now to clean up the town and repair the public property that was damaged? Who did the town belong to now? The soldier in the army jeep broke the silence of my musing by announcing the resumption of the curfew and ordering us to return home. *Beita,* the

Hebrew word for "home," I now heard for the first time. It sounded like a mockery of the Arabic word for "home," *beit*. To our *beita* we returned, just as the soldier ordered.

A short time later, during a longer break in the curfew, I cycled to Jerusalem with a friend, taking pictures along the way. The route was littered with wrecked cars. Some of them had been crushed by tanks that had flattened them almost to the ground. How did it feel, I wondered, to drive a tank over a car parked in someone's driveway and see the owner at the window watching, his face crumbling at the sight of his car being mounted by a tank?

The houses we saw on the way had suffered very little damage. Many continued to look as ostentatious as ever, with their odd trapezoidal windows, blue spiral stairs, and grand entrances. It was as though the war had been between the tanks and the cars, and the cars had lost.

It was a clear crisp June morning as we cycled south. I focused on the metallic casualties by the side of the road, but every once in a while my eyes would stray to the western hills from which the Israeli army had invaded. I knew there had never been any gates to keep the soldiers away, and yet it was as if some previous buffer had been removed, bringing these fields to the west into full view. Where once there was division, now there was an open, continuous, accessible space.

This new perception of space became most evident after I had cycled up the last hill and could see Jerusalem. To the east was Mount Scopus, then the valley of Wad el Joz — the valley of walnuts — then, on a smaller hill straight ahead, Shiekh Jarrah with the Ambassador Hotel at its center, now turned into military headquarters. The view did not stop there; it continued for the first time into the western neighborhoods, with low houses, many with tiled roofs and gardens. How was it that the Israeli side had suddenly become visible? How could it have been that for all these years before the occupation the only Jerusalem I had ever seen was confined to the eastern Arab sector? I had, of course, heard much about the western side that we called New Jerusalem. My mother had gone to school in the Rehavia neighborhood, and I knew many Palestinians who before 1948 had lived in Talbieh, Bekaa, and Musrara. But up until now these were only names. The space had expanded and I could absorb the full range of the panoramic view extending below.

Jerusalem was bathed in a light blue haze. I could see no tall buildings. It looked like a large village with empty green spaces between the houses, more a pasture than a bustling crowded city.

I shot photos until I reached the end of my roll of film. It was not enough to look. I needed material proof. If we were to be separated from Jerusalem, I did not want to be left, like my parents after their forced exile from Jaffa, with only memories.

A few days later I traveled by car with my parents to the new city. As we approached the famed Jaffa Road, there was the strong enticing smell of vanilla in the air. How different the Jewish side was! This Jerusalem had a majesty and anonymity that did not exist in the eastern side. So close were the two sections of the city and yet so apart. All I recognized here were the names: the Generali building, Terra Sancta, Kapulski's, Cinema Edison, the German Colony, Musrara. My mother pointed things out as we went from place to place. I felt her excitement and realized that for her this was a true return to the past.

Several weeks later the Israeli army set up a checkpoint on the road between Ramallah and Jerusalem. Within a few hours, we were visited by our cousin Mary, a very tall woman with a tendency for overdramatizing. She came with her husband, a doctor with a wide sympathetic mouth and froglike eyes.

"We have come," they said, "to bid you farewell."

"Farewell?" my mother asked. "But why? Are you leaving us?"

"No," Mary said wringing her hands, "we are not leaving. But the Israeli army is placing a checkpoint on the road between us. Ramallah will be separated from Jerusalem and we shall never be able to see you again. So farewell, dear friends, farewell."

Both Mary and her husband began to hug and kiss every one of us. Mary's tears did not stop flowing. She bowed to reach the cheeks of our family members, all of whom were too short for her head, perched as it was over legs like stilts.

Of course Mary had exaggerated, and her kisses and tears were wasted. The checkpoint that was eventually erected on the road between Ramallah and Jerusalem did not restrict the movement of people, only goods. And eventually it was dismantled. Our two families were not separated forever. We were able to visit Mary again and receive a detailed account of her experiences during the war. We were told that their house in Beit Hanina had been threatened by Israeli bombardment for the entire duration of the war. She and her husband had to hide themselves in the tiny stairwell, an ordeal no less phenomenal than that of our neighbor's obese wife trying to fit herself in that tiny hole in the wall below our house.

A month after the occupation David Rosenblum, my father's old friend and former colleague during mandate times, came to serve with the legal unit of the Israeli Army Command stationed at the Grand Hotel near our house. One of the first things he did upon arriving in Ramallah was visit my father. They had not met for twenty years and had much to talk about. Before he left, Rosenblum asked if he could do anything for my father. My father only had one request: "Take me to see Jaffa," he said.

I remember how excited my father was to be visiting Jaffa again, and how excited I was to hear his account when he returned. To me it was like a dream come true, for a member of my family to actually travel across these hills to the west and visit the mythic city on the horizon. For my father the trip was more like traversing abandoned space and regaining lost time, going back through the darkness to where the lights shone every evening.

When my father left for Jaffa, I stayed behind waiting impatiently for his return. The prospect of his going into the forbidden, of seeing behind the veil, of going to the point beyond the permissible to the distant, unreachable horizon excited and mystified me.

I remember lying on the couch in the glass veranda of our house overlooking those hills to the west, the point of the lights at night. I listened to Rachmaninoff's second piano concerto and waited. The visit meant a lot to my father and had such an impact that he was never the same. It started the process that eventually led to the affirmation of his new vision for the resolution of the Palestinian–Israeli conflict.

It was midafternoon when they set off. The June sun burned bright over the limestone rocks of the hills around Ramallah. Everything was brown or yellow, dried by the sun, all but the olive trees that stood between the rocks marking little territories, fiercely held to the earth by strong and lumpy roots, thick like the feet of an elephant. If you looked carefully, the hillsides were like natural gardens where the terraces followed the contours of the hills. There were no parallel lines, but terraces of different sizes held in the earth and a few olive trees at the same elevation. Then lower down was another terrace, always with a path for the mule and the hand-driven plow between the first and second levels. There were innumerable little niches, corners, and shy spots where you could picnic on sloping slabs of rock under the shade of an olive tree. As my father looked from the window of the car he must have wondered whether the land had always been so resplendent, or if he was able to see such beauty now because his heart had suddenly opened to what had become so contemptuously familiar these past two decades. Or was this beauty now visible because he was no longer imprisoned within it? Instead he was on his way to another landscape, one he had held up as having a monopoly on beauty.

As they drove to the top and arrived at Beit Ur, the highest spot in the region, my father saw how organically the villages merged with the countryside around them. They stood huddled by the curve in the hills, unobtrusive, unimposing, built to protect against the elements while attempting to cause the least damage to the general sweep of their natural curvature.

They opened the windows and a fresh, dry wind swept through

the car as they traveled down. Balmy, refreshing, and caressing, it couldn't have been a more perfect day for his return visit.

The sun, which had been shining in their eyes, now hid behind the hills as they descended from the heights of Beit Ur. The hills were lit by the indirect glow, giving them a softer, deeper hue as they absorbed, more than reflected, the light. The rocks and the trees stood with long shadows that made the fields seem cluttered with light and shade. And from behind their tops the sky was a pure golden bronze color. How many thousands of sunsets had he seen? — and yet it was as though he had never witnessed one before, never felt that excitement at every shift of light and shade, never admired the power or the colors of the sun, never realized how what you see is not constant. In their slow, quiet, unassuming manner these ancient hills had induced him to think of them as so tediously ordinary and eternally bland that he had no interest in them. To him they had represented the lethargy and dullness of old age, the loss of the dynamism of Jaffa, and the promise of youth.

As the sun descended behind the next range of hills, the golden light became softer and more alluring. The foreground grew dimmer and deeper like velvet, and the horizon was a silhouette that he could follow with his eyes. The skyline had flattened out into a thin, broken line with sharp angles and curves where the olive trees rode over the backs of the hills in processions of camels, donkeys, and mules. They were illuminated from behind with a powerful golden light that became stronger as the foreground dimmed until the hills were transformed into a mass of solid humps as though turned onto themselves, taking in all the light and emitting nothing.

Once they descended, they found the coastal plain spread before them. As it opened up my father felt his heart open with it. His eyes roamed the wide expanse, and he felt as though he had for these past twenty years confined even his sight. For all that time he had not laid his eyes on something so wide and open. A great joy went through him. He felt liberated, as someone who, unknowingly imprisoned, suddenly realizes his freedom. Of one thing he was very sure: he would never again let himself be confined as he had been by these borders and states of mind.

And then they crossed that first plain and moved northwest up a small hill turning a corner, the same corner that he remembered driving around so often in the past. From there they could see behind them the consoling view of the Latrun monastery, with its many arcades and long arched windows, graciously resting in the slight rise just above the hills they left.

They traveled along the old familiar road lined with high eucalyptus trees that the British had planted along both sides of the road as camouflage. The familiar now completely captured my father. He felt at home, as though he had never left. Then the citrus orchards began, with their dark green healthy foliage. The trees were still dotted with oranges as deeply colored as the leaves. The country seemed to him like one resplendent garden and a cry resonated from deep within: how could we have left all this? Tears came to his eyes but he suppressed them. He did not want to indulge in perpetuating the tradition that he disliked so much — that of wailing over loss.

As they passed the familiar towns on their way to Jaffa, he called out their names in an incantation, in confirmation of their bond: Abasieh, Beit Dajan, Yazour, Salameh. The road was the same. The trees were higher but recognizable from twenty years before. The crafts shops were left to crumble, empty, without the buzz of life that had characterized them.

The sun had not yet set when they reached Jaffa and the sea. It hovered at the edge of the water, and he caught a glimpse of it before it sank. He was left alone in his beloved Jaffa, the site of his youth, in the brief twilight before darkness descended.

My father's feeling upon reaching Jaffa was a mixture of joy and disappointment, like a lover after a long and difficult trip to see a dying loved one. The anticipation and determination had been so consuming that he had given no thought to the reality of his arrival.

The loved one was not as he had left her. She had been ravaged by disease and the struggle to survive. She was not at all as he had remembered, but a mere ghost of herself with pale crumpled skin, dead silent.

"Take me first to Nuzha Street," my father told his friend.

They drove down the boulevard, its median-strip garden still preserving some of its earlier charm. All the houses and shops on this street were still there but the Cinema Rivoli, which looked closed. My father looked across the island and saw the house of his mother-in-law, the last place he had seen on his final fleeting visit to Jaffa twenty-odd years ago. It was a two-story house with a pine tree in the corner of its garden. Only two meters high when he was last here, it was a big tree now, one of the few pines in Jaffa, and its towering presence shaded the front porch of the house. He looked at the front gate. It was just as he left it, only now the paint was peeling. Ghosts from the past do not freeze in time: their gardens continue to grow, their walls peel from the ravages of nature and neglect. How gray the houses looked after the white limestone houses of Ramallah! Farther up was one of the few stone houses of Jaffa, the Dajani house and hospital, recessed in a forested garden. Everything had grown big around the house, making it seem closed in on itself, distant, mysterious in repose. Farther still was the Continental Hotel, where he had lived for five years before getting married. It looked gray, small, and charmless. The sign that had proudly declared CONTINENTAL HOTEL had been removed. You wouldn't know it had once been a hotel with a prosperous restaurant, well equipped and hospitable.

When they got to the apartment building where he had had his own flat the light was growing dimmer. My father was now hoping for complete darkness, complete anonymity.

They continued to drive northwest, arriving at the clock piazza. The Ottoman clock still stood, but it had stopped running. The police station remained despite the explosion that had rocked it in 1948. The row of homes along the market street starting from this piazza was still there, dilapidated, blackened, with unpainted metal shutters.

The Magistrate's Courthouse building had been demolished in 1948. But the barbershop where my father had his hair cut, Hinn's, was still standing. His house, his office, his favorite haunts, the shop where he had sandwiches for lunch, the newspaper stand, the little public garden, the mule-drawn cart, the café where the idle *khawajat* with the *tarboush* on their heads sat all day drinking coffee, smoking *nergilehs,* and playing dominoes were all lost to memory. Ghosts in his head confused the reality with the dream, neither cherishing the dream nor dealing with the present.

"Let's drive up to Ajami," he managed to say after a long and involved silence.

The car turned left toward the winding road. The same old bakery was still there. Why had something of the living past remained? Would it not have been easier if it had all gone, better still all crumbled and buried in the ground? Why this half reality, neither fully there nor fully gone? Half tones, shades, lingering twilight, as the taunting sun took its time to sink. The church where he was wed was still there, as they had left it, still with its pink stucco and wrought-iron gate.

A breeze was now blowing as they drove farther up, the breeze that comes before the sun sets. On the Rabieh of Jaffa he could see the houses of the rich as palatial as ever. They seemed to have aged with dignity. He was impressed by how many of these houses the Israelis had allowed to remain standing. They still rested comfortably on the higher reaches of the town. Looking at these villas he could imagine the life of the idle rich that had taken place in them, the parties, the gossip, the fatuous conflicts of the happy and the miserable families who had inhabited them. A whole society, where life had once been.

The sun was just sinking into the sea. Below he could see the port and the beach where he went swimming. He had reached the end. This was the coast, the edge of the land. From here the sea led to the horizon, a straight line now streaked by the rays of the setting sun.

The air was humid and heavy. Not like the dry light air of Ramallah. Here he was finally united with the desire of his heart. He was standing where he had wanted to be. Beyond were the refreshing clear waters of the Mediterranean, the gentle rippling of its waves incessantly breaking along the glittering shore. He felt that he never wanted to move from here. He wanted to drop to the ground and melt into the earth.

When the sun had set, he returned to himself and saw his Israeli friend standing beside him. Two men, of the same age and height, a Palestinian and a Jew, stood side by side in the twilight of a ruined city. They had started their working lives in the same profession before the same courts. But they had moved, along with their people, in entirely different directions. Rosenblum's gaze was turned northward to the emerging lights from the nearby city.

"That is Tel Aviv," he proudly pointed out.

It was at this point that my father must have realized that the glittering lights to which his eyes had been riveted for all these years were not the lights of Jaffa but those of Tel Aviv. For as the sun set, Jaffa lapsed into slumber and darkness. It was Tel Aviv that glowed with the glitter of the night-lights.

They drove down from the Rabieh to the almost destroyed Manshieh quarter, traveling along a long street by the sea now called Hayarkon, toward the lights of the thriving city of Tel Aviv. Leaving the ghosts behind, he now confronted the life that had been created by the new dwellers of this land. The Tel Aviv he had known was but a suburb of Jaffa; now the ghost town was the dead suburb of the living city. His silent companion now came to life, proudly pointing out the accomplishments of his own hometown. He was like a proud father showing off the blooming daughter who had been a plain child when his neighbor had last laid eyes on her.

Rosenblum pointed to the pedestrian bridge overhead, the multi-lane highways, the Mann Auditorium, the Opera House, the public gardens, the museums. The twilight had turned into night and the city was now lit by the electric lights of the boulevards, houses, and shops. My father was impressed with the masses milling about on the street. The place was throbbing with activity. Many new quarters had sprung up. He recognized some of the streets, Ben Yehuda, Dizingoff, Rothschild. But there was a major difference between the Tel Aviv he remembered of twenty years ago and what he now saw. There was a vitality to the place that he could not have imagined: buses as numerous as cars, hordes of young people out for the evening, sidewalk cafés. This was the place he had been watching grow from his exile across the hills. All these years he had watched its development, failing to realize that the home that he had left was falling into decrepit disrepair and being replaced, just a small distance away, by a metropolis.

As he was driven through Tel Aviv my father must have been filled with a deep sense of regret. He had not only left his property but abandoned the whole fabric of his former life. If there was continuity it was in this place, managed by its new dwellers. The Palestinians had deserted not only their houses but their lives and waited for others to manage them. The civil service, the judiciary, the marketplace, the public services, all had been left for others — UNRWA and other relief agencies — to run.

We had been stunned, bewildered, jettisoned across an imaginary border. We remained on the other side, looking at what we left behind, leaving in the process both what was lost and what we had managed to keep. Our dumbfoundedness had been so petrifying that we could not manage to continue the life we had lived before. Because of our loss of the part, we had abandoned the whole. All that remained was a shadow life, a life of dreams and anticipation and memory. We didn't allow the new generation to make a new life for themselves because we continued to impress them with the glory of what was, a magic that could never be replicated. We allowed others to inherit all that had been established because we failed to see any of it as ours. We defined our loss as total, forgetting that we still had something; we had ourselves and a life to live. Why had we allowed others to define for us our privation, our bereavement, and the meaning of our past? Why had we accepted our defeat as total and ourselves as maimed and reduced? With this abandonment we made the same mistakes that had led to defeat in the first place. Learning nothing from our experience, we were doomed like Sisyphus.

The more he saw of the active life of Tel Aviv, the more angry my father became. We had spent these years lamenting, whining, complaining, bemoaning the lost country, turning Palestine into words, songs, poetry, reminiscences, and speeches. We had put our misplaced faith in the armies of our perceived deliverers. How distracted we had been from doing what was positive and real. How could we have expected our shadow life to compare to this resurgence of the real, this formidable reconstruction of a society? Instead of developing a vital life in whatever was left for us, we wandered throughout the world complaining, like the Ancient Mariner stopping every wedding guest to tell our story.

And meanwhile we expected the enemy to remain where we left them. We were willing to believe what we hoped for rather than come to terms with their reality. We were told that Israel was crumbling from inside, crippled by high unemployment, suffering under unspeakable economic conditions. How far we were from the development this enemy had achieved! Would we continue to live by our delusions or would we resurrect ourselves from the ashes?

It was then that my father must have promised himself that he never again wanted to hear another song about the lost country. He never wanted to succumb to the deception of false glory. Never wanted to let words wield their own magic and take him with them to what he now realized was a false world, a false consciousness, a masterful deception and detrimental abandonment of self. My father swore that from then on he would be hardheaded; he would stubbornly confront what only he knew best about his past and his present.

After his trip to Jaffa, my father's life could no longer be the same. One of its fundamental coordinates had changed. His eyes had always been fixed on the horizon of his yearning. Now when he looked in the same direction, he could no longer see only what he wanted to see. Now that he had crossed over, the spell was broken. The war had shattered more than one illusion.

My father saw that we must make a break with the past.

If in the past we were a lamenting people, now we would become dynamic, taking control of our own destinies. We must begin a new way of life, a new social and spatial organization of our society, not cramped but spread out, using the empty hills to establish new communities where those living in refugee camps could move, where the new Palestinian would be created: a forward-looking, bold, assertive citizen able to come to terms with his history, who would challenge the enemy to make peace on the basis of a new division of the land between two states living side by side in peace together.

Such was the significance to my father of his maiden trip to Jaffa. But the trip was no less important to me. It marked the beginning of my deference to my father regarding my right to my own past. From then on I became a hostage to his historical memory. He held the keys to the past, which I could unlock only if he handed them over to me. I knew only what he told me. I had accepted that in his abandoned past was the only real life, the only one worth living and dying for. Now he had gone back. And I waited to hear his account of his return. I knew that I could not go back because to me it was not a reality that had any existence outside my father's mind.

The pattern was set for a long time to come. I did not know it then, but two events took place in my life that were far more important than the fact of the occupation of my country: I lost my father to politics, and I began my search for the man who was my father, a process that would continue for many years after his death.

My father's voice continued to be heard in different parts of the West Bank, but it was quickly becoming muted by another, stronger voice. Every evening I heard this other voice on the radio broadcasting from Damascus. It was appropriately called *Sout el Saaika,* the Voice of the Lightning Bolt, and after I turned it on I felt as though lightning had penetrated deep into my body and made my heart thump with a different pace. The announcer had a deep husky, insistent voice expressing such urgency, I felt that at any moment the most important announcement was going to be made. The theme music was arousing and was punctuated by yelling and thumping of feet from a large group of men. It reminded me of the yelling we had been ordered to do during our marching exercises when we turned a corner and saluted. But this surely was more real. I thought of Munther and Sami from my class, who had left school to join the Fatah Revolutionary Organization that in 1968 had launched a big recruitment drive. Could they be among those whose yelling I was now hearing?

There was much marching music accompanied by large groups of men yelling and chanting patriotic songs. Communiqués were read. They came from the front; they spoke of military victories achieved against Israel. The war was still going on; the defeat was only in our head if we wanted to believe it. And if we didn't, all we needed to do was to turn on the radio.

Everything about this station was different, as it should have been, this being the voice of the revolution. Even the news was not read in the normal boring drone but with a rushed breathlessness, dispensed with quickly so that the most important segment, the bulletins from the front, could begin. They involved coded messages to various people who were cooperating with the revolution and carrying out secret missions on its behalf here. Every message ended with the declarations "Revolution until Victory," and "Long

Live the Revolution." But then came a message that made my blood curdle. It was addressed to my father:

"A. S.," it declared, "you are a traitor, a despicable collaborator. You want to surrender and sell our birthright. We know how to deal with the likes of you.

"A. S. you shall pay for your treason. We shall eliminate you. Silence you forever. Make an example of you for others. Traitor. Collaborator. Quisling."

CHAPTER EIGHT

AS I LISTENED to this message from our revolutionary brethren broadcasting from Damascus, dread came over me. I realized that my father had dared to utter the unspeakable: recognition of Israel. Not only was his life now in danger, but he had become a pariah whose very existence could not be acknowledged. This was why he was only referred to by his initials. It was the same ploy used by the Arab states against Israel. It could not be mentioned by name. It could only be referred to as "the Zionist entity." My father had succeeded in making himself enemy number one to the new rising force, the Palestinian revolution and armed struggle.

Despite the stigma, I remained loyal to my father. He made very few attempts to help me reconcile the contradictions that now marked my life. At a stage when I craved the security of order around me, I felt only chaos and uncertainty. I was now a member of a defeated people.

My father revived old friendships with his Jewish friends, members of the enemy state that now occupied our land. He traveled and spoke at every forum that was available to him. He often took me along, expecting that I would understand simply by listening to his logical explanation of how it was in the past between the two peoples and how it should be in the future. He was lost in his idealistic vision of a new world based on peace and reconciliation. I listened and tried to understand but could not help hearing the revolutionary broadcast from Damascus at the same time. The denunciations of my father's politics increased in intensity as fear of his possible success grew stronger. Secretly I wished not for a political leader but for an understanding father who would pay more attention to my needs as a young man growing up in extremely difficult circumstances. I will never know if he was aware of my needs. I only know that he tried to dazzle me with his activism and seemingly inexhaustible energy and drive. I was strongly attracted to him and, much as I felt dissatisfied by his distance, I could not abandon him. I have spent my life trying to unravel the enigma that he presented as I tried to get close to him.

It helped that I was used to the status of the outsider. It was not a new experience for me to hold unorthodox views. Those who we were taught at school were heroes, my father had told me, were actually traitors to the Palestinian cause. Such was my father's view of Hajj Amin el Husseini, the leader of Palestinians during the Arab Revolt of the 1930s, for example. In fact I was coached to view the whole version of Arab and Palestinian history that I had learned at school with suspicion. I learned what I was given in order to pass the exams but was obedient enough to my father to retain nothing of it. I also knew that we were not Jordanian, as we were taught at school; we were Palestinian. Even when it was not safe to say this to others, I knew who I really was, and this was enough. I believed what Father said: they were all wrong and Father was right. I was thus the traitor's son. But this only sealed my isolation, it did not cause it. The cause was deeper and more personal.

I touched the skin above my upper lip and felt the hair growing there, thick facial hair, evidence of my development from a boy to a man. The world of men was another world, one that I would be ushered into when I was invited by my father. Before I could move into that world I needed his acceptance. But he did not give it.

I remember how mystified I felt when as a young man I stood by the sink and watched him shave. I listened intently to the scraping of the shaving blade against his skin as it plowed through the thick field of hair on his cheek and smoothed it. The ritual symbolized the world of men and I ached for him to take me along. But I waited in vain.

It never occurred to me that my friends did not wait for their father's consent before they bought themselves shavers. I looked with awe at the developing relationship between my friends and their fathers and how naturally they seemed to move from the world of boys. Their voices seemed to change without causing embarrassment, their feet became larger and they wore men's shoes, but my case was different. I tried to conceal every manifestation of masculine growth, hoping that I would come to understand what manhood meant and come to deserve promotion to that special and distinguished status. I seemed to be postponing my growth by suppressing any sign of manhood as I waited for my father's recognition.

Meanwhile, I slipped into the bathroom when my father was not there and used his razor to shave, without any foam, the evidence of my imminent manhood.

"Who used my shaving blade?" my father screamed when he discovered what I had done. He looked at me accusingly. Why did he need to ask? Who else could be using his shaving blade but me? I was the only candidate; my brother's face was still clear and hairless. I tried to deny my crime but he did not believe me. He was the same about the scissors, which I also borrowed for a close cropping of the growing hair over my upper lip. He did not like his things to be out of their place. I wonder now whether I intentionally misplaced the scissors every time so that my father would notice what I was up to. When they were not where they should be, all his pent-up anger would explode all out of proportion to the situation. He seemed to have no clue about my needs as a growing young man. He never said: *Why don't you buy your own blade?* Better still, he could have gone out and bought one for me rather than scold me mercilessly in front of my sisters, confirming my suspicions that he did not approve of my shaving because I did not deserve this promotion to the world of men that nature was thrusting on me despite myself.

I hoped the barber would remember to shave off my facial hair when I went for a haircut, holding a five-piaster silver coin in my hand. I sat waiting for my turn observing the young men. They stretched out on the high chair, their heads resting on the headrest, their Adam's apples prominent with the white sheet tied just below.

The barber gave them a full shave. If they saw one of their friends passing by they yelled a loud greeting, lifting an arm from beneath the cover and inviting him in. There was no surreptitiousness about their getting a shave. They were proud of their bodies and seemed to embrace the developing signs of manhood, hair, acne, and all with enthusiasm and pride. Why could I not do the same?

When my turn came I moved silently to the empty seat and gave my head over to the barber's dexterous hands. He clipped the scissors expertly all over my head as he had done since I began having my hair cut at his shop as a four-year-old. But this was not what interested me now. I was hoping that he would remember my new needs and attend to them. Would I have the courage to ask him if he didn't remember? The tension mounted when he made a final check of my nape and began passing the shaving knife over it, making it clean and smooth. When he finished he lowered his head. I could feel his warm breath fanning my newly shaved nape: "Shall I shave your mustache?" he whispered in my ear. "Yes," I answered timidly, enthusiastically. The barber dipped his finger in the soap ball and then passed it over my upper lip. It felt cool. My heart began to pound faster and I closed my eyes. I could hear the barber sharpen the knife blade on the leather strap hanging next to the counter. He then came back, pinched my right cheek between his two expert fingers, and began shaving from the corner of my mouth up. Closer to my ears I could now hear the same scraping sound that Father made when he shaved. It was finally happening. I was getting a shave. The barber pinched the left cheek and passed the blade up. Then he passed it under my nose, starting from the upper lip and moving up to my nostrils. All the hairs were now properly and professionally removed. For the first time my mustache was fully shaved.

I left the shop feeling proud, transfigured, and acutely aware of a unique tingle both underneath the tender skin where my mustache had been and down my nose into the rest of my blazing being. The air blowing against my skin tickled and energized me. It also smelled sharper. I lifted my hand and passed my fingers slowly over the precious new skin. It felt swollen, smooth, and arousing. It sent quivers through my body. Light-footed I walked home, feeling that my glowing body was cutting through the air and wondering who would be the first member of my family to see me after my first shave. The autumn morning sky was clear with milk-white clouds. Their shadows were darkening parts of the hills and the wadi that now came within sight.

At the corner of our house on top of the hill before the slope, I stopped and looked at the horizon. But my gaze this time was fixed on the hills closer to home. I noticed how round and soft they looked. On top of one was a small rectangular house. I followed the footpath that began there and meandered down to the wadi. Just before the foot of the hill I noticed a tuft of pine trees. Around them was red freshly turned soil exposing the roots. I gazed at them. They seemed to crawl down the path, getting all entwined like giant snakes. The hills on both sides looked like the breasts of a young woman stretched out over the land. I had never noticed any of this before. My eyes had always focused on the distant horizon.

Sometimes I worked up the courage to buy a Wilkinson Sword shaving blade from Abu Yusuf who had a small pushcart on the sidewalk. And then I would go home, unwrap the blade, take it between my fingers and pass it over my skin against the flow of the hair. I would feel great excitement as I performed this dangerous bloody task, which often resulted in many cuts to my skin. But I did not mind. I was promoting myself from one stage of my life to another — albeit still in secret.

One day I forgot the blade in my trouser pocket. My grandmother, in the course of preparing the washing, put her hand in my pocket and cut her fingers. She screamed: "Ya *majnoun,* mad boy, what do you have in that pocket of yours?"

I rushed off to remove the blade while she went to wash the blood away and proceeded to deny that there was anything there.

"But then what cut my fingers?" she demanded to know in her logical uncompromising way.

I had grown up a weak and delicate child. My mother had been an anxious nurse through my succession of life-threatening ailments — diphtheria, hepatitis, pneumonia — and always made me feel that I would barely survive. I never felt confident about my body and learned to treat it as fragile and capricious.

Because of the extended periods of enforced confinement I did not interact with the boys who played in the street by our house. Instead I was exposed to the talk of the women who, during long coffee breaks, discussed everything and everyone. I came to see my father and his life through the eyes of my mother and her women friends. This made him all the more remote and mysterious.

For his part, my father was unhappy with the way I was being brought up. He worried that I would grow up to be a sissy, so far removed from the real world that I would be unable to manage. But every time he made an effort to liberate me from the clutches of my mother, sickness would once again force my return to her care. He could only wait for the next chance.

Now, as a young man, it was the war that isolated me. What a time it was to grow up in! The long hours of curfew meant worse confinement than I had ever experienced. It was several months before the schools opened again, and I suffered acutely from the absence of structure in my life. None of my friends lived nearby; I was forced to spend the long days alone in a house full of women. Because water was scarce, I could not even continue to tend the garden.

My father's penetration of that land on the horizon meant a certain opening and expansion of the world into which I was born. But what was I to make of this new development? Old Jewish friends of my father's began to visit us, and sometimes we crossed over and visited them. I was able to see for myself the developed world they had made of the land of my dreams. But how was I to respond to this? Their young sons, many of whom were my age, lived lives so different from mine. They were engaged in pre-army training. They seemed not to suffer from difficulties of adjustment and had developed a national character. One of my father's friends had a son by the name of Avi who was given a Vespa motorcycle on his sixteenth birthday. He was able to travel all around the country on his bike. How different this was from the life of confinement I had to lead. I was sure it was much easier for Avi. After he finished school he would join the army, become a soldier, a member of an army unit. There was a clear, recognized structure to his life — all he had to do was follow the track. But I had no track to follow.

The world of the PLO fighters seemed too remote to be imaginable, and the narrow world at home too restrictive to be satisfying. Until I figured out what it was to be man and what kind of man I wanted to be, I seemed to have decided to hold on to my boyhood, to keep all my options open. Could I wish to be like Avi when he was my enemy? Should I hate him as my enemy? Father said it was time for peace. But what did this mean? The people around me had a simple solution to all my dilemmas; they hated the Israelis, all of them, without exception. They would spit after they saw an Israeli bus pass by. But this was not something I could emulate. It was just such simplistic, anti-Israel attitudes that Father said had brought us to the state of defeat we were now in.

These new experiences and my father's politics made me feel estranged even from my classmates. I looked with awe at the way they used sexual innuendo to express their developing manhood. But I could not participate in these exploits, which both attracted and repelled me. I wanted so much to belong but interpreted my failure to do so to be evidence of my uniqueness and superiority.

For me, then, politics was like sex. The common expression of raw anger toward the Israelis was not for me. It was beneath me. My attitudes were more differentiated, more sophisticated. No. I would never belong to a platoon and scream as one with the *shabab* when I heard it being broadcast on the radio from Damascus. I would never carry arms. And yet I yearned to be one of the *shabab* even when I despised the collective uniformity that the term implied. Who was I, then? I was going to grow into a different kind of man, a distinguished rational man with a more developed self-consciousness and sensibility than I saw displayed by those around me. I had no role model, though, so I began to write to find my way out of this dilemma.

The Israeli English paper, the *Jerusalem Post,* had a youth page published on Friday. I began to contribute poems and articles and continued to do so from 1969 to 1971, the two years I spent at Birzeit Junior College. The few Arabs who read the paper from my side thought it outrageous that I should contribute to a Zionist paper. This did not stop me. I was following my father in his single mindedness and determination to do what he believed in. Most of the writing was an attempt to communicate with my father. I was so pleased when he read the pieces that were published and wondered if he understood the hidden messages there for him. He often praised what I wrote but never acknowledged my messages.

My father's Israeli friends read my pieces and praised my writing and foretold a brilliant future for me. This must have made my father proud. But I was never able to tell what he made of my talent. My paternal grandfather had been a poet, but my father had not taken after him. In fact he never found writing easy. He always preferred oral pleadings in court. When he did write he pondered over every word. To him poetry and fiction in particular were luxuries he could not afford.

The world as he experienced it was too capricious a place to afford such lapses of attention as applying one's mind to fanciful activities like writing fiction. He repeatedly expressed his dissatisfaction with his own father. He liked to tell the story of how he had advised the poet in the late 1930s to modernize the printing press at New Gate in the Old City of Jerusalem and invest in new machinery. "Had he listened to me," my father always said, "he would have made a fortune."

What always disturbed him was the negative attitude, the resignation implied in his own father's response.

"Whatever I suggested, my father would say no. 'No, we cannot afford this,' 'No, it is too risky.' Always 'No.' 'No.' 'No.'"

These early experiences shaped my father's personality. They made him determined always to be bold, a risk taker, an adventurer. He was going to be a man of action who would change the world — he could not indulge in describing and bemoaning its state in literary writings. This may explain his lack of enthusiasm for my literary ambitions. The last thing he wished for me was to take after his own father and become a poet. He wanted to make me a man of the world, that meant being a lawyer, not a writer.

CHAPTER NINE

AFTER COMPLETING TWO years at a junior college, I was accepted in 1971 to the American University of Beirut, where I was to study English literature. My father was concerned about my safety in Beirut. It was the seat of the Palestinian armed resistance, and given the position they were taking against him he had good reason to fear that they might try to harm him through his son. The university was a hotbed of politics. Several of the leaders of PLO factions had graduated from there. My father wisely never expressed any concern that I would participate in the resistance. He certainly did not warn me against the risks. My mind was set on my studies.

We had visited Beirut on several occasions as a family before 1967. During my father's exile, when I was four years old, my mother and grandmother traveled to Beirut to see him. It was a very unsettling time for my mother. The family was low on funds. We stayed at the Ouan pension near the lighthouse. The tension, the humidity, and the uncertainty caused my health to deteriorate drastically. My stomach could not hold the food I ate; I became very weak. It was decided that I would travel back to Ramallah with my grandmother. As we were boarding the plane, my grandmother stopped me and asked: "Don't you want to say good-bye to Beirut?" I turned and said, *"Tuz ala Beirut."* To hell with Beirut.

In the years prior to the 1967 war, when my father's work had picked up again, we used to travel to Lebanon for vacation every summer. But now we stayed at the Bliss Hotel, which was owned and run by my maternal uncle Emile. It sat opposite the main gate of the American University of Beirut, and from its roof restaurant, where we had our breakfast, I could see the students going in and out of the campus. From there AUB looked like a lush green buffer between the busy Bliss Street and the blue Mediterranean Sea. I dreamed of the time when I would join this university. As I looked at the students carrying their books, rushing with purpose in and out of the gateway, some holding hands, others moving in clusters, I was sure that they had all attained independence and were recognized by their parents as adults in their own right. I knew this would be the place where I would develop into a man — something that would continue to elude me as long as I lived at home with my parents.

But the university of my dreams had to wait until I finished two years at Birzeit Junior College. This was not a delay that I welcomed. My grades qualified me to go directly to AUB, but my mother thought I was too young to leave home. After completing these two years of enforced stay at home, I could not be held back. I was sent to Beirut, the freest and most exciting city in the Arab Middle East. And I was going to make the most of it.

Beirut was a city, and I had never lived alone in a city before. It was the cultural center of the Arab world. It had a free press, the best universities, theaters, cinemas, places of entertainment, and it was home for the most celebrated Arab artists, musicians, writers, and free thinkers. There was nothing you could not get in this city. Downtown were the attractive, bustling covered markets, Souk Sursuk and Souk el Taweeleh, where you could find every spice, confectionary, and accessory. Close by was the famous red-light district in what was known as the Bourg. On the peripheries were the clusters of Palestinian refugee camps with their narrow alleys and cramped houses in Sabra, Shatila, and Tel el Zaater. Beside abject poverty you could see the height of affluence and luxury, the posh hotels and apartment blocks overlooking the sea where food flown from Paris was offered at private parties. But wherever people lived they took care to look at their best. In the evening, sitting at a seaside café and watching the sun setting into the blue water, I watched people who dressed like royalty even though many lived in destitute conditions. Appearance was everything in Beirut; this was

how you were judged. You also had to be street smart. The perils
were many in this large and confusing city, and the driving was
chaotic. In the old days, when we had visited as a family, the red
electric tramcars — called *trumwhye* — added color and danger to
the street traffic. Amid the chaotic flow of cars, the tram would
surge forward, and we were supposed to cross the lines of traffic to
get on or off it, its bells jingling. The tram's stops were never long
enough for a safe entry or exit. My mother would scream at us to be
quick as she looked back to make sure no one was left behind. Then
we would walk down the famous Hamra Street and stop at
Temptation, a small corner boutique where Lora, the wife of my
mother's maternal uncle, worked. She was Egyptian with an attractive round face. She spoke Arabic with a clipped Egyptian accent,
punctuating her words with carefully chosen French. It was a
pleasure to watch her passing her small elegant fingers through the
colorful silk scarves that her small shop was famous for. Like her
husband she came from a well-to-do background. She was a good
saleswoman, treating her merchandise and customers with the
same seriousness of purpose she gave to everything in her life.
When we got tired of watching Lora, we went out for the special ice
cream, called Merry Cream, that was softer and creamier than what
we got in Ramallah at Rukab's. The round sesame bagels also were
of a different shape and taste, pencil thin and crispy on one side and
thick and soft on the other.

Beirut's was a mercantile urban culture. It was the last city in
the Middle East with such a cosmopolitan and mixed population.
There were Armenians, Greeks, Jews, Christians, Moslems,
Syrians, Egyptians, Palestinians, Circassians, Turks, Americans,
and Europeans all living in precarious balance. It was all so different from the semidry rural life of the West Bank that I was used
to. Here people had a unique zest for life. They liked to show off,
to spend money, to live well. It resembled life in Jaffa as Father was
fond of describing it. The pleasures the city offered were not expensive. At a reasonable cost I could eat at many of the city's good

restaurants, from Uncle Sam's at the corner of Bliss Street, where I could eat pancakes, to Maroushe and its famous chicken sandwich with garlic sauce. Chantille for chocolates, Bourgoise for pastries, and Mixed Nuts for the best fresh nuts in the Middle East. There were famous sidewalk cafés — the Horse Shoe, Strand — and the more exclusive restaurants where the best Middle Eastern food was offered. I had never seen better presentation of food. I felt so welcomed. It was in such contrast to the casual manner of Palestinian restaurateurs. And what did it matter that the proprietress of Zenna restaurant on Bliss Street where I often had my meals did not find me special? It was enough that she acted as though I was, giving me sweet eyes and complimenting my new shirt. No one seemed to care what lay beneath the surface. Many of the political leaders who were destroying the country had been known to be involved in murders, but as long as they presented themselves well and looked and spoke eloquently, they were accepted. One politician never appeared in public without a fresh white carnation pinned into the lapel of his jacket. It was a culture of appearances. I was dazzled but remained ill at ease. Beirut was a city bursting at the seams.

Many suspicious characters loitered in the streets of Beirut. Spies posing as eccentric artists manned the corners with easel and brush pretending to paint watercolors when they were in fact observing the movement of the next target for an Israeli hit squad. There were new recruits for the intelligence departments of Western countries who studied Arabic and specialized in Middle Eastern studies at AUB; evangelists and other religious fundamentalists working to bring about a moral revolution to redeem the virtuous and punish the corrupt; occultists with headquarters in the high mountains of Lebanon, where they spent mysterious weekends; hustlers, drug addicts, prostitutes, genuine artists, performers in the many plays that took place in the Theatre of Beirut and at the international festival at Balbaak. Beirut was famous for its posh cinemas — and they were rarely empty. Nowhere else did people worship the world of make-believe as in Beirut, or mixed their language as here: *Merci kteer. Bonjour aleekum*. Beirut in the early 1970s was exciting, arousing, corrupt, vulgar, refined and dangerous.

I often thought that Lebanon closely resembled the cedar tree on the country's flag. There is no center to a cedar; no main branch out of which subsidiary branches take off. Every branch is a main branch. The tree takes up a huge space, its branches spreading sideways on every side almost parallel to the ground. It is an attractive tree if planted in a spacious terrain: Its existence, like its beauty, depends on its branches having enough room to spread out. But Lebanon is a small land. The diverse religious communities that make up the country did not seem to come together in any strong center; nor did they show much tolerance toward each other. As long as the contradictions among the groups could be contained, the diversity made for an attractive mix of people. During my time in Lebanon I was constantly aware of a violence simmering just below the surface. Fortunately for me I had already left when in the latter part of 1973 this violence erupted into a brutal civil war that raged for fifteen years.

Amid this bustling chaotic metropolis lay the orderly and well-functioning campus of AUB. It stretched down the hill from Bliss Street all the way to the sea. Once you left the noisy street and entered the campus you found yourself in a different world of open spaces, greenery, attractive buildings, and strategically placed wooden benches where lovers sat beneath the huge cedars and looked westward to the Mediterranean. Upon leaving the university library, on the stretch leading to the main gate building, you could see the Lebanese mountains with the white snow on the one side and the deep blue sea on the other.

The tranquility I experienced during my first few weeks on the AUB campus was not to last. One morning, a few weeks after classes began, I entered the campus to find a student handing out leaflets declaring a strike. The student politics on campus were a reflection of the complicated situation between the right-wing Christian phalange and the left-wing Lebanese and Palestinians outside its well-protected walls.

My friends from Birzeit and I had joined AUB in midstream, during our junior year. All of us had done very well at Birzeit and were serious students. But Beirut and AUB offered many temptations. We all lived in one of the two dormitories, Penrose and Newman. The rooms were small, and it was difficult to study in them. For me the experience of living with friends in such close quarters was new. It was expected that we would all take part in student political activities. After all, we were Palestinian; we must therefore be politically active. I tried going to the meetings held in the dormitory but soon gave up. Despite the chaos of the strike and the occupation of various buildings, I continued to concentrate on my studies.

"How can you possibly disregard everything else and read Locke?" Khalil Mahshi, my roommate, wanted to know. He believed that we had a responsibility as students to support Palestinian politics. In his eyes I was alienating myself and losing out on important experiences. The pressure to participate increased when my friends began volunteering as teachers at the Palestinian refugee camps. Even then I stayed away. The student strike ended with the dismissal of more than a hundred students, including several of my friends.

The initial storm of strikes and student violence soon subsided, but the political discussions continued. Important seminars took place on campus involving such thinkers as the Syrian Sadiq Jallal el Azem, who had written a critique of the PLO's revolutionary thinking. I attended these but found that I could only be a passive listener. I didn't know enough about revolutionary thought to be able to participate actively in its analysis. The only positions I espoused were those of my father — I had none of my own — and these were too unpopular and conciliatory to be shared with the extremist student body. I held on to my homebred political truths and concentrated on my studies.

I was convinced that my interests lay outside the realm of politics. I welcomed the chance to be away from the influence of my parents. In the silence of my own mind, I knew that I would eventually form my own opinions about myself and my world. Geographically, Beirut was only a few hours' drive from Ramallah, yet I felt much farther from home than that. There was no telephone communication, and travel was only possible through the most circuitous route. The written word would now be my only means of communication with my father. I knew that this had many advantages. Through my letters I could communicate with him in a way that I had been unable to do face to face. I relished the fact that I would finally be able to share my innermost thoughts in a fuller and more profound way than I had ever been able to. I now had the opportunity to establish a deeper and more direct communication with my father, unmediated by my mother. Beirut provided me a temporary respite from the old patterns that had characterized our relationship.

The letters I wrote to my father were always in English. His to me were sometimes written in English, sometimes in Arabic. For me English was an easier medium for communication. All the examples I knew of the father–son relationship, whether in real life, in Arabic films, or books, were formal, respectful, and distant. The only models for the relationship that I aspired to could be found in English, hence it became my preferred language for communicating with Father. When I returned from university I found that he had filed all the letters I wrote to him. I had also kept his. These letters provide a full record of my time in Beirut. Going over them has made me realize that this was the golden period of my relationship with my father.

The first letter I wrote upon my arrival in Lebanon set the stage. I rather loftily cautioned my father:

> Now our only means of communication will be through letters. Therefore I intend to make my letters long and introspective. I shall write as though I were writing for my diary. So be tolerant.

In this first letter I wrote about an incident that had occurred at Ben Gurion Airport on my way out of Israel. What happened then had almost prevented me from leaving.

Most of my friends had come to Lebanon by land, crossing the Allenby Bridge over the Jordan River, then traveling from Jordan to Syria and on to Lebanon. My family did not think that this would be a safe path for me. I left via the Ben Gurion Airport to Nicosia, and from there took another plane to Beirut.

I took a taxi to the airport along with my mother and a few of my friends who were following the same route. My mother came to wave me off. At the outside entrance to the airport we were stopped and subjected to a thorough search by a young female soldier who insisted on emptying all our bags and going through our entire luggage piece by piece. The Ramallah taxi driver began to complain to me: "See how they treat us? We have to go through this every time. Can't you do something about it?"

The driver was taking all this passively but was trying to instigate me, a young man of twenty, to react.

At first I remained calm and decided I would limit my subversion to helping my friends rearrange their clothes in their suitcases. But as I did so I began to feel my blood boil. When my turn came she took everything out of my bag. When she got to my electric shaver she asked: "What is this?"

"An electric shaver," I said.

"Take it apart," she ordered.

I began to dismantle the machine piece by piece as I would when cleaning it, all the while growing more nervous and angry. When I finished I held all the pieces and threw them at her, saying, "Take them," then muttering: "*Ya kalbeh,*" you dog.

I had not expected that she would hear the last two words, but she did. To my surprise I saw her drop the pieces of my shaver and march off to her officer, saying that I had insulted her; she wanted me detained for insulting a soldier in the course of her duties. Promptly I was packed into the army jeep that was parked nearby and taken to the police station at the airport. My mother insisted, of course, on going with me.

My mother wanted me to apologize. I refused. I argued that I did not care about going to the university anymore. What use would it be to return holding the highest degree if I allow such a young woman soldier to insult me? My mother said that this was nonsense and I should not make a big issue out of this and that there was no time for philosophizing. Just apologize and let us avoid any further trouble, she said. She finally prevailed, and I was allowed to leave.

The first letter I received from my father referring to this incident was based on my mother's account, which he had accepted unquestioningly. His words reveal his pride at my principled stand before injustice. And yet this was moderated by his paternal concern over the vulnerability I had exhibited. He began the letter in an uncharacteristically indirect way and only later referred to the incident, to offer me advice. He used flower arranging, which he took as evidence of my love of beauty, as an example. This was a unique validation of an activity that at the time he could not have approved of — and one that may have increased his worries about my orientation. Now he used it as evidence of my love of the country and hoped that it would not be a passing phenomenon. He said that he had recently watched a television documentary on the life of Van Gogh:

> The announcer was showing us the beautiful paintings of this great artist. His love of nature was evident in the colors he used to represent the fields, the trees, and the rocks. He used color in a way that no other artist had done before. As I watched, you came to my mind. I remembered your interest in dried flowers which you picked, dried and mounted over the piece of olive wood and decorated with carefully picked rocks to make an attractive arrangement to decorate our house and attract attention to it. And I said to myself: is this love simply a passing romantic wave

which will eventually abate or is it a deeper entrenched love which shall not be swept aside by the winds of change and be eradicated by emotions. I asked myself this after your mother told me of what happened between you and the soldier at the airport and the comment you made before you traveled: do I return holding a doctorate just to be oppressed by a girl like this and be given such a harsh treatment? No my dear Raja. Such an incident shall not be the first or the last. You will be subjected to harsh treatment in your life whether from a girl like this one or from others or even from the closest people to you here in your own country. But this should not prevent you from returning to your homeland or influencing your attitude whatever success you may win and whatever glory you may achieve. I do not tell you this out of selfishness. I may not be around when you complete your education. I say this so that you will believe in what I have believed in and so that you will also assert these values in your children and grandchildren.

In this first letter my father opened up in a way that I had never known him to do when I lived at home. I took this as a sign of approval of my intention to send him what amounted to excerpts from my diary framed in the form of letters. I was not circumspect and included in these letters whatever I happened to be thinking about. If I happened to be contemplating the effect of each of my parents on me, I wrote about this. At the time I believed I was exercising extreme honesty. Now I have my doubts. I suspect I was offering rationalizations. In one of the letters I spoke of the "perfect balance" my parents offered in their influence on me. Father motivated me to pursue my ambition, while Mother offered the security of a return home after my ambitions were fulfilled. I used the occasion of making this discovery to declare my love to both of them equally.

I also shared with my father my thoughts about my past and my society. I wrote that I was distinguishing myself from my society, which I believed "kills the spark in people." I declared that I would not succumb to these lethal tendencies. "As you can read from my letter," I said, "I am struggling against all the despair and deadliness that the West Bank has put in me. Now I am an optimist."

It is clear that I was wary of going too far down this track of self-exposure without getting assurance of my father's approval. "In your next letter," I wrote, "I want you to tell me how you feel about the changes that are occurring in me."

My father responded:

> Do not expect me to write you a long letter dealing with what I think about the formation of your personality that you have long been discussing in your letters to us. The reason is that I want you to create for yourself what you wish for yourself. This is on the one hand; on the other I believe that you have laid out to yourself a good path, which shall lead to glory that will make us proud of you. This is my hope and my vision for you. I only have to pray to God to support you and help you fulfill your dreams.

This was the assurance I needed, and I now went ahead with confidence. This positive development in our relationship must also have encouraged me to choose the profession that would bring me back to Ramallah to work with him. When I told him of my decision to study law, my father's response may have been his most heartfelt:

> Your decision to go for law was a great relief to both your mother and myself. We both believe that you have finally arrived at a correct and wise conclusion. So carry on and do not hesitate to obtain the highest

degree in this line whether from a u.s. university or a
British one, though I prefer the latter.

The several objective changes that had occurred in my life all
seemed to put my father more at ease with me: I had decided to
follow his lead and study law; I was living in Beirut, a cosmopolitan
city where I was bound to learn the ways of the world; and I was
away from my mother and her direct influence on my character. He
no longer needed to use a stern, didactic tone in addressing me. And
his letters began to reveal another side of him. They read more like
the letters of a younger man with unfulfilled passions and aspirations. They helped me understand him better. My urge to express
more of myself to my father meant that I also wrote to him about my
doubts and confusion. Rereading such letters now, I am struck by
how unusual it was for a son, particularly in Arab society, to write so
openly to his father. But to me then, this was the chance to let my
father really know me. I told him of my concerns, about myself, my
studies, the way I was conducting my life, whether it was normal to
be enjoying my education so much, my rebellion and refusal to conform, even the nightmares from which I awoke screaming.

Yet my initial promise to share my innermost thoughts to my
father was not boundless. Once I fell in love, it seemed to flag.
Whether this was because my long and involved letters reflected my
initial loneliness after coming to Beirut, or because my assumption
that I was truly able to address my father as a friend and confidant
was illusory, it is difficult to know. What is clear is that for a long
time I kept my love for Carol from my father and made no reference to her in my letters.

Carol was an American woman a few years my senior. She had
bright brown eyes, light brown hair, and long, well-articulated fingers. She was a good piano player. She had a face that expressed
both strength and vulnerability. Her upper lip often seemed on the
verge of quivering. It was the face of a victim who had learned to
endure. Growing up she had been through difficult psychological

ordeals with her mother. Her parents were small-town factory workers. She was the only member of her family to have attended college. From our first encounter I recognized that behind her soft and vulnerable exterior lay a strong defiant will. I fell for this, and soon she left her apartment and came to live with me. Love had a profound effect on me. The AUB campus began to seem a very romantic place. The grass became greener; the benches beneath the trees overlooking the sea turned into enchanted niches made just for the two of us. We began to spend all of our free time together. The security that this relationship gave me enabled me to look back at my past with new eyes. I began to realize how confining and frustrating my life had been, and I promised myself that I would never again allow myself to be captured by my family in the same way. I often discussed my thoughts with Carol, who listened sympathetically and refrained from passing judgment. She must have been disappointed to hear of my negative attitude toward marriage and family life, but she probably thought I was passing through a rebellious phase.

I did not mention these emotions and reframings of my past in any of my letters to my father. What I now left out of my letters was just as telling as what I chose to include. But at the time I was not aware of my evasion. I took the frequency and length of my letters to my father as a sure sign of the depth and thoroughness of our communication. My idealism was so confining that it prevented me from realizing my own limitations.

My letters also reveal little interest on my part in learning about the life of my father, his work, and his political activity. And there was scant reference to the political situation that was engaging the interest and time of most of the students at AUB. My few references to the long and crippling students' strike reveal how little political sophistication I had and what little sympathy I showed to the students' positions. I was an outsider to the game of politics being played on campus. It was through such political involvement that students were developing their knowledge of how things worked in the Arab world, but I regretted the loss of precious time every time a strike kept us from class. I could see no reason why students should be involved in political struggles on or off campus. I believed that if we all worked hard to improve ourselves, our society would be better off. I saw all the political struggles as a flexing of muscles, unbecoming to university students. So I took myself to the library and immersed myself in my books.

One of my few exceptional references to political questions comes in a letter written during my second semester at AUB. I mentioned the proposed municipal election in the West Bank, which I knew my father was supporting.

> I must say that the trend here is very adverse to the elections. But that doesn't affect me. I believe what you are doing to be the right thing. In any case you should not be worried that it is in any way dangerous here for me. It is perfectly safe. The people here completely misunderstand.

Reading the letters and my father's responses to them I now realize that I too had an impact on him. I never suspected that my letters were encouraging, if not instigating, my father to go ahead with his project for the establishment of an Arab university in the West Bank. It is very likely that this idea came to him after I complained about my education at Birzeit, which I believed did not give students their due. I stressed how important it was for Palestinians to have a university with a liberal tradition, one that encouraged excellence in students.

In the years to come this project, like all the others he pursued, was opposed by the nationalists, who immediately declared that it was not proper to establish a university under occupation and that it would certainly be one dominated by the Israeli authorities. By this point he had worked hard for many years on the project and had succeeded, after strenuous efforts, in obtaining the required license from the authorities. He registered the Foundation for the Establishment of the University, rented offices, and so forth — but the university was never established. Recently I found among my father's papers stationery printed with the name of the foundation. Testimony of yet another of my father's dashed hopes.

Despite the difficult financial situation that my father had found himself in after the 1967 war, and the decline in his legal work, he never left me without money. He also never objected to any of my plans to travel on trips organized by the university. When I declared that I was intending to visit the Soviet Union, he wrote back that while my mother disagreed, he encouraged me to go and wished me a journey that would revive me mentally and physically after the hard work he knew I was doing. In the same letter he noted how encouraged he was by reading my letters with their lengthy descriptions of my personal and mental development. He said that I was *"on the right track."*

It was only toward the end of my second year at AUB that I told my father about my relationship with Carol. This must have worried him. He wrote back from New York, where he had traveled for work:

> Before leaving we received your long but very inter-
> esting letter. We were all happy that you are in good
> health and spirits. Your mother and myself were
> however a little worried about your friendship with
> the American girl, not that we have any objection to
> that but we are afraid that this may finally culminate
> in some matrimonial relation — a step which we
> both believe is premature as you have a long way to
> go before you take such a decision. So please son, be
> careful.

That summer of 1973 I was due to graduate from AUB. But I knew that my father would not be able to attend my graduation in

Beirut because his Jordanian passport had been withdrawn, and he could not enter Lebanon on an Israeli travel document. So I decided to skip the graduation ceremony. Carol had hoped that we would go together to Canada to continue our education at her university, McGill. She was working on Kafka and Mallarmé; I would work on Joyce. But this prospect never appealed to me. It would be a false life, I thought. Mine was another sort of challenge: to combine writing and the life of a professional lawyer, to find myself in my father's country.

So I came up with my own plan: I would accompany Carol to Europe. We would first go to France to visit an old friend of hers and then to Dublin, where I was anxious to visit the James Joyce Museum at the Martello Tower. There I would bid Carol farewell and return to London alone to start a second phase of my journey, which I believed I had to experience without her. I was able to convince myself that this was my own decision, not at all influenced by my father's words in his last letter to me.

CHAPTER TEN

AT DOVER I was stopped by the British border police and taken for questioning. Carol stood aside waiting for me.

I had then a long dark scruffy beard, long black hair, and piles of papers. The policeman wanted to know the true mission of this suspicious-looking Palestinian coming to Britain.

"Sight-seeing," I declared.

"And what about all these papers?" the immigration officer asked, his slightly open mouth resting on top of his folded hands as he tilted back in his chair to keep a safe distance from me.

"These are my diaries."

"I must examine them."

"I can't let you," I protested. "They are my private papers."

"I must examine them," the policeman repeated.

I was baffled. What about freedom of thought? How could a British officer not respect the privacy of my personal papers? I refused to hand them over and kept them close to my chest.

"You will not be allowed in unless I can look through these papers," he said with a tone of finality.

I was sure that I had the right to refuse to share my most intimate thoughts with a public officer, certainly in the West, in a country that celebrates civil rights. And yet unless I complied I would not be allowed into the country. I had no choice.

I put the papers on the table and the officer began to leaf through my illegible jottings. It was obvious that he could not make anything out, which only increased his suspicions. These must surely be secret messages.

"Read them to me," the officer ordered.

Why not? I felt that I now had the upper hand since without my help he would not be able to get anywhere.

"All of them?" I asked mockingly.

"No." He looked piqued. He flipped through until his eyes fell on a section that had the largest number of words with triple underlining. "This part here."

I took a chair next to the older man and began to read:

> Cold water surprises the skin of my face to life. My face exists as a part of me when will the rest of my body awaken? I must undo the process of subjugation and unleash the locks placed at the time when I could not allow myself to experience the new sensations because of fear. I am at the point of no return. I either work hard and complete the run now or never. I must explore to the end what I have begun.

"That's enough," said the officer. "Remove your papers. You can go now."

Carol was relieved to see me again. She had been worried that I would be turned back. We stayed in London for a few days and then traveled on to Dublin where we stayed at a bed-sit in Sandycove. That same afternoon we walked down to the Martello Tower. From this tower we would part ways. I had planned it this way. From where Joyce's hero, Stephen Dedalus, began his famous day, I would go off alone into the world.

A steep road curved down to the sea. The weather had started bright and clear but was beginning to change by the time we reached the tower. Perfectly round but short and stumpy, the Martello Tower was well preserved; it stood in repose on the shore a short distance from the sea. Both Carol and I were quiet as we approached. A fast-moving mist by now blocked the sun and turned the sea gray. As I walked toward the tower, I could hear the words of Joyce describing his companion: "Stately plump Buck Mulligan coming down the stairs bearing a bowl of lather on which a mirror and razor lay crossed." As I walked up the metal stairs to the iron door, I thought of the milk woman who "had darkened the doorway by her entering form." We were greeted by a young bearded Irishman with thick black hair. He said very little and left us to our own musings as we walked quietly and reverently around the circular room, examining the objects behind glass in the display shelves in the middle and all around the walls. We could see Joyce's round glasses, a few of his letters, some handwritten pages from manuscripts, and at the end, on the right-hand side of the iron gate, his death mask revealing a tense expression with tightly closed thin lips. After making this respectful, silent round of the objects on display, we climbed up the circular stairs, examining as we went up the round gun rest. When we got to the top the sun was completely concealed behind the mist, and the air was cold and moist. As I stood under the light drizzle looking out at the gray sea, my cheeks felt cold and dry, my lips were bloodless; only my eyes kindled with the energy of the promise of the glorious future that I believed awaited me.

My head felt heavy with words. I was aware that verbalized reality was more accessible to me than sensual experience. The rain was getting stronger. I tilted up my face and let the cold rain pour down my cheeks. My voyage back to a full life was beginning just as I had planned.

"How austere," I heard Carol mutter as she stood alone looking out to the gray and mist. She was in a somber mood. This made her face seem longer than usual. The mouth seemed to lag, creating a wide space between the upturned nose and upper lip, increasing the look of vulnerability on her face. Her long brown hair clung to her coat as she stood on top of the tower as though in mourning, looking westward to the invisible horizon and exclaiming again: "How austere!"

I could hear her weeping. I thought of going over to her, taking her in my arms and consoling her, but decided against it. I knew why she wept. We had been through this before. She had told me that what I called the rational path, the practical thing to do, was a cruel choice. She could not understand how I could so easily brush aside emotions with the mind. How could I be so indifferent to the pain she was feeling because of our parting? Why could I not allow myself to feel sorrow? Her tears flowed and I stayed away, loveless and cold, like a tower enclosed on itself, refusing entry to anyone.

She wrapped her arms around her body and seemed so alone, so distant, so vulnerable. I walked around and stopped on the opposite side from where she stood.

I left Carol at the tower, walked down the spiral stairs and on to the seashore. There were silver slithers of water on the beach with black soil like soot between. After walking a short distance I stopped and looked back at the tower.

The image of Carol standing alone in the tower crying stayed with me. As I took the ferry back after saying my good-bye I watched the receding shoreline in the drizzle and mist and wished I too could cry.

It was four-thirty in the morning when I reached London. Too late to find a hotel. I walked out of the train station at King's Cross into a city cold with smog. I found a bench in Euston Park and sat like a derelict with the homeless and drunks, waiting for the first light of day. Soon I was visited by a policeman whose mouth was almost gagged by the black strap of his helmet. He looked at me with suspicion then demanded to know who I was and where I came from. "Can I see your passport?" he asked.

I didn't have one. I only had a travel document issued by the Israeli military authorities. I handed it over to him.

He flipped through it then turned it over to examine the covers. *What sort of document is this,* he must have been wondering. Then his eye fell on the entry stamp given to me at Dover. He closed it and examined me once again.

"You're not supposed to be here in the park at this hour," he said with his warm breath seeping underneath his gag.

"I have just come back from Dublin and will find accommodation as soon as it is light," I said.

The policeman's towering presence lingered for a moment. Then he slipped away and I was left alone with my luggage on the wet bench in the mist.

My first year in London proved very difficult. I was following two programs: my father's and my own. In the first I was to study law in order to return to the West Bank to practice my father's profession. Nothing could be more conventional. According to the second, however, I was a liberated, progressive young man who believed in personal freedom, in free love, in living outside society. The conventional man would dwell in the profession of law, the nonconformist in the world of letters. It was important to do both to preserve the two sides of my character. In order to write, I had to pursue my research into aspects of myself that remained mysterious to me. This research would be done through the study of philosophy, which I would pursue alongside law. The law would prepare me for life in society, the writing for the life of the mind.

But my life in London did not turn out as I had expected. I had been ill advised. I was studying law at a college that prepared students for the bar examinations. This meant that there was no room for a social life. I also enrolled at University College, where I was reading philosophy in preparation for a master's degree. This was a time when empiricism and linguistic analysis were supreme in English philosophical thought. It was generally agreed that Continental philosophers were not proper philosophers. Sartre was dismissed by most as pretentious and unworthy of the attention of serious students. Some went as far as to call contemporary Continental philosophers charlatans. It was the philosophy of these charlatans that interested me more than that of the respected logical positivists, but I had come to the wrong place to pursue it.

I ran between the College of Law and University College and had no time for either. I found London an altogether cold and uninviting place. The popular slogan was sos (Shut Off Switch), and the villains were my fellow Arabs who in 1973 had begun the oil embargo. I found it very difficult to make friends and spent most of my time alone with my books and my sterile thoughts.

In one of my letters from London, I complain that Father was typing his letters to me. This meant that he was dictating them to his secretary. I was missing the communication we had established through our correspondence when I was studying literature in Beirut. I had come to London with great expectations, hoping to find acceptance, the community that had escaped me in Lebanon. I didn't. I was in the wrong place. The students at the college of law had one goal: to return to their respective countries with an English legal qualification and concentrate on making lots of money. Those at University College were passionate about analytic philosophy. So I remained more alone than I had ever been. Something was wrong and I did not know what it was. In my encounters with colleagues, I would mutter aloud my introspective monologue and would puzzle and embarrass my listeners.

As I was going through these difficult times, Carol persisted in writing from her university in Montreal. Her letters were full of love and a yearning to be together again. Despite my loneliness, I remained stubbornly resistant to her appeal even when I was starved of love, companionship, and caring. Her letters were like a persistent banging on the windows of my solitary existence, and yet I found myself unable to respond. They failed to move me. I put them aside and suspected that she was trying to trap me. By the third term, she gave up.

Was I incapable of love? Most likely so. Love does not grow under conditions of prudence, and everything in my life now was programmed, including my human relations. Carol was writing to me about breaking away from the life of her family in Middle America. And she assumed that I too would eventually be capable of doing the same. She took no account of the great pull my family and society had on me. How could she not have realized that I was so immature, so dependent, so emotionally stifled; that I came from an insecure society that was claiming me? I had to plan for my future in a conventional career. I could not continue my relationship with Carol, because it was simply not practical. I had been warned so often by my family against falling for a Western woman. And by my grandmother against falling for any woman: "A woman may not be what she seems," she used to warn me. "One woman I knew would bite hard at the table when the man was gone to keep down her anger and stop herself from screaming. She did not want him to know how she really was. She wanted to appear mild and soft. It all came out after they got married. This is why you should be very careful. You are too naive. Don't take women for what they seem. Be very careful. Don't be deceived." It was indeed unlikely that I was capable of love.

It was as though I was living my life on two levels. On the one hand I was a Palestinian who came from a place riddled with insecurities. I was considered fortunate to be able to pursue legal education in London. My father was anxious to get me involved in his practice before his retirement. From the outside, I had everything going for me. I was getting the best legal education and I would be returning to join the foremost legal firm in the country. Palestinians cannot take chances with their lives. It would be unheard of to take a year off to travel and "find myself." There was no time to waste.

My profound need for my father's acceptance made me do much to please him. There was no doubt that what I cared most about was my relationship with him. Now that law was my main course of study and I had severed my ties with Carol, I was redeemed in his eyes and could be abandoned by him. Our brief period of communication in Beirut was over. My pursuit of law would make of me a pale reflection of my father's external self. Had I disappointed him by yielding to his expressed desire and abandoning literature and my friendship with Carol? Was it his cherished secret hope that I would pursue the nonconformist path that he was denied and fulfill him through my success as an artist?

I was so alone, so confused, so profoundly sad. I had abandoned all I cared for to win over my father and he was sending me short typed perfunctory letters. My psychological anguish began to express itself physically. I suffered piercing pains in my stomach. During the summer I spent in Ramallah after my first year in London I consulted a physician, who diagnosed the pain as a symptom of tension and gave me an analgesic. But this provided only temporary relief. When I returned to London in September the pain increased. I did not know what to do. I had abandoned Carol, who had been the only person who understood and loved me and with whom I had felt physical fulfillment. The flat I returned to in London had been in use the year before by a family friend who had partied there before handing it over and had left all his garbage to rot for the month between his departure and my arrival. He had also bashed in the bathroom door. The state of the apartment increased my sense of confusion, loss, and despair. I did not know who to turn to. I desperately wanted to make a fundamental change in my life but I did not even know how to start.

When I was in Beirut I accepted that the kind of questions that interested me could not be shared, but I thought it would be different in London. This was the home of my favorite authors, people who had written on the questions that interested me. But I could not find like-minded people. I tried going to poetry readings but was unable to forge any friendships. My unresolved psychological difficulties were progressively turning my body into a tangle of nerves, preventing me from eating or even breathing properly. I tried abandoning my body by imitating the behavior of those who seemed to be leading normal happy lives. I went out to bars drinking and smoking. But I always knew that I was only mimicking.

I began to blame my predicament on the West. All I could see was drabness and rationality. There was no poetry, no lyricism, no flair. My mind could not take flight the way it used to. It would be called back to the ancient blackened buildings of Lincoln's Inn, where barristers were rushing to the court in black gowns and gray wigs. I began to realize how much I despised this place and the people in it. How could such a culture have produced such great writers? I knew that the artists I was interested in had been rebels. But my own rebellion was focused on another place and a different set of problems.

I went back in my mind to the beginning of the Israeli occupation of my country and analyzed its effect on me and on my relationship with my father. I understood that I had suppressed my true feelings for the Israelis because of my father's position, which I now began to realize was not necessarily my own. One day I surprised one of my philosophy teachers, an expert on Marxism, by declaring that I finally understood what evil meant. Perhaps I should allow myself the freedom to feel the hate I had always denied. I pursued emotional exercises and learned to give free rein to all the feelings I had prohibited myself. All this made me even more strange and distant from the other students.

I was going out disheveled, uncombed, with circles around my eyes from sleeplessness or hours of light sleep when I would dream of myself dreaming. One part of me would refuse to lose consciousness and carry on with the reel of words that now accompanied me day and night. I longed for just one other human being who had gone through similar experiences. Perhaps one of my professors at the university was right when he insinuated that I was having a nervous breakdown. And yet consulting a professional was not something I was willing even to consider. To do so would mean to declare my failure.

Then Muneer appeared.

CHAPTER ELEVEN

MUNEER WAS MY cousin, son of my aunt, Julia's adversary in the border struggle who was guilty of planting the passionflower in the disputed territory. He was a few years older than me. I had met him at his parents' house when we were growing up, but we were never friends.

Muneer's background was similar to mine but he had responded very differently. He too had attended the American University of Beirut, where, like me, he had been a loner. He had a particular attachment to his grandfather, who had fathered six daughters along with Muneer's father and had passed all his property to his son. Muneer, too, was an only son until he was fifteen, and his grandfather had always assured him that all the property would pass to him. When his brother was born he went into a rage. He felt it was a plot by his mother to disinherit him. He never forgave his mother and believed she was the cause of all the problems at home. His mother and father had different temperaments. The father was soft spoken and a peaceful conciliator; the mother a highly intelligent, angry, unfulfilled woman with a kind heart and a sharp tongue.

Muneer was always given the best. As a student at AUB his father gave him enough money to live in a luxury apartment, to the dismay of his mother. He boasted to his colleagues that he was going to make his first million before he was thirty. After university he had worked for a short period in Saudi Arabia, the only two years in his life when he held a regular job. Afterward he pursued get-rich-quick schemes and began his perilous sojourns in the world. When he came over to London to see me for the first time he had been roughed up in a bar in Colombia. He stood in the middle of my small bed-sit and announced in his deep husky voice: "I was mugged. I could have been killed. They converged on me in the bar in Colombia. Fifteen of them and hit me with glass bottles. It was a miracle that I escaped alive. Look at my hand. See the stitches. There are nine of them."

It was the first time that I had heard the word *mugged*. And the first time that I had been with someone who had been mugged.

"But I've had enough of violence. *Ya zalameh,* man, I'm tired. I tell you I'm tired. I want to rest. Go home and rest. Just live simply in my grandfather's old house in Ramallah and rest. I cannot go on like this anymore."

His plan was to take up employment again in Saudi Arabia for a year or two, after which he would return to live in Ramallah. He had come to London this time for an interview with a man who worked for a Saudi company. Muneer was an elegant man, short, slim, and well proportioned. He dressed well and had an expensive taste in clothes. He always wore Bally shoes and stamped his feet as he walked in small stiff steps. His movements were sharp and angular. His voice was deep but he blurted out his words in a commanding tense way. He spoke and acted in the raw manner of a young man whose voice had just broken. He could be very gentle and a pleasure to be with when he was happy but without warning could switch into a brittle, vindictive, combative man. His voice would become sharp and go into a falsetto as he asked in a pleading manner expressive of deep hurt, *"Leash? Leash?"* — Why? — and move away without waiting to hear a response.

When he came to visit me at the beginning of my second year I was living in a flat in Beaufort Gardens in Knightsbridge. It was not big enough for two people. But before we could find Muneer a place to stay, he got a message that his businessman interviewer was delayed and would not be coming to London for another ten days. Rather than wait in London, I suggested that we drive up to Dublin, where I would have the chance to again visit the Martello Tower. I viewed Muneer as a reckless adventurer who would make a good travel companion. But I was wary of him too, and felt that I must help him put his life in order.

Muneer rented a car. We traveled through the green Irish countryside along small meandering roads. He drove as if he was sure of the road. But I had no fear. I had put my trust in him despite his erratic driving. He never anticipated curves, but like my father he had firm control of the wheel.

When we reached Dublin I headed straight to the Martello Tower. Unlike my last visit this time the sky was blue and cloudless. Everything was open and sparkly. I could see how green the area around the tower was and wondered if it had once been a moat, the tower a fortress. I walked down the slope to the apex of the curve, to the tower. How beautiful it was, enfolded between the curving slope and the sea; how austere, Carol had said. Now it did not seem austere at all. Or was she thinking of me? I realized what a heavy price I had paid for my ruthlessness. But I did not speak to Muneer of Carol as he did not speak to me about many aspects of his life. It was better this way. In our different ways we had both had hard blows and were on the verge of a change. Our past was our own. In the case of Muneer I preferred not to know about the work he was involved in. I was doing my best to be non-judgmental, but this would be more difficult if he confirmed what I suspected. We stood in silence under the clear sky on top of the tower, each with his own thoughts, just as I had stood twelve months earlier with Carol.

We arrived back in London a few days before Muneer's interview with the Palestinian businessman. We now had to find a place for Muneer to stay. We put our bags in my apartment and went out to search.

There was a sign on the building opposite mine: VACANCY. Muneer rang the bell, but no one answered. He rang again. No answer.

"It seems there's no one there," I said. "Maybe it isn't vacant anymore."

"Then why keep the sign?"

Muneer put his hand on the bell and kept it suppressed. Hurried nervous steps could be heard approaching the door.

"Bastard. Son of a bitch," a man cursed as he opened the door. "What do you think you're doing, eh? You should be ashamed of yourself."

"The sign says you have a vacancy," Muneer said in a low monotone voice, looking at the man calmly with his head tilted sideways.

"Even if there were vacancies I would not lease it to you. You get out of here right away or I'll call the police. You hear?"

"Kharah alik," shit on you, Muneer responded. We left as the man slammed the door behind us.

This then is how my quiet well-to-do neighbors in Knightsbridge can behave, I thought, absolving Muneer of any blame. Ultimately we succeeded in finding a place for Muneer in the area and continued to meet for meals. Over one I asked Muneer whether he would ever get married and raise a family of his own. His answer was: "If I find a good woman, I will live with her. But I will not bring up children. My seed has passed. I've fulfilled that obligation. Continuity is assured."

"Do you have a child?"

"Yes, somewhere in this world. I have not seen him and he wasn't conceived with a woman I loved. It was an accident. I was in Denmark and a young girl was staying in the next room. She came over to me and told me that after a night with her boyfriend she wasn't sexually satisfied, and she was afraid she would become frigid because it was her first time. I told her, 'When you are starting you need an experienced man. Your boyfriend is still fresh. He doesn't know how to satisfy you.' That night she knocked at my door. She wanted me to fuck her. I did and my seed passed that night. I am sure of it. I have a child by her. Now I need not worry. My seed has passed."

He saw that I was puzzled and continued: "My karma is not family life. I've tried many lives. In Thailand I lived on the hill with two women. Each was as beautiful as the sun. I called one sun and the other moon. I had a motorcycle and whizzed down the hill at a hundred miles an hour. It scared the shit out of the little Thais. They were afraid of me, the poor people. Such gentle people. So kind. The place was like a paradise on earth. But I got tired of it at the end. I left. I didn't want to be bogged down. Then I went to South America and was mugged. Now I'm sick of this whole business."

I wondered what my karma was.

My family didn't like Muneer and I knew what they would think if they knew I was befriending him. But the more I came to know him the more I believed that he was a good man. Perhaps he was misjudged. Of course he had gone astray but he was determined to change and to conform. And because I cared for him I was going to help him. I knew my having faith in him would be beneficial. I did not need to fake this. I *had* faith in him. I was even proud of him. He had come from a similar background and had managed to break all the rules. In my mind he was a self-made man who rejected the burden of the past and had re-created himself.

As I listened to Muneer's experiences, I began to put my own into context. For the first time I saw how I had made Ramallah my whole world, and the political conflict between the Arabs and the Jews my only reality. Muneer was helping me accept that Palestine was but a small part of the larger world. Why was I blocking out all the rest?

Still the voice of my father told me to beware. Muneer went against everything that I had been told was good and right. He did what was bad. He lived dangerously. He did not do proper acceptable work. He was not living as society expected. He was not married, as a man of his age should be. He did not have a job. He was not settled. He had been in dangerous situations and had associated with the worst elements of this world. He was not a good man. He was the kind of man I should avoid. He would lead me astray if I stayed with him. "He will utterly destroy you," I could hear my father say.

But Muneer was bringing me out of my loneliness and I was grateful. He was very gentle with me. I was aware of how different we were and yet I appreciated his honesty and his friendship. When I spoke of myself Muneer would listen and not comment. Through his silence I could hear myself justifying the choices I had made, and they were beginning to sound false. The more I tried to argue my case to Muneer the more hollow I sounded to myself.

The day of the interview Muneer had a lot to drink. I was unhappy about this but I could not stop him. I had tried to stay with him for most of the time before the interview because I could tell that he was nervous. But a nervous man can consume a lot of drinks in a brief period of time. Muneer went to the Ritz, where the interview was to take place, heavily intoxicated. I remained in my room in Beaufort Gardens waiting for his return.

He was gone for several hours and I waited anxiously. At eight-thirty the bell rang. I opened the door and saw that Muneer had that look of resignation and peace about him. "How did it go?" I asked.

"He is an elderly man. It turns out that he knew my father. He is soft spoken and is the personnel manager at the company. He asked me about my life and I couldn't lie. He advised me to become steady and to change my life if I wanted a job in Saudi Arabia. He thinks I can trim myself to size in order to qualify for his job. I don't want any advice. I don't want anyone telling me what to do. I could see it started even before I took the job. I too had things to tell him. I had advice to give him. It isn't for me, *ya akhi,* my brother. I am beyond it already. I cannot go back to what I left ten years ago. I was there for two years, playing the role of the young manager making money. But I left. I cannot go back now. To hell with it, man. I will go to India. I sent a cable to Sri Pandit to book a place for me. It is time for India now. This is the present cycle in my life. I know it. I want to go to Auroville. *Khalas. Khalas.* Enough. I am done with this cycle."

There was nothing I could do now. Muneer had obviously not been offered the job. He had no other interviews lined up, and perhaps he would never interview again in his life. Now he was determined to go to India. All I could do was listen to his plans for a new life before losing him and returning to my lonely existence in the apartment with the bashed-in door.

Muneer repeatedly described himself as a water kettle that, from excessive boiling, forms scales. If the scales are not scraped or dissolved, they clog the nozzle. "I need to go back to India periodically to scrape the scales produced by life in the West. There I unclog the paths to my soul so that my soul can take flight again."

During our trip to Dublin, Muneer had talked about authors like Hermann Hesse, Ouspinsky, and Madame Blavatsky. When we got back to London the first thing I did was to buy some of these books. I began to see that the writings addressed some of my deepest concerns. They treated the body and the mind as one without the artificial division found in Western philosophy. Then I learned of hatha yoga, the yoga of the mind, in which breathing integrates the soul with the body. The breath, passing through the various organs of the body, revives them. I began to suspect that such practices might solve many of my problems.

India was not in my worldview at this time. My two worlds were the Middle East and the West. There was nothing else. Yoga had always seemed to me magic and acrobatics. When I was young an Indian man who claimed to be a yogi was brought to the Grand Hotel in Ramallah to perform at the Casino in the evening. I was taken to attend the show. He was a very thin man with a shaved head. He twisted his body in the most astounding manner. His performance that evening was shared with a trapeze artist who swung her body in the air. The Indian dazzled us with his stunts on the ground, writhing like a snake and rippling his stomach. And she made dangerous jumps in the air. This was a yogi to me: a performer with complete control over his stomach. Because I had long been suffering from stomach disorders, the possibility that the stomach could be controlled and moved around in this incredible manner fascinated me.

When Muneer spoke of India now, I listened. He told me about Aurobindo, a very different kind of yogi than the acrobat I had watched at the Ramallah Grand Hotel. And he told me about Auroville, the city of dawn, a utopian experiment in new living.

On Muneer's last evening in London, we went out to an Italian restaurant in Knightsbridge close to where I was living. Muneer ordered fresh oysters for both of us. He wanted me to try them. He also ordered chilled white wine. It was a deluxe restaurant. We were well served. We sipped luxuriously at the wine. Muneer told me to suck the oysters into my mouth and keep them there until they melted. The taste of the sea was in them, he said. I felt the slimy live animal in my mouth changing its texture. One living body acting on another to assimilate and consume it.

"How do you like it?" Muneer asked.

"It's very good."

"Shall we order another bottle of wine?"

"Why not. You know, Muneer," I said, "being with you has meant so much to me. I feel so much better. My breathing has improved. I feel myself more alive."

"Yes I know. I have also felt the change in you. I feel you very deeply. You have a very special relationship to your body. You have a sensitivity that I have never seen in anyone else. You must be careful about yourself. Be kind to your body. Give it attention. I set aside one day a week to take care of my body. Spend time checking it. Cutting the hair and nails and washing it carefully."

I wished I could do the same.

"You must be aware you are a special man. You are like a little Buddha, *ya akhi*. Your body is still pure. It has not yet been defiled. I feel you with my body. I know what you suffer. You are close to me. My body feels you. Do you hear?"

Tears began to rush down my cheeks. I was so touched. I raised my hand and Muneer raised his and we held hands over the table.

"I love you, man," Muneer whispered.

Following the gloom and despair that I was living through just a month before, I had now felt the loving care of a new friend. I was learning about a new experiment in living and about the different kinds of yoga. I learned that the breath is the soul. Was this not what I had been seeking: a discipline that did not deny the body or the mind; one that integrated the two and cherished the physical without denying the spiritual?

I calculated how much it would cost to live in India for a few months and what the plane fare would be. Even with the airfare three months in India would cost less than what I spent in London in two weeks. I could afford to leave my studies for three months without losing the year, and I would take my law books with me and continue studying.

But would I dare take such a trip with Muneer? I knew very well what my father thought of him. He was a failure. He was a rebel. He was up to no good. He squandered his father's money. He was not kind and considerate to his mother. He had not taken care of his sisters. He did not measure up to or fulfill any of his father's hopes and expectations. He was bad. Bad. Bad. With nothing to redeem him. I knew exactly how my father would react if I told him that I was leaving my studies in London to go to India with Muneer to practice yoga. *Yoga?* he would scream. *Yoga? Sitting down immobile in meditation like a fool. Is this why I spend my money on you? To go and practice yoga? What good could it bring you? What would be solved by it? The Palestinian–Israeli conflict? How would you be able to take care of yourself? Is this what I brought you up to become? It is all the bad influence of this evil man on you. I am sure of it. He has always despised me and is now getting back at me through you. This is it. He finds a good steady boy getting on with his life and his studies and he corrupts him, revels in corrupting him. This is all we need: India and yoga and ashrams. This is all that a people like us who are suffering under occupation need.*

For weeks the voice of my father and the voice of Muneer struggled within me. But while I listened to both and considered both I also felt the difference my relationship with Muneer had already made on my life. I was happier than I had ever been. I stopped seeing myself as a complete failure. My body was beginning to come alive again. This must be good. *What use is my education and my success in life if I am miserable? When does a man go after experiences if not when he is still a student? If I don't do it now then when? I will only be leaving for three months and will come back and resume my studies. And it will be less expensive than life in London. I will not be abusing my father's resources. I have followed father's ways long enough. It is time now to follow my own heart and try this out.*

In the end, India won. But I had not been rash about it. I had been deliberate and conscious. I believed I would be able to explain my reasoning thoroughly to my father. I also believed that once I explained my father would understand and would support me. I decided not to phone him, however. I did not want to hear him tell me not to go and then have to disobey him. And anyway, I was better at explaining things in writing than over the telephone.

The evening after Muneer left I stayed in my room intending to compose the letter to my father. As I started, I remembered that I had been invited for dinner by the Palestinian family that owned my flat. I decided not to go. I wanted to concentrate on the letter. At a quarter to ten I could hear heavy banging on my door. It was Sami, their son. He must have been sent by his family to check on me.

"Raja," he howled, "are you there?"

I started to jump up to open the door and then sat back. I listened to the incessant knocking. He must have sensed that I was hiding in the room and this made him more persistent. I was lying doubled over on the bed. There were two possibilities: opening the door and joining the party, or remaining silent, invisible. The tension caused a familiar sharp piercing pain in my stomach. I had experienced the same pain when my own family forced similar choices on me. Now I had a third choice, one that this Palestinian family in London could not possibly understand.

My father had urged me to stay on good terms with this family; they were from Palestine's aristocracy and friends of his from Jaffa.

When I saw them, I was forced to listen to their stories about their life in Jaffa and was never able to talk about my own experiences in Palestine. In their eyes, Palestine was Jaffa, and Palestinian history stopped in 1948. They had plugged themselves into London's aristocracy and continued their frivolous, empty life. I often felt fake and depleted at their parties. Initially I was innocent enough to try for genuine communication. Their door would be opened by a butler, who ushered me into a world of display and pretension. Drinks were served by swerving waiters, already intoxicated, dressed in white. Amid the expensive pieces of tasteless decor I would look for someone to talk to without affectation and posturing, but it always proved futile. These people had long lost their ability to act as genuine human beings.

I was finished with this sort of self-denial. We may both have been Palestinian but their values were not my values. They had learned to survive in London through pretension and hypocrisy. I decided to stay away from their parties. Other parts of my being craved expression. I needed India for that. *India?* I could hear them gasp. *That dirty place? What do you want to go to India for?*

I remained still, hardly breathing as the knocking persisted. I was determined not to open the door. This time I would not seek validation from my father or his friends. But I would write a letter explaining my decision to my father. I would not ask for his permission or his blessing and I would not mail the letter from London. I decided to mail it from India after my arrival.

Soon the knocking ceased and I heard Sami's footsteps going down the stairs. Once again the apartment fell silent. I was left alone bundled on the bed with Sami's garbage and the door he had once smashed. I resumed my writing, explaining to my father the absurdity of my life in London and my hopes to heal my body and redeem my soul practicing yoga. The next morning I left London for Bombay.

CHAPTER TWELVE

I CARRIED THE letter with me on the plane to Bombay the next day. From there I transferred to Madras, where Muneer was waiting for me in the airport lounge. He plopped me into a shabby taxi, which took us to the headquarters of the Theosophical Society at Adyar two miles away from the teeming city. Muneer thought that it was best for me to take India in stages, otherwise I might be overwhelmed.

In London we had visited the offices of the Theosophical Society and became members so we could stay as guests in its Great Hall in India. The headquarters included a large park with representations of all the great religious figures in low relief: Buddha, Christ, Zarathustra, Krishna, Nanak, Moses, Confucius, and Orpheus, among others. The park extended between the ocean and the estuary of the Adyar River.

We were given rooms adjacent to each other on the second floor. I had a large airy sitting room with my own bathroom. The bedroom had a tiled floor inlaid with the mystic star and a four-poster bed with a mosquito net. The room opened onto a veranda where every evening Muneer and I sat on wicker chairs reminiscent of those on my grandmother's balcony in Ramallah. The long, wide veranda overlooked the Adyar River, and from where we sat we could hear the low murmur of the water in its slow flow to the sea, the gurgling of the frogs, the sharp continuous buzz of the crickets, and the general humid breathing of the lush growth of bushes and trees that enveloped us. It was the perfect way to begin my India trip.

Every evening we sat late into the night talking about the past and common family members. We were in a perfectly protected world of our own. London, Ramallah, and the world of my father seemed remote. Now I could concentrate on my body and meditate on the state of my diaphragm. Nothing else was more important. My father's voice was receding. I was coming to my own. We had memorable evenings on that enchanted verandah, I sat in the lotus position doing my breathing exercises and meditating, and Muneer in his own faraway world. When I thought of my father I focused on how I could communicate the significance of my experiences. But I was no longer troubled by his expected cynicism. I no longer needed his validation. I was no longer reluctant to delve farther into the world of my own being.

The next morning I walked down a narrow winding footpath between the large thickets that lined the banks of the river. I could hear the scratching sound of a crawling creeper and the whiz of the twig as it snapped straight after a bird flew away. I was alone in the mudflats, but I felt that all the plants and animals had noted my presence. I bent my head to avoid a branch stretched in my way and when I emerged from the thickets saw the gray ocean spread before me. Without thinking I ran to it. I did not stop until I was immersed in the water and my linen gown was floating. I was pleased by the spontaneity of my action, until the wet pajamas clinging to my body reminded me of those times when as a four-year-old child I involuntarily wet myself in bed as I dreamed of water.

I stayed in India less than three weeks. During the first week, my father remained present in my thoughts. For the first time in my life I began to get some perspective on his personality and was able to see him as a separate individual. I realized how he had limited himself by identifying so closely with his role as a lawyer. Muneer believed that he played games. "He hides behind a veil," Muneer declared. "I could see his mask. I fought it out with him on several occasions and he didn't like it. He became defensive and would not listen to me. I lost him."

"He's a great man, the top of his profession," I said in his defense.

"Aziz may be a good lawyer, but you are the better man. You have good vibrations. I love you more than I love my own brother."

I accepted Muneer's special love for me. I depended on him to help me challenge the voice of my natural father who claimed me through what I now believed was emotional blackmail: I could not be a man until he declared me one, and he would not do so until I satisfied his standards. I knew very well what these standards were — completing my studies, qualifying as a lawyer, joining his practice, marrying, begetting children, and building a house. It did not matter what state my soul was in as long as I doggedly fulfilled these obligations and conformed to the norm. But would I be happy following this traditional course? My father had expressed no sympathy for my physical problems. He continued to believe that my ailments could be treated if I subjected myself to a good physician. Yet by reducing everything to the physical, he was denying the best part of me.

Muneer took me on the second stage of our journey, to the Sri Aurobindo Ashram at Pondicherry. During my second week there I grew dissatisfied with the lack of structure. A good student, I felt the need for more formal instruction in yoga. Muneer investigated the possibilities and found an ashram not far from Pondicherry that offered instruction in yoga, Sanskrit, traditional Indian medicine, and a whole range of things I was interested in. I would join for a month and hoped I would gain a deeper, more formal understanding of yoga and ancient Indian philosophy and culture. I wanted Muneer to join me, but he said that the discipline would kill him. He did accompany me on the first exploratory visit, though.

We both rode in a rickshaw driven by a young man with powerful leg muscles. It was late in the evening and the sun was just beginning to set. It gave the rice paddies a deep orange glow; there was a light refreshing breeze. As I looked at the fields on both sides of the narrow road I wondered if I was making the right decision. The worst part was that I would be away from Muneer.

The new ashram was in a large lush tropical garden. We entered through a metal gate into the main building, which had a

Julia, standing on the right, with her mother, father, two brothers, and sister at the Nassar Hotel in Haifa around 1920.

My grandmother Julia and grandfather Justice Saleem Shehadeh in their garden in Jaffa before 1948.

Julia, on the right, with Azizeh, the woman who was her live-in housekeeper for many years. This photo was taken after 1948.

Aziz as a child with sister Mary and cousin in
Jerusalem around 1920.

My mother, Wedad, and father, Aziz, in Jaffa in
1945 during their engagement.

My parents wedding in Jaffa, 1945.

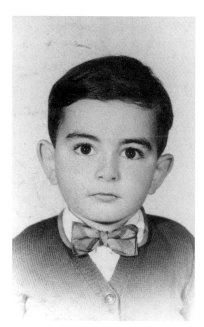

A studio picture of me at six.

At Lincoln's Inn, London, after I was called to the English Bar. With Lord Denning, the Dajani family, and my parents.

A recent picture of the summer house in Ramallah where my parents vacationed after leaving Jaffa in 1948.

On the Ramallah–Jerusalem Road. A picture I took after the 1967 war. How did it feel, I wondered, to drive a tank over a car and see the driver at the window, watching his face crumbling at the sight of his car being mounted by a tank.

The King Abdullah murder trial. The accused is turning to face the camera. My father can be seen at top right of center.

At the King Abdullah trial. My father is in the center.

Typing a letter to my father at my room in the Penrose Dormitory at American University of Beirut, 1971.

Brooding in Jericho, 1983.

Me in 1990, making a point at a human rights conference.

My father in 1984, before his death.

With President and Mrs. Jimmy Carter at the U.S. Consulate General in Jerusalem. Also pictured are the Consul General, Philip Wilcox Jr., and his wife.

deep stairwell. On the walls were large posters of the human body with symbols from ancient Indian culture. We climbed a spiral staircase up to the second floor where the yogi had his office. We entered an expensively furnished office and waited for the yogi. I realized that I was holding my breath. This would be my first encounter with an authentic yogi since the spindly showman I had seen at the Ramallah Grand Hotel when I was a child.

A large portly man wearing a flowing robe entered the room. I was taken aback. How could such a fat man be a yogi? How could he possibly move his stomach or control his breath? Was he an authentic yogi or was he a fake? The man had presence and flair. He spoke quickly and with authority, although he was breathing heavily. His wife was with him, a young tall American with long smooth brown hair who silently stood back watching us, her head bent to the side. Without wasting time he told us what was offered at his ashram and said I had to join for at least three months. The tuition was four hundred dollars, but if I paid in advance I would get a fifty-dollar reduction. I could start right away. Before we left, Muneer asked the yogi to take special care of me, and the yogi promised that he would.

But now that I had seen the yogi in person and was confronted with the practical arrangements of my stay at this ashram, I was uncertain. I could not afford to stay here for three months, and I did not take to this yogi. After we left the office I asked Muneer what he thought. "Try it out," he advised.

We walked around the ashram examining the place more closely. It had a lovely garden. I would be happy staying in such a place. All the students were Western: most were German and the rest English, French, and American. I saw students in one class lying flat on the ground while others stepped on their bodies with bare feet. We stopped to speak to one of the teachers and as we did a tall bony Frenchman came by with a large swelling on his ankle. He had been bitten by a scorpion. He came to get advice on how to clean his stomach. His teacher told us that he had been fasting for three days in preparation and when I asked how it was done I was told that he must swallow a rag, which would then be slowly pulled back up through his mouth. Even as the teacher was describing the procedure, I felt like throwing up. "Are such practices mandatory?" I asked. "No, not at all," said the teacher, who could see that I had turned pale.

Until this visit to the ashram, India and yoga had been mysterious and magical experiences directed by Muneer. Now I was sure that I needed more formal training. The next morning, after saying goodbye to Muneer, I hired a rickshaw and took my small bag to the ashram.

I was led to my room by one of the students. On the way I asked her what she thought about the ashram. She answered in hushed tones that it was generally all right but there were things that she did not like although she would not say what they were. My room had a metal bed with a thin mattress, nothing else. The single window had a few bars but no glass. A large animal might be prevented from entering, but cobras, scorpions, spiders, and all other sorts of creeping things would be able to wander in and out at will. I thought of that swollen ankle of the brave emaciated young Frenchman and wondered whether I would be able to sleep. I was told that when I heard the bell in the evening I should proceed to the roof of the main building. Another bell would ring before dawn; I should quickly dress and be ready to start the morning exercises. Until the first bell I had some time to myself, so I walked in the beautiful garden.

I was not quite sure how to get to the roof when the first bell rang, and I lost my way in the narrow lanes with overhanging climbers and palms. One of the attendants discovered me and asked me why I wasn't with the others. He led me to the roof where I found all the students sitting in the lotus position under a star-studded sky. In front was a couch that was mounted on a raised platform with lanterns on either side. I found a place on the far right and sat with the others and waited. Forty-five minutes later the portly yogi entered solemnly and with pomp and took his place on his small throne that had been prepared for him between the two lanterns. He eyed all of us and began a long monologue about the corrupt West and his various experiences there. I listened with astonishment. Periodically I turned to look at the other students trying to gauge what they thought. No one reacted, not even when the yogi told the most bizarre stories. In one of these the smell of cooked bacon that the carnivorous English have for breakfast made him think of his father. He proudly recounted how his father's body at its cremation had burned to ashes by the very fat it bore. The smell it emitted was like the bacon he smelled as he walked in the morning in London. "How I loved my father," the yogi sighed.

Two hours later as we were walking out, the yogi came over to me and asked what I thought.

"Great," I lied. "Great stuff."

I was afraid to say what I really thought. As soon as we left the roof I asked the students whether it was obligatory to attend these evening sessions and when they said yes I knew that I could not stay. I began plotting my escape and that night lay awake in fear, thinking that even if I survived some sort of sting, I would be made to stay here for a long time against my will.

I lay on my back on the hard bed keeping watch over the open window wondering what was going to come through. I yearned to be once again with Muneer at the house of Sri Pundit. I had hardly fallen asleep when a loud bell rang and I heard nervous commotion outside as everyone began to go to the single toilet and put on their clothes without showering. I too put on my clothes and walked with everyone else through the dark mysterious garden, stepping gently with my sandaled feet so as not to disturb any sleeping creepers. There were ten rickshaws with sleepy drivers waiting outside the gate. They drove us to the Indian Ocean, where we were lined up along the shore and did the morning breathing exercises of welcoming the sun. I enjoyed this very much. When the sun made its successful ascent in response to our bidding, we rode back to the

ashram and had a breakfast of thick gummy rice pudding decorated with a large number of black ants. The morning hatha yoga
exercises might have convinced me to stay, but the morning breakfast tipped the scales and I knew that I had to leave. Too scared to
announce this, I thought that I would first fetch my bag, stand by
the gate, and there, close to my escape route, announce my decision.
To avoid any violence I would declare my great appreciation for the
ashram and my intention to support its work by making a generous
contribution of fifty dollars, which I considered to be my ransom
money. Then I would dart out.

When I got back to Pondicherry and entered Muneer's room,
he was not surprised to see me. "I knew you would not stay," he
said. He seemed happy to welcome me back.

That night I experienced a waking dream. I thought I had been
awakened by the tired, sleepy voice of a woman praying. At first I
thought the sound came from the floor above me, but then I
remembered that there was none. It was not morning: who could be
up in the middle of the night praying? But my thoughts were
silenced by a sound whispering to me, comforting me with its warm
breath, silencing my mind, assuring me that I was accepted in this
house. The comfort penetrated deep into my body. Then I realized
that this was Sweet Mother, Aurobindo's companion, praying for
me, giving me strength and comfort, assuring me that what I was
doing was right, encouraging me in my quest. I understood her
even though I could not make out a single word. The murmur continued to blow comfort over me and then, as I calmed down and
went deeper and deeper into myself, it began to recede until it
ceased to be audible.

When I awoke next morning, it was from a very deep slumber.
I went over to Muneer's room and told him about the experience.

"It's the Mother," he said with confidence. "She often makes an
appearance to newcomers, if she is glad to have them as her guests."

"Has she ever appeared to you?" I asked.

"Me? Oh no. I have never been favored by mothers."

After this, I went back to my room, which had become a comfortable cocoon that I was loath to leave. Outside, children were banging against a tin. Their bangs were rhythmic and constant. Boom. Boom Boom. Oddly enough I did not find their noise distracting. I incorporated it into my reveries and it took me back to another experience in my childhood. As I returned from school I would stop at the blacksmith and hear him pound at an iron bar with a heavy metal hammer that bounced up after every bang. The blacksmith then held up the bar and looked into it to check if it had straightened. He would then place it down and start all over again: Boom Boom Boom.

Through meditation I began to return to that young boy and be reunited with my body. I was starting a long process that I now felt certain was to be the path of my liberation, a sweet illusion I held with all the certainty of a twenty-three-year-old.

But then a different banging sound began, this time closer by. Someone was banging on my wooden door. Who might it be? It took me a moment to get up.

"Who is it?" I called.

"Mr. Shehadeh," the caller shouted back, "there is a telephone call for you."

CHAPTER THIRTEEN

THE CONNECTION WAS bad. All I could hear was the faint pleading voice of my sister, Siham.

"Raja, come home."

"Why?" I shouted into the receiver. "Why?"

"Your mother."

"What about my mother?"

"Your mother wants you."

"Why?"

"She is ill."

"What is the matter with her?"

"Very very ill."

"Is she alive?"

"Come back. Come back quickly. Don't delay."

"Please tell me the truth. Is she alive?"

"Come back as soon as you can. Come back."

The voice trailed off and the line went dead. I was in tears. I was sure my mother must have died and my sister did not want to tell me the news in one blow. I had only one thought: I must leave. I must leave immediately.

The people at the office were very concerned. They had heard me shouting into the telephone. They saw the tears in my eyes.

"What's wrong?" they asked.

"My mother," I answered.

They tried to comfort me but I couldn't listen. I had lost my head. "Where can I find a travel agent?" I asked.

"We'll send someone with you," the man said kindly.

I went back to Sri Pandit's house and found Muneer waiting to hear my news. I told him that I must leave.

"Don't be rash. Maybe she's all right, why leave so suddenly without finding out more? Take a breath. Wait. Don't be so rash."

"I must leave. I must."

"I think you should wait. I'm sure of it. Don't be impulsive."

"I must leave. I cannot stay."

I had sent my clothes for washing and was left with only one peach-colored linen shirt, which to this day I still have. It was the only thing I brought back with me from India.

I left Muneer standing despondent and perplexed and put myself in a cranky old cab hoping that it would not break down on the way. It was a long drive. The driver tried to speak to me but soon gave up. I wanted to be left alone with my thoughts. Most of the time I cried. I thought of Mother and felt a part of me dying. My mind kept returning to the fairy-tale reality she used to paint for me in her stories. Now she was gone and I would never fulfill her expectations. I had not cried like this for years.

But how did my sister know where to find me? When I wrote the letter to my father I did not know my address in India. Although I had said that I was only staying for a few months, my father must have read my letter as an announcement of a long-term abandonment of my former life. Siham later told me that it was this absence of a forwarding address that had upset my father most of all. He also told Siham that he was very busy with the case of Hilarion Cappuci, a Syrian Catholic bishop whom he was defending against an arms smuggling charge and that he could not be distracted at this time. She told him that he did not need to worry. She would find me and, if need be, she would go to India to look for me.

The giveaway had been the postmark. Because I did not want the letter to arrive until I was well into my trip, I had waited until I was settled in Pondicherry before mailing it. I was sure that the Indian mail was slow and it would be a few weeks before the letter arrived in Israel. I was wrong. Within a week the letter was received in Ramallah with the Pondicherry postmark. This was the first hint. The second was that I had mentioned in the letter that I was going to be in an ashram. But what is an ashram? No one in Ramallah knew. There was an English Anglican priest who lived in the Old City of Jerusalem who had been to India and was interested in Indian mysticism. Siham went to see him.

She later told me that they sat together by the wall of the Old City, close to where he was living, watching the sunset. He was a tall, simple, attractive middle-aged man who was a searcher and had stayed at ashrams himself. He wore the Franciscans' long robe and sandals and had long unruly hair. He was one of those men of religion who was obsessed with Jerusalem and with trying to dis-cover where religion had gone wrong in this city. He knew of the Aurobindo Ashram in Pondicherry and thought that I must be staying there. He spoke positively to Siham of the ashram and said that my family should not be worried. There was nothing wrong in being at an ashram, and Aurobindo was a serious guru. But Siham was on a mission and was not prepared to listen. She had to get information to find me and get me back. Day and night my mother was ranting that I was lost and would never come home. I had to be brought back by any means. Once she had the name of the ashram, Siham got the telephone number.

My mother was exhausted from worry but she was not sick. When I returned and found her alive and well I was relieved. So relieved that I felt no resentment at being called back. I remember how dazed I had been from the long journey and my constant weeping. I felt like someone who had awakened from a deep slumber. When I got to the house it was as if I was seeing it for the first time. I felt very alone. My short but profound experience in India separated me from the rest of the family, and I no longer experienced my life only in relation to my father.

I started to see life in the occupied territories with new eyes, the life of Arabs and Jews. I saw how distant people were from their own selves, how petty their struggles and ambitions were. I tried to help them reconnect with the larger world but whatever I said made no sense to them and they looked at me with shock and pity. *India,* they seemed to say, *has turned the poor man's mind and made him even stranger than he was before.* But I did not mind their skeptical looks and spent many hours wondering how they would change if they too meditated and took up the practice of yoga. As for myself, I knew where my happiness lay and sat alone in my room at my family's house for many hours in the lotus position.

In all I had been in India for less than three weeks, but this short visit had left an indelible mark. It showed me an alternative to the kind of life that I had been living, and this I have never forgotten.

My father was happiest when he had lots of work. When I returned from India he was immersed in the Cappuci case. Naturally he had no time for me and was more inaccessible than ever. He worked day and night preparing. I was met with silence, without complaints, and without questions. It was as though I had just come back from any ordinary trip. I found this both comforting, because I did not relish his judgment, and disappointing, because I had tried hard in my letters to him to reach out and he was not responding. I remember that we had only one evening alone when we stayed up after everyone else had gone to bed and he did not need to work. I asked if he had any questions for me. He said no and added: "I don't understand what you did or why, but it is your affair." He was unwilling to say any more or to hear about my experience. We sat in silence for a few minutes, and then turned to our rooms.

During the day I accompanied my father to the Israeli District Court in Jerusalem where the trial was held. He was doing splendidly. Every day the papers would report on the front page everything that had taken place at the trial the day before. His courage in defending a supporter of the struggle was also admirable and gave him credit with those who had thought the worst of him.

As I followed the case I realized what a long way I had before I reached my father's level. "The law," he always said, "is like a sea. You can swim and swim and never reach the shore. There is a lot to learn and you will never find that you know everything; there is always more to learn." I was still learning to swim.

I continued with my yoga in the privacy of my own room in my parents' house. It was an odd experience to sit in yoga positions there, but I did it anyway. Then one day when I was alone in the house sitting in the lotus position with the smell of incense wafting into my nose, the doorbell rang. I unfurled my legs, stood up, and walked falteringly to the door. It was an Arab policeman, who handed me a summons to appear the next morning at ten at Captain Yossi's office at the military headquarters at the Tegart in Ramallah.

"Sign here," he said and left me standing at the top of the stairs in a state of great agitation.

The twelve hours until the time of the interview were twelve too many. The next morning I carried the summons and presented myself at the gate of the Tegart. It was a fresh autumn day in November and I waited outside with the crowds of other young Palestinian men who had been similarly summoned. It was well past ten when I was allowed into the gray cement building with its high walls and small, arrow-shaped windows. Inside this forbidding labyrinth uniformed Israeli men and women carrying guns walked comfortably. The officer who took me to Captain Yossi was eating a tangerine. The refreshing citrus smell contrasted with the blandness of this military compound.

When the interview began with routine questions I suspected that this captain was only updating my file. Perhaps someone had alerted him to my recent travels and the authorities needed to know why.

I responded to Captain Yossi's questions with clenched teeth. I could almost hear the agitated beat of my heart. After taking my particulars he asked me what I had done in Lebanon. I answered that I had studied literature and philosophy.

"What else did you do?"

"Nothing much," I answered.

"Who were your friends in Lebanon?"

I blanked. I couldn't remember.

"You had no friends?"

I did of course.

"Can you name them?"

I couldn't. I felt that I was being asked to betray my friends by informing on them. Not a single name came to mind.

"Surely you must remember the names of your friends."

I tried to think of the names of those who were least involved in politics, but couldn't. Every time a name came to mind, I remembered some political involvement of its holder.

"Why do you want to know about my friends?" I asked.

"For no particular reason. Can't you give me any name?"

I tried hard. I knew I must come up with at least one name, but whom could I betray? I began to sweat.

"Well, who was the head of the student council?"

I knew the name, of course I did. He had been my classmate at the Friends School in Ramallah. I told myself that the name of the head of the student council was not a secret. Everyone knew it. I would not be revealing any secret if I gave it: "Maher Masri," I blurted out.

"Tell me about him."

"He was the head of the student council."

"Why did you travel to India?"

"To be in an ashram."

"But why?"

"Because of my interest in yoga."

I began to feel more comfortable and thought that maybe I could tell this man something that could do him some good. I began to tell him about yoga. He looked at me strangely, reached for his pack of cigarettes, and offered me one.

"I don't smoke," I said.

He lit one and inhaled, deeply scrutinizing me as he did so.

Someone knocked at the door. Captain Yossi cried: "I'm coming. I'm done."

I realized that I no longer interested him. He motioned to me to leave. As I left I wondered what he had written in my file.

Ten days later I returned to London and was able to concentrate on my studies. I made up the missed work without difficulty and was able to pass all my exams and finish in the assigned time of three years. In October 1976 I was called to the English bar at Lincoln's Inn. This time my father was able to attend my graduation ceremony, which was presided over by Lord Denning, the master of the rolls.

The picture taken at the sherry party after the ceremony shows me with a rather silly boyish expression. My father stands with a wide, proud smile on his face. Next to me is Lord Denning, looking like John Gielgud.

I was full of uninformed excitement about what was ahead of me. I had chosen my father's path and was going to try to live up to his expectations. He had been fond of repeating that I would never complete my law studies in his lifetime and that he was doomed to a life of drudgery in his law office without any help from me. On the first score, at least, I had proven him wrong.

I knew that I would not be a traditional lawyer. I was going to be a lawyer in the daytime and a writer at night. For this I needed to live a special life. I certainly was going to leave home as soon as I could afford to. I was going to live simply and not be concerned about material possessions. I was going to be an example of a new sort of a Palestinian professional. I would live close to the people, using my advantages as a Western-educated lawyer to interpret the law and contribute to the community so that it could better resist the occupation and prepare for a more democratic future. This was how I would contribute to the struggle.

While I expected difficulties practicing law under occupation, I had no doubt that I would be a brilliant lawyer. And on my own terms. I was unaware of the extent of the opposition I would encounter and did not know what I was getting myself into. But I was soon to find out.

CHAPTER FOURTEEN

WHEN I RETURNED to Ramallah in 1976 to practice law, I was the first Western-educated lawyer to come back to the West Bank since 1948. Under the British mandate the judiciary had attracted the brightest of the middle classes. After 1948 most of the more successful Palestinian lawyers and those who served with the judiciary left and established new lives outside Palestine, either in the West or in the emerging newly independent Arab states. Among those remaining in the West Bank a number assisted the Jordanian regime as advisers, judges, or members of government. Only a few, my father among them, continued to practice. They had to adjust to the new and deteriorating conditions. But after the Israeli occupation the deterioration had become far worse.

With the Israeli annexation of East Jerusalem, the Arab courts were moved to Ramallah. The building chosen as the Ramallah courthouse was the former municipal vegetable market. I remember visiting this structure years before when it had first been built. I went with my father to see the vegetable market, and an official from the municipality took us around and proudly explained how the stalls were built from concrete; water was available to keep the vegetables fresh. The new courthouse was next to the chicken slaughterhouses, which gave their name to the street. The court was said to be on Chicken Street.

My father was not discouraged by any of these moves. He functioned with the highest professional standards whether he pleaded before the advanced Israeli court or the underdeveloped court on Chicken Street. When we went to court together, he always charged ahead; I had to run to keep up. If I became distracted he would disappear into one of the rooms and I would lose him. I was careful not to do this during our first visit to the courthouse in Ramallah. He introduced me to the various officials and judges. I remember what several said when they met me: *"Farkh el bat awam,"* the offspring of a duck can surely swim.

I still remember the first case my father defended after the Israeli occupation. The courts were closed; the judges and lawyers were on strike. The daughter of my father's close friend Dr. Akram Nuri was charged with (and ultimately convicted of) offending the Israeli flag. Aida had been returning from Jordan over the Allenby Bridge across the River Jordan. When she saw the Israeli flag she became belligerent and declared loudly to the Israeli soldiers there, "This flag you have hoisted up here should be brought down and burned." Aida was promptly charged. She had not yet turned sixteen and was unaware that she would be held criminally liable for her declaration. Dr. Nuri entreated my father to defend her: "You cannot abandon me at a time like this," he told my father. "I need you to defend my daughter." The military court was convened in a makeshift courtroom. I sat just behind my father and remember him looking larger than usual in his black robe with puffed sleeves. Then suddenly a young soldier entered, stood to attention, lifted up his head, looked straight ahead, and declared: "When I shout everyone must stand up."

There was something raw, Spartan, even animalistic about this sentinel standing by the door of this makeshift court dressed in a tight-fitting khaki uniform. He must have been a year or two older than me, but his was another unfamiliar world. He was as forward as I was reserved. I concealed my body; he utilized his to impose his authority over us. His thighs were thrust forward. His neck muscles were taut with the Adam's apple looming large and prominent; his chest was held high. He had hardly made his announcement before three middle-aged military reserve army officers stomped in from a side door. In contrast with the young soldier they were relaxed. They seemed to saunter toward their seats at the far end of the room. Their entrance was accompanied by a startlingly loud scream from the enthusiastic but nervous young soldier by the door. It was a cry more fitting for the open air than for such a closed space. But it effectively established the intimidating atmosphere that has characterized all military court sessions since Ramallah fell under Israeli occupation.

Typically my father was a forerunner. Very few Palestinian lawyers dared practice their profession. Those who did continued to do so surreptitiously, in defiance of the decision of the bar association in Jordan to boycott the courts and strike until the end of the Israeli occupation. Only in 1971 did a few of the more prominent lawyers who were already practicing meet at my father's office and openly declare their position against the strike and call for its suspension. The next day someone came up to me at Birzeit College, where I was studying at the time, and whispered his sympathy for my father. I had not seen the papers and did not know what he was talking about. The news item in the local paper said that a number of lawyers had gone against the decision of the bar association, and the disciplinary committee of the bar had decided to disbar them. But not all were given equal punishment. With the exception of my father, all were disbarred for the maximum period of five years; he and my uncle were the only two disbarred for life. My father was also further punished by having his passport withdrawn once again, thus leaving him effectively stateless.

The strike continued for thirty years and was ended only after the Palestinian Authority took charge as a result of the Oslo peace process. It was the longest strike in history. The self-exclusion from the scene by the legal community gave Israel a free and uncontested hand both in the administration of its new judiciary and in the changes to the laws that it began to implement soon after the occupation. For the first decade of the occupation, none of Israel's actions were challenged by the local legal community. The Israeli-appointed judges ruled that the local court would not accept cases that contested Israeli-issued military orders amending local laws. In this way they proved more uncensorious of Israel than the Israeli High Court itself.

Over the years, the number of lawyers willing to end the strike and resume their practice increased in response to the increasing demand for legal services. Eventually the profession was split between striking and working lawyers. A newly qualified lawyer could choose which side of the profession he or she would join. If they joined the striking lawyers, they received a stipend without being expected to work. The training was carried out at the office of a striking lawyer, and the new member was sworn in to a profession that he or she never practiced nor was ever expected to practice.

There were several attempts made by the working lawyers to organize a new bar association to look after their interests, but these efforts failed. Jordan, Israel, and the PLO, each for its own reasons, were not interested in a new independent force arising from within the occupied territories. The state of the judiciary was deemed to be of no importance to the PLO struggle; neither were the changes that Israel was bringing about in the laws and the public administration structure. The general position was that it was an all-out war with Israel, not a piecemeal one. When the war was won, all the transformations Israel had brought about in the territories would be undone and life would resume as though nothing had ever happened.

I was unaware of the consequences of such a position when I began practicing as a lawyer in the West Bank. I soon realized it was an emasculating existence. The prevailing local Palestinian politics were of the crudest kind. In essence they involved control — at any cost. The Palestinian political factions that wielded power were not accountable. No attention was paid to society's need for a properly functioning judiciary. Those like my father, who tried to respond to society's need for legal services, were condemned. It was feared that if they succeeded they might use their position to challenge the political hegemony of the PLO. The crippling use of negative power, so frequently resorted to, was an easy and successful weapon against those like my father who saw what society needed but were prevented from providing it. Even a project such as the organization of the legal profession, which was undoubtedly crucial for the life of the community, was opposed because the political forces outside the occupied territories were concerned that it could lead to the development of a new political force. The choice available for people living in what was called the "inside" was either to give allegiance to one or the other of these forces, or to mind their own business. This naturally brought about a general atmosphere of apathy at best, and paralyzing demoralization at worst. These were the conditions that prevailed when I returned from England to join the legal profession in the West Bank under Israeli military occupation.

The law required that a new lawyer train for two years before qualifying. I did my training at my father's office. I accompanied my father to many of his court appearances and was sent to the different departments to carry out various transactions on behalf of clients. When I was with my father all the court clerks were on their toes. He made them scurry about doing work as he requested. There were a few old-timers whom he knew from the mandate days, and they often reminisced about those better times. But when I went alone to the court I met a different attitude. Only in retrospect do I realize how their attitude was colored by jealousy: who did I think I was, coming with my Western education, thinking I was better because I had my father's office behind me? I could not understand then why they made it so difficult for me to get anything done. My own mind was full of the lofty ideals of service; I was looking for ways to be useful and make the most of any opportunities to improve the system. But it would be a few years before I would find a way to use my talents for the public good. For the time being, I endured the hardships without the consolation of finding a public role for myself.

For the first two and a half years I was still learning about the situation. I took a part-time teaching job at Bethlehem University to supplement my income and spent my days at the courts and in the office, and my nights writing. I rented a one-bedroom ground-floor apartment. Its entrance was dominated by birds of paradise and a fig tree. I furnished it with simple furniture, some of which I made myself. I never aspired to own a fancy apartment or to live beyond the level of my neighbors.

It was during this period that my father assigned me to a job that would greatly affect my life: He asked me to prepare a subject index of the hundreds of military orders that the Israeli military government had issued since the beginning of the occupation. They were stacked in one corner of the office, serially numbered, loose sheets of yellowed paper typed in Hebrew with a poor translation into Arabic, headed: THE ISRAELI DEFENSE FORCES COMMAND OF JUDEA AND SAMARIA.

I began to go through these tattered sheets. As I read I became aware of the extent of the Israeli legal changes. The legal unit of the Israeli army at the headquarters in Beit El near Ramallah had been extremely meticulous in studying all the laws in force in the West Bank — Jordanian, British mandate, and Ottoman — and had canceled, amended, and supplemented them as it pleased. This went contrary to international law, governing the powers of an occupying state — this much I knew. Why then was no one protesting?

I spoke to other lawyers, but they showed no interest. No one paid attention to these military orders anyway — many lawyers used the back of these sheets as scrap paper. These amendments to the law were treated as though they did not exist, just as Israel itself was treated by the Arab states. But it did exist, and we were living under its domination. These military orders also existed, and one day their application would be forced on us. I was sure of this. We needed to tell the world that the Israeli claim that the occupation was the most benevolent in history was not true; that the reality of life under occupation was very different from the one portrayed to the outside world. I knew all this but I did not know how to expose the situation or how to do anything to change it.

The lawyers I came in contact with did not share my sense of being slighted by the conditions imposed upon our profession. They were impervious to their surroundings. Anyone passing the squalid lawyers' room at the courthouse could hear mirthless hollow laughter followed by the stamping of feet and clapping of hands that smacked of bitterness and frustration. They learned to place a powerful divide between their work and their lives. Their work was not what gave them their identity. It was just a job. They were resigned to practicing under such abysmal conditions. Those who were more politically minded joined the ranks of one of the factions of the PLO. They did what they could to serve their faction and received a stipend to supplement their income. None of these factions supported work that would improve the conditions of the judiciary. Such activity was seen as reformist and implied an acceptance of the occupation. Under these conditions the fate of the lawyer was simply to endure.

Palestinians under occupation withstood different degrees of suffering. Those who were caught carrying out military actions were tortured and had to suffer many years of imprisonment in Israeli jails. Others suffered the denial of vital permits because they were marked as PLO activists. But most just suffered the restrictions on economic activities: underdevelopment, land confiscation, collective punishment, and general despair that made life so intolerable. I empathized with the pain of the various sectors of society with which I came in contact, but I refused to be driven to despair. What saved me was my divided allegiance: lawyer by day, writer by night. I could observe and interact with the members of my daytime profession but I could not allow myself to be completely absorbed in it. I had to remain aloof to be able to write. My father observed my behavior and could never understand or accept what he interpreted as my ambivalence toward the law and the profession. But divided allegiance was as far as I was willing to go to accommodate my father.

Another source of hope was the small success I was having in starting a new organization to deal with the deteriorating legal conditions. During my stay in London I had learned of an organization called Justice, the British section of the International Commission of Jurists, whose headquarters were in Geneva. This was an organization dedicated to the promotion of the rule of law. I began to dream about the creation of a Palestinian section of the ICJ, to promote the rule of law in the West Bank. It was my good fortune that I then met Charles Shammas, a Lebanese American graduate of Yale University who had come to the West Bank to try out new ideas. He was exceptionally bright with a highly developed ethical sensibility. He had a broad royal forehead, weak chin, mischievous smile, and bright sparkly eyes. Together we began the difficult process of creating the first professional nonfactional organization in the West Bank dedicated to working on issues of an essentially political nature. We were soon joined by a third partner who proved of immense help to us, Jonathan Kuttab, with his thick black Afro and his black intelligent eyes. He was an American lawyer whose family had emigrated after he finished high school in Jerusalem. He was looking for ways to serve the Palestinian cause through the law and had written to ask me for ideas. I told him about the new organization and he soon left the law office in New York where he had been working and came to help us with our new project.

We were an enthusiastic trio. We put all we had into our work, writing letters, meeting people, and devising strategies. With Charles's meticulous mind and Jonathan's flair I was in very good company. My earlier pessimism began to turn into optimism. I could see the difference that the return of a single competent professional could make. I was sure that we could reveal to the world the true nature of the occupation while promoting an appreciation for the principles of the rule of law among Palestinian society. My enthusiasm revived my self-confidence and made me defiant. My father viewed the change in me with apprehension and disapproval. My attempts to win his support for our new cause proved unsuccessful. He warned me not to waste my energies and become distracted from my main work at the office.

The three of us volunteered our time for the West Bank affiliate of the ICJ, which we called Law in the Service of Man, later Al Haq. I did so while continuing with my legal practice and my writing. Now that I had completed my training and registered as a lawyer, I began to go to court on my own.

My name echoed through the vestibule of the Nablus court. The caller with the booming voice was the same man who had been at the court when my grandfather Saleem served as a district court judge in the mid-1940s under the British mandate government. When I climbed the stairs on my way to the courtroom, he greeted me kindly. I may have reminded him of Saleem. I looked up at the door leading from the judge's chambers to the courtroom and saw that it was still covered with the black velvet cloth that must originally have been placed there by the British to add pomp to this otherwise unimpressive room. Now the cloth was frayed and flaking; it had lost its former sheen. The door stood bereft of its former dignity and mystery as the entrance to the chamber where the Honorable Justice retired. Its haggard unkempt appearance was more in accord with the rest of the place and those who now inhabited it.

Our law office also represented clients in Jerusalem whose work had to be undertaken in Israeli courts and official departments — East Jerusalem had been annexed to Israel in June 1967, and Israeli law applied there. The experiences I had on the Israeli side contrasted with those on the West Bank. The courts operated efficiently. They were clean and well administered. The officials were helpful, at ease, comfortable. I remember how I felt when I entered the office of the head of the Execution Department at the Israeli court in the Maskoubiyyeh (Russian Compound) quarter in Jerusalem and heard a Brahms piano sonata coming from the Israeli Broadcasting Service. A sense of calm and order emanated from the office. We spoke in hushed voices. The officer of the court, gray haired with sloping shoulders, had time for me and every effort was made to expedite action, not to find excuses to postpone it. The judges were self-respecting people who had inherited the system from the British

mandate and had worked to develop it. Some of the sitting judges
must have worked with my grandfather Saleem. This must be the
kind of atmosphere my father referred to when he talked about his
practice in Jaffa. Why could we not have something similar? Surely
this is what we should aspire to. But how should we go about it? The
Israelis had continued from where the British left off, but in our case
the continuity had been severed. Jordan had continued to apply
some of the British laws, but Jordan was not Palestine — and now
we were neither Jordan nor Palestine. We were a nation under occupation, with the majority of our efforts dedicated to liberation from
occupation. Why had I come back if nothing could be done to bring
about change as long as the occupation continued? Had I unwit-
tingly condemned myself to a doomed professional life under the
most difficult working conditions conceivable?

I was beginning to have serious misgivings about my decision to
return to the West Bank. I knew that the longer I stayed in Ramallah
the more difficult it would be to practice law in the West. I was
depriving myself of options as I began to lose touch with legal developments in England. Was I condemning myself to turning into the
image of those lawyers I saw around me? Father said not to worry. I
would always be different. I would never become like them. But how
could I be sure?

Such worries occupied me only during weekdays. On the
weekend, I pushed them aside. Throughout the winter months I
would leave Ramallah on Saturday at noon after the office closed
and in the company of a few friends would go to the family house
in Jericho. In forty-five minutes we were in the shabby flat town of
Jericho with its mud houses and water canals. The shared taxi
dropped us in the center of town and we would walk or cycle down
toward the Jordan River to the winter house. There were no street-
lights on the potholed road lined with citrus groves — orange,
pomelia, and lemon. During February and March the delicate
caressing fragrance of these blossoms filled the air. Jericho's mild
refreshing weather blew on our faces. The light would slowly give

way to darkness and a vast sky. The flatness of Jericho, the lowest town on earth, made the starlit sky seem vaster than anywhere else I've been. We grilled meat and chicken on skewers over a charcoal fire in the garden and sat late into the night around the bonfire drinking, eating, and smoking, leaving the occupation and the courts and the hazards of life in the occupied territories far away in the mountains of Ramallah and Jerusalem. Here in this flat oasis everything operated at a different pace, and no soldiers bothered us or ever came by to spoil our mood. We slept late and the next morning did some work in the garden and had the entire day for ourselves. I gave thought to my writing, keeping in my mind whatever section of the book I happened to be working on, thinking of my sentences like Gertrude Stein did when she posed for Picasso, albeit in different circumstances. I had just completed a draft of the autobiographical novel that I had been working on since my time at AUB. I planned to travel to the United States to show my book to a few people there.

In the evening we went for a long walk through the sand dunes, crossing a shallow stream that collected from the springs in the mountains of the central ridge that ran down through Wadi Kilt and eventually into the Jordan River ending in the Dead Sea. As the light dimmed, magic returned to the world. The dying light of the sun reflected off the rose-colored rocks and accentuated the mosaic of rock, soil, pebbles, and greenery between bits of cracked mud. It was like a gigantic jigsaw puzzle put together by a mighty hand, so quiet and peaceful.

I sat on a rock and dangled my feet in the cool water. I looked down and saw a nymph, her shape ever shifting yet with a firm bottom in the rocks, the black pebbles her vagina and heart. Constantly changing into wings and feathers and lovely, alluring shapes, blending into each other, undulating in gentle ever-moving ripples. Where was Carol now? What had become of her? Why had I ever left her? I decided to look for her on my upcoming visit to the United States.

CHAPTER FIFTEEN

I ARRIVED IN Washington, D.C., on the third of November 1979. This was my first trip to the United States and the contrast with the restrictive life I had endured under occupation was dramatic. I will never forget the sense of freedom I experienced when I walked out of Dulles Airport. Leila, a childhood friend from Ramallah, met me and drove me in her Cadillac to her house in Maryland. It had all the features of a dream house, but it was not one. It had a brightly lit attractive kitchen, which we entered through the garage with its remote-controlled door. Then we went into the sitting room with a fireplace; cushions with Palestinian embroidery were bunched on the floor. The bedrooms were upstairs. My room was too cozy for comfort. I knew that Leila like many Palestinians had dreamed of the pleasures of life in the United States. But I could tell that she was not satisfied. She showed me around her little kingdom and it occurred to me that she was confined to it by a conservative husband who did not allow her to work.

Outside my friend's house I felt an admirable American energy. The sheer abundance of space was inspiring. This was the land of opportunity. The people I met seemed open and expansive. At home, one person's victory is regarded as another's doom; as though the land cannot afford more than one success. Here people seemed to worship winners. At home society conspires to destroy, discourage, and bring down by rampant corrosive jealousy those who triumph. It's a society that encourages you to cringe. Most of your energy is spent extending feelers to detect public perception of your actions, because your survival is contingent on remaining on good terms with your society. You have to be attentive to your extended family so that you can continue to count on their support. You must spend inordinate amounts of time at dull and senseless social occasions, because absence would be interpreted as unforgivable, offensive arrogance. Mine may be the land of prophets but it is certainly not the land of benevolence.

I phoned Carol's family to find her address and immediately mailed her the manuscript, making sure to add a return address. I remained hopeful that I would hear from her, but she did not call. During the six years we had been out of touch I had not sent a single letter. I should not have expected any response, and yet it distressed me that I would never know what she felt about my description of our time together.

From D.C. I traveled to Houston, where one of my classmates had become a wealthy businessman. He was very happy to see me and threw a large party and invited many of the people from Ramallah who had emigrated and were eager to hear about life "back home." I was impressed with the attempt of these Palestinians to maintain the way of life they had been used to. They made much more food than the number of invited guests could possibly eat, and to show respect the main dish was stuffed lamb. The slaughtered animal sat over a mountain of rice studded on every side with lightly browned fried almonds. The rice too was fried with minced meat. The amount of meat was proportionate to the host's respect for the guest. The men stayed in one room and the women in another. Very few mixed, and the dialect was an old one that I now rarely heard in Ramallah itself. It was as though time had been frozen in Houston and the emigrants held on to the ways and patterns of speech that they had had when they left. And yet it was only an illusion that they were still Ramallah people, that Ramallah was still home to them, and that the occupation was the only obstacle to their return. They were settled here. Compared with how they had lived in Ramallah, their lives in America were luxurious. They worried about the future and the alienation of their children, but very few had taught their children Arabic. The American children mocked the ways of their Palestinian parents, their bad English, awkward manners, and constant boasting about the glorious life they enjoyed "back home," where every other person was a cousin.

After we all ate heartily and drank a considerable amount of alcohol they wanted to know about the situation in the homeland. What could I tell this intoxicated group? How could anything of that life come back to me now in this Texas living room? Even after a brief absence the reality of life under occupation seemed so bizarre and distant. How must it be to those who had gathered to honor me, who had been away for decades without ever having returned to visit? I knew what was expected of me: an inflamed passionate denunciation of the Zionist enemy as the source of all our troubles. Yet I somehow could not oblige. Why, I wondered?

Only later did I realize that to do so would have been a betrayal of my own existence. To simplify my life and paint it in black-and-white terms was to deny my own reality, which I mainly experienced in tones of gray. If my countrymen really cared about me they had to see me as a human being, one who did not exist only in those heroic moments of struggle against the occupation as they liked to imagine. They had to realize that I was like them; my society had an integrity of its own that was not derived from the negation of the existence of the Zionist enemy. It was a living viable society, always changing and developing with a multiplicity of needs; a society that had to survive under difficult and trying conditions. If they really cared they could learn about these conditions and would try to put themselves in our shoes. Only then would they begin to be able to understand our needs and contribute to our struggle. I was not booed when I finally spoke, but I was not tolerated for very long either. Side conversations began to proliferate and slowly spread like a cobweb here and there until I was edged aside and reduced to speaking to a few of the more open-minded and polite guests. Soon they too excused themselves, saying they had to get up early next morning to go to work at their grocery stores.

Most of the Palestinians I met were anxious to hear about life in the occupied territories. But the gap between what they expected to hear and what I had to say was immense. Their impressions were formed by the media. But our lives were not a series of the dramatic points the media reported. If they had been, our nerves would have snapped under the strain long ago.

Our lives were in fact much less dramatic and more staid than these emigrants imagined. I almost felt that I needed to apologize for a lack of tragedy in my life. There was a similar strain when we spoke about Israel. In their view everything about Israel was evil. There were no gradations, no exceptions. All the Israelis were wicked people. But of course this is not true. There were aspects of Israel that I admired. But the moment I opened my mouth to speak about these, I was silenced. My listener would look at me with pity. I could imagine him thinking that the occupation forces must have terrorized me into losing my senses. When I insisted that I was not speaking out of fear, he would become suspicious. Could I have been recruited to the side of the enemy? Perhaps I was a spy or an Israeli agent who should not be trusted. The conversation at this point would trail off.

How could I tell them that we were heroic not because of the great risks that we were taking but because of our perseverance in the face of small, daily harassments and obstructions to our lives, none of which on their own amounted to much? Just bureaucratic hassles that everyone, even in the best of democracies, encounters sometimes. But in our case they were not random, occasional, or intermittent. They were persistent and constant, part of a policy to make the life of Palestinians so difficult that it would seem better to leave than to stay and suffer. Our heroism lay in our determination to stay, not in our acts of daring or even in military operations taken in resistance to the occupation. These were carried out by the smallest minority. The majority was resisting through staying put. This was the truth about life under occupation and this did not make for very exciting news or a narrative that could hold the attention even of the most ardent listeners.

I also wanted to speak about what our society needed to do to sustain itself, to adapt and develop in order to be able to withstand such powerful neighbors. If we didn't keep up with the Israelis, we were not going to survive. We needed to do more than aim for mere survival; we had to develop into a society that could reorganize itself and be ready to live as a democracy, respectful of the rule of law, when the occupation finally ended. After I spoke, I realized how much like my father I sounded, and the responses to my arguments made me more appreciative of his difficulties. It was as though people felt I had no right to speak in these terms. I realized only later, when I thought more about it, that for the Palestinians outside we did not constitute a society that had any right to a voice or to pursue political, social, or economic objectives. The Palestinian society that was outside had grouped itself under the umbrella of the PLO and felt that only this organization could speak on our behalf. But I did not want to rival anyone for political hegemony; I was speaking about social development, about the reorganization of society, about learning from Israel how it had become so effective. But then by bringing in Israel as the example to be followed, I clearly discredited myself. I was revealing my ignorance and lack of exposure. Of course I would admire Israel: I live under its rule. Do not the colonized always eventually come to admire their colonizers?

These experiences brought me closer to Palestinians in Israel. I had not been able to appreciate how difficult it had been for them to communicate their experiences to other Arabs. Now I was encountering the same difficulty. I remembered hearing about a Palestinian youth from Israel who was enthusiastic about being part of a delegation visiting some Eastern Bloc country because of his chance to meet with other Arab youth. He introduced himself to a fellow Arab from Syria, but he was spat at the moment he mentioned that he came from Israel.

I was having a drink with a Palestinian writer who had lived in the States for many years. He had the longest of beards and long disheveled hair, which he tied behind his neck like a Greek Orthodox priest. He had a wild look in his eyes. He took me to a restaurant in Georgetown called The Tombs. We went down a long staircase underground to the restaurant and my host impatiently asked me a few perfunctory questions and then immediately began to preach to me: "You should resist the occupation. You should not let them get away with it. You should not accept anything that they have as good. This is an important temptation to resist, otherwise you will find yourself dragged into their way of thinking. It is all propaganda. They are very clever at propaganda. We know this. You should know this too. You should never forget this."

You should. And you should.

I sat opposite him at the thick wooden table in the dim yellow light looking straight into his darting eyes, nodding and saying nothing. I wondered if he had ever considered that he did not know what he was talking about. How could someone who is a writer, who should be concerned about the consciousness of others, not want to know? This was an opportunity for him, I would have thought. Here I was ready to tell him everything I knew and to describe my experiences under occupation. But he didn't want to listen. He presumed to know everything about Israel and about us, the Palestinians living under its military rule. He did not have to worry about being stopped and harassed. He did not have to be concerned that soldiers could enter his home and do what they wished under the authority of the military law. He did not live with the constant news of bombs exploding here and there and injuries and deaths and bloodshed and collective punishments and hatred and fear and no certainty from day to day whether you can go on with the education of your children or with your business or profession.

There was one person who really listened. This was the artist Kamal Boullata. He was the only Palestinian in the States who took my work seriously and bothered to read it and give me his sincere reaction. In his kind and considerate way, he tried to gently convey to me that I had taken upon myself to write in a Western Joycean style when I should be doing something entirely different. My investigation should not be into my subjective self but my objective reality, which remained unrecorded in any book. I heard what Kamal said. He at least had bothered to read my manuscript. But we write about what we are most concerned about, and my internal reality then was more real to me than any external life. As an artist Kamal could understand this, but he still tried to steer me in a different direction.

We sat for long hours talking in his small two-room apartment on Dupont Circle. I looked at his round face with dimpled cheeks and thick curly hair and knew that he was listening and feeling. My pain was his pain. He had an exceptional capacity to empathize, to put himself in my place and imagine how it would feel if he went through the difficulties I described. At the end he told me:

"Why don't you write down what you told me? Just write it as you said it. It will make great stuff. People here don't know what you go through. Even I did not and I try to keep up. Think about it."

From D.C. I traveled to New York, where I stayed with Beth Heisey, the reserved and highly efficient friend of Jonathan Kuttab who later became his wife. She worked near the UN Headquarters. When I told her of my experiences with the courts and the extent to which Israel had changed our local laws, she organized a meeting with John Pace, the secretary of the UN Committee to Investigate Israeli Practices in the Occupied Territories. I explained to John what I knew about the illegal changes and suggested that the investigation into Israeli practices should also include the legal aspects. He was interested in what I had to say and promised to keep it in mind.

It was an edifying month. Afterward, I returned to my former life in Ramallah carrying the copy of my manuscript, now cluttered with Kamal's scribbling.

CHAPTER SIXTEEN

I DID NOT spend much time revising the manuscript. My law and human rights work claimed me.

Even when I had little time to spare I continued to think that this period of intense activity would eventually end and I would be able to return to my original interests. I considered this period a voyage out of my traditional introspective concerns into the real, outside world of my father, a way of being in the world with which I had always been secretly and distantly fascinated. My life had always seemed like a pale reflection of the "real life" of my father. No more. Now that I too was engaged in the real world, I no longer had to defer to him. I was an equal and could speak back and challenge him.

I knew that the time would come when I would use the experience won through my engagement in the world in my writing. Meanwhile I would write about the actual stuff of life as it happened to me and to others, recording daily experiences spontaneously in a diary style. It would be a kind of documentary writing that didn't demand much time, for I didn't have time. What it lacked in literary merit would be compensated for by its value as documentation for future generations or anyone else who cared to know what life was like under occupation.

I remember standing by the gate of the military government office waiting for a permit to travel across the bridge to Amman for work. It was my third attempt at securing entrance to the office. I had gone to court in the morning and finished my work as quickly as I could to get there in time and yet I was still refused entrance. As I stood in line I thought of Kamal. How can Palestinians living in the United States — where you can go about your work without obstruction and harassments — understand how it feels to have your day punctuated by these useless, frustrating activities that involve pleading for vital permits with officials who create all sorts of trivial excuses to deny them to you? I thought of this day and of the day before and of the day after. I had very little to look forward to. I just had to go on without reluctance or despair. On and on and on doing what it takes to keep my life going under the impossible conditions of military occupation. I decided to write a letter to Kamal Boullata in which I would pour out the pain and frustration of my day, from morning until evening. I signed the letter Samed — the steadfast, the persevering — because this was how my experiences had made me feel.

One letter followed another until it became a habit for me every evening after my work to write my letter from Samed to Kamal. I was worried about mailing these letters because of the censor, who checked all mail and could confiscate my letters or copy them and use them in a case against me. Writing these letters replaced writing in my diary, which I had previously done every evening. After several months I reviewed the letters and realized that they gave a graphic sense of the reality of daily life under occupation. Eventually a selection was published in *The Middle East* magazine published in London. They were signed "Samed."

Just after the publication of these letters I was having coffee at the National Palace Hotel in Jerusalem with the Israeli journalist Yehuda Litani, who covered the occupied territories for the Israeli newspaper *Haaretz*. Yehuda, who spoke with a hushed inquisitorial voice, had a way of scrutinizing his companion in the manner of an interrogator. He suggested that I write a piece for an Israeli newspaper about daily life in Ramallah. "The average person in Israel has no idea of the difficulties someone like you has to endure," he said.

I thought that the timing of this suggestion was curious, coming as it did in the wake of the publication of my letters about daily life. Could Yehuda have seen or heard about the unsigned article in the London magazine and wanted to know whether I was its author? Was this his indirect way of finding out? At first I didn't want to tell Yehuda about my Samed letters. But then I braced myself and said: "Let's go around the corner to Taha bookstore on Salah Ed Din Street. There's something I want to show you."

We walked around and I picked up the magazine on display and gave it to him to read.

Yehuda Litani introduced me to his friend Yehuda Meltzer, the Israeli publisher. We met at the newly renovated Notre Dame Hotel opposite the Old City's New Gate on the hill between East and West Jerusalem in what had formerly been no-man's-land. We sat on a terrace overlooking the Old City, the Arab section of Jerusalem, and on the top of the hill to the east the newly expanded Mount Scopus campus of Hebrew University. It was a clear crisp winter morning. Yehuda wore a cap. He was a jaunty man who looked younger than his years. He had an engaging way of speaking that immediately created an atmosphere of friendship and trust. A lifelong friendship began between us from that early meeting.

Through Yehuda I met Naomi Eilan, an attractive young philosophy student at Oxford and a brilliant editor, who helped me turn the letters into a book. Two years later the book was published in England as *The Third Way: A Journal of Life in the West Bank*. It was translated into Hebrew and published in Jerusalem. The Hebrew edition of the book published by Yehuda's company gave rise to a number of letters from Israelis of different walks of life and political leanings. Many wrote that my book had opened their eyes to the reality of life in the occupied territories.

But this was not the only writing I was engaged in. Upon my return I received an invitation from John Pace to appear before the Committee Investigating Israeli Practices in the Occupied Territories at its next meeting in Geneva. In the course of preparing for my testimony I reviewed hundreds of military orders. I ended up taking with me material that required three full days to deliver. My testimony was eventually published in four long volumes of a UN document in which, upon my request, I was referred to as Mr. M.

"UN documents end up on the shelf," said Niall MacDermot, the secretary general of the International Commission of Jurists, who I met in Geneva for the first time and with whom I established a friendship that lasted until his death. "Why don't you consider expanding your testimony into a book? The ICJ would be willing to publish such a book."

I took up his suggestion. While I was working on *The Third Way,* I also worked on *The West Bank and the Rule of Law.* It was a joint publication of the ICJ and Al Haq (then called Law In The Service of Man). The publication of this book gave the fledgling organization a boost. And it also opened the door to immense opportunities. Al Haq was the only organization documenting human rights violations and reporting on the legal changes brought about by Israel in the occupied territories. To cope with the work the organization needed to recruit field-workers, legal experts, and writers. We tried to recruit lawyers practicing in the West Bank but found scant interest there. So we began to train young university graduates with no experience in law or human rights. We also accepted volunteers from outside the West Bank, who proved immensely helpful in advancing the cause of Palestinian human rights. Slowly the organization was acquiring an international reputation. Its information was trusted and began to be used on a large scale.

I was one of two volunteer codirectors. As the full-time staff of the organization grew in number, eventually reaching forty, the administrative burdens increased considerably. I was constantly writing more reports and booklets for publication, reviewing and editing the work of others and participating in meetings that went into the late hours of the night. All of this was in addition to my office work. My father was not pleased by this.

He could not see the point. Instead of concentrating my efforts on advancing in my profession, making money, getting married, and bringing up children, I was wasting my time on documentation and analysis of human rights violations. What was the use, he asked, of condemning Israeli practices when the Israeli policies of settling the land were continuing? The right response was a political one: a diplomatic initiative for peace with Israel on the basis of the partition of the land. This is what would end Jewish settlement of Palestinian land. What was the use of wasting time diagnosing the disease when we already knew the remedy?

I shared my father's frustration and felt his sense of urgency for a solution. I also could see what was happening to our land. But the role I saw for myself was as an advocate of human rights, not a political activist. My legal practice only confirmed the need for speaking out on human rights issues. One of the cases that left a strong impression on me was that of Khalid Ameereh.

I will never forget Khalid with his high, bony cheeks and tense, wiry body. He introduced me to the reality of the Tegart and gave me a new vision of human rights work, which I now took up with renewed commitment.

Khalid's mother, a simple village woman, came to see me and asked that I take her son's case. I was impressed by this woman who had lost her husband and had to work as a domestic servant to support her five children. She had high hopes for her eldest son, Khalid, whom she had succeeded in placing at the University of Birzeit, where he was studying to become an engineer. Her son had shown strong academic potential; she must have been dreaming of the time when he would qualify as an engineer and save the family from their financial difficulties. But like many of his peers Khalid had joined the resistance against occupation and began to neglect his studies. As long as the land was under occupation, he believed that all his energy should go to the collective effort of liberating it. I first met my client eighteen days after he had been arrested. I should have considered myself fortunate to have been given this opportunity: In most such cases many months passed before the court would allow an interview between a lawyer and a security offender.

The Tegart is a large compact rectangular cement fortress built in 1936 by Sir Charles Tegart as part of the effort to suppress the Palestine revolt against the British rule in Palestine. Dozens of

similar structures dot the Palestinian landscape. The driveway from
the main Ramallah–Birzeit road leads up to the main gate, which
faces the hills to the southwest. I walked around to the back, passing
the northern door of the military court, and turned another corner
until I reached the prison gate. I rang the bell and waited behind a
high, formidable-looking metal gate. Soon a little slit was opened
and I was asked who I was. I declared my name and my purpose; a
small door opened and I stepped in. There was a small open court-
yard in the middle with alleyways all around leading to the prisoner's cells. On one side were the interrogation cells, which I came
to hear a lot about but was never allowed to visit. Khalid was
brought to me in a small room where a soldier remained standing.
I objected to the presence of the soldier, claiming the right to a private audience with my client, but to no avail. I had brought cigarettes with me, because I knew this is what most prisoners crave. I
offered the pack to Khalid. He refused, saying that he was not a
smoker. This was most unusual among detainees, but then Khalid
was not a typical detainee. He was not intimidated by the presence
of the soldier and was willing to describe to me his ordeal since his
arrest eighteen days ago. It was then that I learned about Barzali —
the word is Hebrew for iron — the officer who seemed to be in
charge of Kahlid's interrogation. I realized that my client's world
had been reduced to a challenge between him, the Palestinian
resister, and Barzali, the agent of the occupation forces. The two
men were engaged in a deadly game in a world that could not
encompass the two of them. It was Khalid or Barzali.

"After my arrest," Khalid told me, "I was blindfolded, thrown
into a jeep, and brought to the Tegart. It was late at night. I was
awakened and was not told why I was being arrested. Once in the
Tegart my ordeal began. I was brought before interrogators who
concentrated their blows on my face and chest. I was asked to confess. I said I had nothing to confess. But they said they knew everything about me. I said if this was the case why are you asking. They
did not like this and continued to beat me until the early hours of

the morning when I was returned to my cell. I then heard an electric motor, which I eventually realized was turned on every
morning at daybreak. This became my way to keep track of time,
because my cell did not get any light. Part of the strategy was to dis-
orient me by depriving me of sleep and food.

"'If you don't want to confess,' I was told, 'we will keep you
here until you change your mind.' But they didn't know who they
were dealing with. Judging by the times I heard the motor turned
on, two days and two nights had passed before I was given food.
Then they shoved me into a dirty toilet with shit smeared on the
walls and floor and there I was made to eat my miserly meal. I did,
anyway, because I was very hungry. I had hardly finished when I
was taken to another room and subjected to a cold shower. While
still wet I was put under a fan. I tried not to shiver; I did not want
to give them the pleasure of seeing me suffer. But I could not control my body. It shivered, like a leaf, as it had never done before."

"'Now will you talk?' they said.

"'What about?' I answered.

"'You think you are too smart for us,' they said, 'we shall see who
will have his way at the end.' They dragged me to a corridor where
other prisoners were handcuffed and hung by the hands to a peg in
the wall with a coarse stinky burlap bag placed over their heads. I
joined their line and became another suffering body denied light and
clean air, concerned only with the excruciating pain in my limbs. At
one point I called the guard and asked to use the toilet. I got no
response. Eventually I could not control my kidneys and the urine
trickled down my dirty trousers making me stink. When it splashed
on the floor I was slapped and cursed and called a filthy animal."

At this point Khalid turned to me and asked: "How long have
I been at the Tegart?"

"Eighteen days," I said.

"It feels like months. After the first week I lost count. I had
thought I was in for months. But you say it's only been eighteen
days?"

"Have you signed any papers?" I asked.

"They brought me a confession in Hebrew to sign, but I refused to sign it. It was then that they brought me Barzali. It was he who subjected me to the worst beating on my face. He tore the skin of my cheeks. Can you see it?"

I could see a scar. But it could have been from an old wound. I knew they would not have let me see my client while any sign that could prove torture was still evident.

After hearing Khalid's story, I felt awkward about advising him not to sign any confession under torture. Would I be able to resist the temptation to sign anything to end such an ordeal if I were in Khalid's place, knowing as I did that any confession would become the basis for an indictment? Still, I felt it was my duty to tell him this, and he received my advice without a sneer. But I noticed that he wanted to tell me something that he found hard to say. I put my head close to his so that he could whisper, but all he said was: "How is my mother keeping?"

This I was able to comfort him about. Otherwise I am not sure I was of much help to my client. He was living a distant and cruel reality and so far had not been broken. I wondered how much more beating those bony cheeks could take before despair and pain would break his resolve. But I was determined to do my best to help him.

After my interview I walked around to the northern entrance of the Tegart and into the office of the military prosecutor to check my client's file. I found that he had already been indicted. This was why I was allowed to see him. I also found in the file a confession written in his own handwriting and realized that this was what he had found so difficult to say. I quickly read the confession and copied it in full. My first assessment was that there was not enough evidence in it to support an indictment. Khalid had been clever enough to remain vague and avoid giving his interrogators any self-incriminating evidence. This raised my spirits and made me believe that I could possibly win this case, even before a military court.

I arrived early on the day of the trial. It was a cold damp day in February and a cold wind swept over the high hill, chilling us to the bone. A thin haze of fog obscured the gray cement walls of the Tegart. We all stood without shelter, wrapped in our heavy coats. I looked at the motley crowd that had gathered in the driveway and thought about how used to waiting we had become. Palestinians under occupation have had many years to learn to wait, to suspend all other activities and come to one of the many Tegarts in the West Bank and wait.

Some had come because their identity card had been confiscated by an officer in one of the military patrols in the streets. It was illegal to move around without an identity card. This then was the only legal place to be, and the person whose card was confiscated had no choice but to wait until he had gotten a chance to meet with the officer, who might return the card if he was satisfied that he got what he wanted. Others had come seeking different kinds of permits. So many of the normal activities of life and death required permits, whether it was travel, or work in Israel, or renewal of car or driving licenses, or the transport of the corpse of a relative who happened to die while on a visit to Jordan. The rest of the crowd was waiting for the military court session because they had a son or brother or friend whose trial was scheduled that day. Most of those waiting in this driveway were villagers. Um Jamil, an extremely nervous well-dressed middle-class woman, was an exception. She was accompanied by her brother, who had a long face and wore a long blue cardigan with low pockets. He seemed wealthy and urbane and was being very solicitous to his sister, trying to calm her down and give her confidence. Every so often she would burst into a loud scream: "Why, why is this happening to me? What have I done wrong? I gave everything to my children. Why should my son do this to me?"

"It will be all right," her brother would whisper in his deep, velvety voice. "Stop worrying. The judge is sure to take into account that Jamil is only a child with no will of his own. Children make mistakes. I am sure it will be all right."

I could not help contrasting this mother's attitude to that of Khalid's mother. I was sure that her loss was even greater. Khalid was her only hope of escape from abject poverty. Yet I had been impressed by how nonjudgmental she was. She did not claim to understand but deferred to the better judgment of her son.

"Khalid always knew what he was doing," she told me. "At a very young age he was very responsible. He took care of his four brothers and was always kind and attentive. I don't understand what is happening, but I have a strong belief in God and in my son." Then she would add, looking directly at me, "And in you. I can tell you are a good man and will do your best to help my son."

I was not going to let her down. I refused to take any money from her, had spent many hours preparing the case, and was prepared to make a plea of no case to answer. I had high hopes that Khalid would be released.

It was already ten o'clock, the time the court was scheduled to begin, but there was no sign of the judge or the prosecutor. As I waited, I passed my time observing the other people in the crowd.

Not far from me sat a *mukhtar* [village elder] from the village of Khirbatah in the Ramallah area. He had found himself a high stone where he sat cross-legged wrapped in a warm, light brown *aba,* the color and texture of goat skin, which it probably was. Unlike the others in the driveway he seemed content. He was surrounded by people from his village on whose behalf he had come. His good relationship with the military governor gave him access to the ear of the governor, into which he whispered good words about those villagers who had come with him. The villagers were either in some sort of trouble with the authorities or had failed on their own to obtain a needed permit.

One of them peeled an egg, sprinkled it with salt, and offered it to the *mukhtar* with some home-baked brown *taboon* bread. He accepted this and a red tomato offered by another villager. From his higher position on the stone he watched his fellow villagers spread their food on the wet ground, inviting everyone else to join them. The *mukhtar* started reminiscing.

"My association with the Tegart goes back a long time," he declared. "I used to come here in 1950 to meet with King Abdullah of Jordan. In those days I was still a young man. I also met many times with His Excellency Glub Pasha the British commander. *Wallah,* by God, he spoke good Arabic. Then the years rolled and the Jews came and I started to come to meet every new military governor who took charge. God be praised I always managed to keep good relations with the masters of the Tegart. One comes and one goes, some good some not so good, but I always have to be there for your sake. God be praised. How the years roll!"

"God keep you and preserve you" one of the villagers said. "You have always served us well. Some green olives?"

He handed the *mukhtar* a few olives wrapped in wet newspaper. He ate them one by one in silence, throwing the pits across to the empty field behind him.

A Druze guard came to the gate from the direction of the military court carrying a piece of paper. He stood behind the gate and declared: "The person with the name I call must come forward. Only two relatives are allowed for each case at the military court. Get that? Two relatives only."

As I learned later, this Druze guard came from the village of Isifia near Haifa, which like the Tegart lay at a high altitude and was surrounded with pine trees. This was his second year of service in Ramallah and he had come to like his job. He was in his midforties and seemed to have cultivated a stern expression, which served him well in his difficult work guarding the troubled crowds. But underneath his sober facade was a softer interior. He never used foul language or force. The expression gave him an air of authority that served him well, and made it appear that he meant what he said and would not be otherwise persuaded. Those farther down the driveway could not see his face and refused to obey his command. As soon as he called the first name the whole crowd pushed against the bar in front of them. It was at this point that Captain Moshe, one of the officers of the military government, drove up. He blew his horn to get the crowd to move away and as soon as he got to the guard, shouted: "How often must I tell you that I don't want anyone in the driveway? Let them stand on the side. It is not a parade here."

The guard ordered the crowd to move aside and explained to the officer that he had told the crowd but they had moved up when he began to read the names.

"What do they think this is? A game of bingo, or some sort of park?" he said, addressing the crowd.

The officer's eye fell on a young well-built man leaning on a tree, smoking a cigarette. He didn't like his open and bold expression. "What are you standing there for?" he asked.

"I'm waiting to collect my ID," the man said without removing his cigarette.

"Take away your cigarette when you speak to me. What's your name?"

"Mahdi Hammad."

"I will remember your name and we'll see if you get your card today. You must learn manners first."

With this the military officer stepped on the accelerator. His car zipped forward with a shriek of tires and disappeared around the corner. He was on his way to another day of work at the Tegart prison.

"You heard what the officer said," the Druze now declared. "Stay back. Only the person whose name I call may come forward. Ahmad Abdel Rahman. Who are the relatives of Ahmad Abdel Rahman?"

Three people approached the guard waving a piece of paper over their head. "It's us. Us."

"I said only two are allowed."

He began frisking the first two and let them through. The third approached with his hands raised. He was a respectful-looking old man.

"Only two for each prisoner," I said.

"But I am his uncle."

"Go back," the guard said, motioning with his hand.

"You must let me in," the old man with the goatee said, his eyes shining. "I am your guest."

"Stay on the side," the guard said, mellowing. "I will see at the end if there are any places left. Sami Abed Mahmoud."

And so it went, on and on and on.

I did not want to take anyone's turn, but after a while I announced to the Druze that I was a lawyer coming for a case and he let me through without frisking. As I walked toward the prosecutor's office, I saw Um Jamil walking uncertainly toward the court ahead of the crowd. Before I left them, I heard her confide to her brother that she was trembling so hard that she could hardly walk. He held her by the arm and led her into the courtroom.

The court was not going to start at ten as scheduled. Two witnesses for one of the offenders on trial had not been summoned. It was the responsibility of the court secretary, Estee, a young Israeli doing her reserve duty, to make sure that all the witnesses were summoned.

Back and forth between the rooms Estee raced, making one telephone call and answering another in the next room. Estee was a conscientious officer who was trying to do a good job in a confusing and erratic system. She was determined to correct whatever mistakes were made and was trying to get the police on the line and arrange for the witnesses to be sent before the arrival of the judge.

It was eleven when the court was finally called to session. I began to worry that there would not be time for Khalid's case. The thought that there would be an adjournment angered me, but there was nothing to do but to wait.

Jamil's case was the first to be heard. The court heard the last witness, the judge asked the sides to sum up, and he adjourned the case for judgment and sentencing after the lunch break. The next case had a dramatic start. The mother of one of the accused made her way to the bar. She was short and emaciated. She wore small plastic blue shoes. She stood on tiptoe, stretched up her neck and looked at the judge with small pleading eyes. Her frazzled face was drained of blood. In a low choking voice she begged him to be lenient with her son. The judge begrudgingly allowed her to say a few words before he called the guard and asked him to expel her from the courtroom. Then with great dispatch and efficiency he went through the case. Before long the prosecutor was summing up and the judge looked as though he was calculating the fate of these four accused. The little boy of one of the mothers began to cry.

"Stop this child," the judge ordered. "Take him out of the courtroom. I said I didn't want any children here."

The defense lawyer sitting next to me was carving FATAH — the main PLO faction — with his ballpoint pen on the side of the witness stand facing us. The judge asked the accused to stand and read his verdict: guilty. He asked if they had anything to say. There was a moment of silence, which was broken by someone in the audience who advised the accused in a whisper: "Ask for mercy." One of the accused answered in a loud voice. "I don't want any mercy from this court."

"*Shakeit,*" Silence, the judge screamed and declared that he was sentencing each of them to five years of actual imprisonment and three suspended.

Together the accused shouted: "Long live the revolution, long live free Palestine. Revolution until victory."

"Take them away," the judge said.

I looked to the back at where Um Jamil sat and saw that her face had turned yellow. She must have been thinking of her son.

As the accused were being taken away, their families followed. Some approached the Israeli lawyer. "You said it would not be so long," they told her.

"I told you they give harsh sentences when wounding takes place. What can I do?" she declared without emotion and walked out.

Now the judge decided that there wasn't time to start another case and declared the start of the lunch break. We all had to stand up as he stomped out. Then we ambled outside to wait some more.

When the lunch break finally ended, the judge came back. I hoped that his lunch had made him mellower for the sake of Jamil and Khalid, but there was no evidence of this. He found Jamil guilty and sentenced him to three years of actual imprisonment and one suspended. I expected that pandemonium would break out, but I was not prepared for what came. Um Jamil did not break into loud screams. She became passive and was adamant that as long as her son was going to be kept in this place, she too would stay with him. Her son seemed embarrassed by the scene his mother was making.

"Don't worry about me," he told her. "I am not alone here. I have many friends around me. I will be all right."

She tried to hang on to him but the soldiers separated them and took the son away. The mother refused to move. She had to be physically dragged out of the court.

There was a short break as one prosecutor and set of lawyers left the court and the judge waited for the next prosecutor to arrive. I took this opportunity to leave the court and breathe some fresh air. I stood away from the door of the court in the cold wind and watched Jamil, who was still in the small room just outside the door, waiting to be transferred to prison. He held the bars of the tiny window and put his head between them, calling on his mother to leave. He looked positively embarrassed. His uncle leaned down over his squatting sister and was trying to talk her into leaving.

"It's no use," he said. "The boy has been sentenced. Your sit-in will do him no good. No good whatsoever."

The soldiers who were passing by on their way to their offices stopped to check the scene and then walked by. I heard the judge announcing the start of the next session, still not Khalid's, and moved back into the courtroom.

The next case was what is called in Hebrew a *zoota*, a mini trial within a trial, which the defense lawyer had requested to prove that the confession taken from his client was extracted under torture. The protagonist of the show was none other than Barzali himself.

I had a chance to examine this man. He was tall and bony with much pent-up nervous energy. He walked with his head high and took the stand looking at no one but the judge, as though he would not condescend to acknowledge the existence of anyone else. Even when the defense lawyer questioned him he did not turn to face him. He answered very briefly, always looking straight ahead. Usually his responses were brief and in the negative: No I did not use force. No I never practice torture. No I did not keep the prisoner from sleeping. No. No. No. A straightforward, unequivocal denial of every claim made by the defense lawyer.

Soon Barzali began to fidget and look at his watch and then at the judge as if to indicate that he had wasted enough time on this charade. Surely he had other more important work to do. He wanted to be released.

I tried to think of Khalid alone with this man but the thought was too horrible. I grew anxious about the time left and was not unhappy when this little trial finished and the judge opened the last file in his pile of cases for today. But to my dismay it was not that of Khalid.

I stood up and protested but got nowhere. The judge asked me to check with the court's secretary. I stomped angrily out of the courtroom and found that Um Jamil was still in the same position with her patient brother leaning over her looking wasted and exasperated.

As I walked toward the secretariat, Barzali walked in front of me. He beat his feet on the ground with his heavy boots as if he owned the world. He was walking toward the jail where Khalid was incarcerated.

I followed him until he turned the corner and stood before the formidable prison gate. I heard him bang heavily on the metal gate, calling to the guard with a loud commanding voice: *"Tiftakh Tiftakh,"* open up. The guard approached, his keys clicking on his side, and I heard the key turning in the lock. The door was opened and Barzali entered and disappeared behind the heavy metal gate, which was shut and locked behind him.

I waited beneath the window of what I assumed were the torture chambers straining my ears to hear a sound from behind the wall. I could hear none, but in my mind I followed the angry steps of Barzali down the prison corridor. No one could speak to him when he was in such an angry state. He went straight to the cell where Khalid was kept. Khalid was still hooded so he could see nothing, but he could hear the heavy footsteps approaching his cell and he knew from their sound that it was Barzali. The steps approached and Khalid knew he was soon going to be alone with his tormentor. But he did not think of shouting. There was no one to call and no one to stop Barzali. Khalid, the Palestinian detainee, and Barzali, the Israeli interrogator, were alone in the deep labyrinths of this old Tegart. *No one will hear Khalid. No one will see what might happen to him. And no one in this Tegart prison will come to Khalid's aid. He and Barzali are alone.*

And I, who now knew about the torture that was taking place inside these walls, could no longer remain silent. I knew what I had to do. I left the Tegart precincts and returned to the office of Al Haq to plan with my colleagues a new campaign to combat torture.

It was Khalid, and cases like his, that inspired me to turn to human rights. My activity in the military courtroom was not enough. There I was on the turf of the Israelis, who were free to reject my pleas without censure, no matter how eloquently I presented them. I knew after this case that I needed to be a witness, to stand between Khalid and Barzali and to bring others to be witnesses as well. Our fight was to reveal the pain and dehumanization that the occupation was inflicting on the oppressor no less than on the oppressed.

CHAPTER SEVENTEEN

ONE EVENING AFTER a long day at the military court and the office I went to the office of Al Haq to meet with the staff. One of the field-workers gave me a tape recording of an interview that he had conducted with a fourteen-year-old shepherd from Jenin who was recuperating in hospital. This young man had been out grazing his sheep when a demonstration took place. He had not participated in the demonstration; nor had he thrown stones at Israeli soldiers. Nevertheless he was arrested upon his return to Jenin and taken to the notorious, newly established prison for young people in an old British army barracks in the Faraa Valley. The interrogator kept pushing the boy: Confess, Confess! But he had done nothing except graze his sheep. He had nothing to confess. Whoever enters Faraa leaves either with a confession or broken limbs. From his hospital bed, this was how the young man described on tape his ordeal:

> They dragged me to the room of the interrogator. "You are going to confess," the chief interrogator told me and gave me a blow on the groin. I started shouting and screaming. They dragged me into a room, took off all my clothes and put me under a hot shower. Then they threw cold water at my naked body and left me to shiver. Leave me alone, I screamed. I have done nothing. What do you want me to confess? But they didn't leave me alone. They continued to beat me until they broke one of my arms.

What I heard did not surprise me; such scenes are repeated again and again. It is estimated that a third of the young males in the West Bank have been humiliated or harassed by the authorities. But hearing the strong voice of this young man describing his ordeal made me think that behind prison walls was a truth that exposed the lie so many of us live.

I thought of my own experiences when I had gone to prison to meet with clients. The guards bring the detainee to the lawyer's room — which is itself an embodiment of a lie. Unlike the rest of the place, it is quiet, orderly, with a desk and chairs. It is a show-piece in a place of squalor, violence, and injustice. The prisoner would be brought in kicking and shouting at the guard. Before the guard left him in the tidy room, he would hurl one last obscenity at the guard, the prison, and the occupation.

"These people are heartless, racist, cowards," he'd say to me breathlessly.

The detainee can say what none of us can. He has more dignity in his prison uniform than I do in a suit. The prisoner has made a decision to fight for his beliefs. He is not afraid of declaring them and taking the consequences. His life has become simpler and more honest. The rest of us hold our beliefs back. We are experts at exer-cising restraint. And most of us feel guilty. We are guilty.

In the early 1980s I was exposed, for the first time in my life, to people who lived and acted unlike the people I had grown up with. Many of my convictions were challenged; I began to belong to more than one world. In my commercial practice at the office I behaved normally. But when I went to the military court I had to deal with a different world, one that my background had not prepared me for. The movement between these contrasting worlds and the con-stant need to adjust took much out of me. I was exhausted by the end of each workweek.

I learned to escape from this heavy workload by walking in the hills around Ramallah. I walked in winter, when the hills were full of mist and rainwater flowed between the folds of the hills down to the wadi, where it collected and rushed with great force tum-bling over the smooth boulders and pebbles. I had been at home for three days writing and I wanted to be outside in spite of the rain. Penny had come to visit me. Idealism, love of the land, and interest in writing had brought us together a few years earlier. The strong friendship developed into love and in 1988 we married and lived in a house not far from the hills. That wet winter day we braved the cold and the rain and rambled all the way to the wet valley, amazed at how changed the hills were from their usual barrenness in the dry season. We continued to walk along the rushing stream, stopping to admire the slowly seeping mist that covered the hills with a gossamer film of diaphanous white until it got dark and we lost our way. The wind and the rain started again and we were drenched. We started climbing but lost the easy path that we had used to get down. We continued to climb the steepest side of the hill, our shoes heavy with thick mud, the cold wind blowing against our wet bodies. But we had the hills all to ourselves. Rain to most people here means staying indoors. The colloquial Arabic word for "winter" and for "rain" is the same. Winter/rain is the time you spend indoors. When we finally made it up to the road it was pitch dark.

We also walked in spring when the hills are at their best. Then the birds are out in force, partridges, sparrows, orange-tufted sunbirds. The springs gush out and the hills are covered with myriad colors. The cyclamens nestle in every rock and make a home in every nook. Red poppies spread their bloom on the flat areas between the stones, and yellow mustard seed and yellow broom come in patches bunched up in large luminous bushes at the borders like drunken hedges. Blue bugloss, miniature iris, and wild orchid punctuate the carpets of red and yellow.

Nor is the beauty any less striking in summer when the different shades of brown predominate, the rocks scattered in the fields like large scabs between the green and silver leaves of the olive trees that dot these ancient terraces.

For rest during our walks we would sit on the roofs of the ancient watchtowers, old structures built out of stone by olive growers several hundred years ago. Next to one of these structures someone had dug out of stone a royal throne for himself. After a long walk it felt so comfortable. We took turns sitting and relaxing and admiring the undulating rolling hills that spread as far as the eye could see. But this quiet and peaceful paradise was not to remain ours for long. Soon surveyors began to appear with their tripods and theodolite. They were followed by Palestinian laborers, who put up barbed wire to fence the expropriated land. Before long bulldozers came and sliced and turned and leveled and destroyed the ancient terracing, uprooting the trees and flattening the tops of the hills and turning the slopes into wide level stretches where soon ready-made homes with sloping red-tiled roofs were deposited. They looked like plastic Swiss chalets that did not belong on these dry ancient hills. The first settlement to be established in the area where we walked was Beit El northeast of Ramallah. Then came Dolev to the northwest. Neither of these turned into cities, as was the case with Givat Zeev southwest of Ramallah. It was established on low hills where I had once driven at the end of my workday to watch the sunset. The wheat swished with the twilight breeze before the sun set, then, green in spring and golden yellow early in the summer. Now when I drive to Jerusalem at night, I see the lights of this settlement. It has spread over several hills, lacing a landscape where few houses had been.

My days alternated between hard, tense work and intervals of tranquility and romance. My father tried to restrain me while some of my colleagues at Al Haq lobbied for escalation. For four years the organization had been documenting and analyzing the Israeli policy of land acquisition. It was time to do more. They decided to squat on some land threatened with confiscation and refuse to move. This new practice was first tried on a plot next to Givat Zeev. The settlers threatened and shot in the air but my colleagues refused to be intimidated. Eventually one of them had to be picked up by the blade of the bulldozer. But nothing was to retard the settlement program, not international condemnation, not human rights organizations, and not obdurate activists who were willing to risk their lives to stop this aggression.

The Al Haq activists did not get hurt in this scuffle. Others were less fortunate. One woman from Beitin whose land was claimed by the nearby settlement of Beit El was tilling the soil with her children when she was shot and killed. Close to Givat Zeev, Sabri Graib refused to budge from his house. He continued, whatever the risk, to work his land. Al Haq supported his legal challenge before the military court and the Israeli High Court. We visited him, took his statement, and included it in a book titled *In Their Own Words,* which was published jointly with the Human Rights Commission of the World Council of Churches in Geneva. His children reported to us how the struggle to save the land had consumed their father.

"He cannot work, he is constantly going from one lawyer to another, taking papers, giving testimony. At night the settlers and the army come to our house. They try to pressure him to sell. They shoot in the air. Now they have built a fence around our house."

We saw the fence. It surrounded the house on all sides, leaving only a narrow passage. For many years this brave family remained in their house as the dynamic settlement spread around them on all sides. They were an exemplary demonstration of Palestinian *sumoud*, steadfastness, in the face of the determined ideological onslaught of the Israeli settlers with seemingly unlimited means at their disposal.

The physical development of the settlements accompanied the development of the legal structures governing these foreign enclaves. They were not part of Israel, which meant that Israeli law could not be applied. And yet they could not exist under the same restrictive laws that had been imposed on the Palestinians. A way had to be found to allow the settlers to enjoy the benefits of Israeli law without formally annexing the areas. The evolution of the legal resolution to this dilemma interested me, and I followed every step of it. By now the military orders began to be properly published. Yet those pertaining to the settlements were made as regulations and were not made available to Palestinians. I had to find a way to get them, so I befriended the Druze translator who worked at the legal unit of the Israeli Command in the West Bank where he was doing his military duty. He gave me copies of these regulations and I studied and wrote about them. I could see that an apartheid-type system of law was developing before my eyes. Two parallel unequal legal systems, one applicable to Palestinians, the other to Israeli Jews. I believed that if this was pointed out there would be many, in Israel and outside, who would oppose this development. I spared no effort to write and speak out, to alert those who stood for the principles of the equality and inalienable rights of all human beings. More was coming to be known about the reality of life in the occupied territories, but the settlers continued to pursue their objectives unabated.

There was also something intellectually intriguing about my human rights work. Perhaps I was compensating for the paucity of intellectual stimulation in my professional work, which tended to be formal and routine. I was intrigued by the Israeli usage of law. They were calling their activities in taking the land legal, and in accord with local and international law. But they were not. I was sure they were not. Yet those who had developed the legal arguments were serious judicial minds who could not be easily discredited. I worked hard until one day it all fell into place.

I was checking on property that had been declared state land by the Israeli authorities. I had always assumed that such transactions were recorded at the special register in the military headquarters in Ramallah. They were not. They were registered instead at the Israel Land Authority in Jerusalem, where close to 93 percent of Israel's lands were listed as public lands. This discovery clarified the ideological basis of what was taking place. By occupying the West Bank the Jewish state was reclaiming Jewish patrimony over the land. When the occupation began, only one-third of the land in the West Bank was registered in the name of Palestinian owners. For the rest, if the owner ceased to use the land for a period of ten consecutive years, he was deemed by the military authorities as having lost his right to it. The Israeli authorities were then justified in declaring it state land. It now reverted to the exclusive ownership of the Jews. We, non-Jews, were no more than squatters with no inherent rights to our land. The Jewish state was willing to allow us to keep land that we were actually using, but the rest went back to its "rightful owners," not through force but through legal strategies justified by distorted interpretations of local land law.

Other legal ploys were used to achieve an administrative and legal separation between the fledgling Jewish minority in the West Bank and the Palestinian majority there. The former would be administered directly by Israel, the latter through the so-called Civil Administration created in compliance with Israel's interpretation of its commitment in the Camp David Accords reached in 1978.

The Israeli military government was to be withdrawn but not abolished. It would delegate its powers to a civilian administrator who would head a structure that took responsibility for the civilian aspects of the lives of Palestinians. Upon its establishment in 1981, this administrative structure was headed by an Israeli military officer. The declared plan was that his powers would eventually be handed over to the local Palestinians. The new political group, which it was hoped would assume these, was to be composed of village leaders. This was the idea of Menahem Milson, an Israeli professor who argued that since 75 percent of Palestinians live in villages, then village leagues should be established, armed, and empowered to assume control over the life of the society. In this way the urban centers, whose elite was tied to the PLO, would be controlled by the rural areas. A new alternative leadership would emerge that would be willing to cooperate with Israel.

My father felt particularly distressed by this new development. It was a perversion of what he advocated. The only alternative to the PLO that Israel was willing to accept was a criminal collaborationist grouping. In the spring of 1982, several months after the establishment of the Israeli Civil Administration and the inauguration of the Village Leagues, violence broke out. In the chaos that ensued the settlers saw an opportunity to exercise vigilantism and consolidate their control over the land. In the village of Sinjil near the settlement of Shilo, settlers kidnapped a schoolboy whom they said had thrown stones at their buses and cars. They also shot randomly, causing boys walking home from school to run to the hills for cover. I went to the area to investigate and found one distressed mother whose son had not returned. She had been to the prison in Ramallah where she was told he was kept. She took with her a sweater for her young son; the prison guard took it from her and promised to give it to him.

"But I have a bad feeling in my heart. I do not believe that Rasheed is in prison. I fear for him. Will you help me find him?" she asked me.

I did my best, and kept up the pressure until three days later a shepherd found the boy in the hills above his village. He had been killed by the bullets of one of the settlers, who was never made to pay for his crime.

That spring there were many demonstrations. Young men were shot and in some cases lost their lives. Schools and universities were closed; checkpoints were placed at the entrance to all towns and many villages. There was widespread rejection of both the Civil Administration and the Village Leagues. The protests continued unabated. The Village Leagues were eventually disbanded, but the Civil Administration remained in place, later to become the basis for the political arrangement between Israel and the PLO.

My path was clear: Faced with the knowledge of torture, my responsibility was to bear witness and urge others to do likewise through documentation of the torture cases. My response to the land expropriation was to expose the process and point out how it violated local and international law. In doing so I assumed that for the process to succeed it had to appear legal. Exposure of the legal violation could embarrass Israel into changing its ways.

I knew that I shared my fear about the loss of our land with my father. He too was very concerned about the long-term consequences of the widespread establishment of Israeli settlements in the occupied territories. He may even have been the instigator of my sense of foreboding. What we didn't share was a response to our common apprehension.

We often traveled together to the court in Hebron, where my father was respected for his skills and dedication as a lawyer. On the way we saw how quickly the land in the southern part of the country was being transformed. The first settlements to be established after 1967, Gush Etzion and Kiryat Arba, could not be seen from the road. When we traveled from Bethlehem to Hebron, all we could see were low, rolling, terraced hills planted with grapevines. In spring the young twigs began to appear on the spindly, fibrous, twisted brown stems that had seemed so dead and lifeless. Vines would fill with leaves, and new branches would cascade from one terrace to another. The grapes hung low over the stones, yellow green and eggplant blue.

But then slowly this countryside began to change. The twisted vines were uprooted and lay mangled on the ground. The earth was turned over, sliced and cut, and reconstructed. The terracing disappeared and in its place wide expanses of flat land were created on which ready-made houses would be perched. The assault on the land was severe.

Ideology and the bulldozers are the bane of this land. The first inspires and the second implements and makes possible in a day what used to take a score of men a month to accomplish. It had not been possible for Palestinians to build on these remote, intractable hills. They simply lacked the means to level the ground. Possession of a bulldozer by Palestinians required special permission from the military authorities and substantial material resources. Only the Israeli side had the means to turn a hill into a plain. Not that Palestinians necessarily had a more developed aesthetic sense or stronger ecological concerns; they simply lacked the means to restructure the land as the Israeli settlers were able to. They had to follow its contours, build along the lines of the hills. Their villages and their gardens were in harmony with the land, organic out-growths that pleased the eye. But now architects prepared designs in remote offices and heavy machinery was brought to execute them. Hills were removed if they stood in the way. They had their tops flattened; they were gouged and sliced to produce new leveling totally out of proportion with the gentle curves of the surrounding hills. All the land was at the mercy of the huge mouth of this rav-enous machine.

But the gun has also played a role in the destruction of the land-scape. The owners of the land were kept at bay with guns. Those operating these bulldozers, as well as the surveyors and planners who came to determine the future shape of things, always came armed. In a normal situation, no government would be able to execute plans on this scale on the property of such large numbers of people who received no compensation without risking mass rebellion.

Most of these hills had never been smitten by the curse of machines. They have remained more or less unchanged since the time of the prophets and ancient Jewish heroes like Elazar, Einav, and Emanuel, for whom the Jewish settlements were being named. My father and I looked at one particularly noisy machine as we drove down to Hebron across the hills. Its chain wheels scaled up the hill like a tank, destroying everything in its path. When it reached midway it stopped. The driver moved his lever; the ripper tooth dropped and the drilling began. Then the blade scooped whatever could be scooped. The fibrous rubble composed of rock, soil, and the stems and roots of the ancient grapes and olive trees was lifted triumphantly up in the air before being dumped into trucks raising clouds of dust in the air. The trucks carrying their loot drove down the new path that had been opened by the bulldozer.

On one of my trips with my father we saw several large

bulldozers hard at work destroying the landscape. When we drove back at the end of the day we saw that eight ready-made housing units had been placed on the leveled areas. A new settlement was in the making. The speed in which it had come to be constructed clearly indicated how quickly it could be removed.

My father sneered at my naïveté. But then he had experienced the transformation of the Palestine of 1948 into Israel. He saw the way a small settlement that never seemed threatening had developed. They stayed and prospered while the ancient city in which he lived dwindled and shrank. "Once these communities come to be established," he said, "it will be impossible to remove them. Children will be born who will know no other home. This is why I have been saying that we must find a political solution now before it is too late."

"I agree," I said. "We must not allow these settlements to be built."

"How do you propose to do this?" he asked.

"By exposing what is happening and proving that the process is illegal."

"And then what?"

"Then the world will condemn the Israeli practices."

"We are not lacking in resolutions condemning Israel. There are scores of them at the UN. What good did they ever do us? In 1948, the UN resolved that the Palestinian refugees should be allowed to return or be compensated. Did this happen? It is already thirty years since this resolution passed. And you tell me we need more resolutions."

"Should we then give up?" I challenged my father.

"Neither war nor your human rights activism will solve our conflict with Israel. Only a political initiative. And soon. Before there is no land left to speak of."

As I listened to my father I could not help thinking how often I had heard him repeat the same words: *political initiative, peace, two-state solution*. Then I said: "I am not a supporter of war."

"Your support of human rights uncoupled with a political solution will get you nowhere."

Why could I never agree with my father? Was it just a son's rebellion? Why did I content myself so myopically with human rights and steer away from politics? Was it, as he claimed, political immaturity, or were there other psychological reasons? I know I had a blind spot. Whenever I spoke to my father about these matters I would close up. After a certain point I would be unable to listen. And he would stop listening to me after I started repeating my convictions as a catechism. We were at cross-purposes. We had many discussions but never had a meeting of minds. Why did I close my mind to my father?

Because this was the compromise I made. Human rights activism was how I would serve the cause to which I was committed. I concentrated on what was achievable. For years I had seen how my father had suffered for his political activism. His integrity was questioned, he was denounced and accused of treason, his life was threatened. Jordan withdrew his passport and he became persona non grata in that country. Whatever public activity he undertook was looked upon with suspicion. Everything he did was suspect. When he tried to get a group together to establish a national university the project was vehemently opposed. When he called for municipal elections he was accused of calling for the entrenchment of the occupation and supporting the Israeli proposal for the creation of a Palestinian civil administration. Even his efforts at organizing the legal profession were condemned. His advocacy of a Palestinian state in the occupied territories turned him into a traitor in the eyes of the political leadership. He was an energetic, public-spirited man who was never allowed to succeed. He had become a marked man, excluded, isolated, and depressed. It was very likely that my choice of human rights activism and my aversion to politics were ways of distancing myself from my father's path.

And yet only my father thought my work in human rights was nonpolitical. All other quarters — Israel, Jordan, and the PLO —

saw this work as a suspicious form of subversive political activism
disguised as human rights activism.

Israeli security could not believe that there was a Palestinian
activist who was not engaged in politics and, consequently,
involved with the PLO, then the bitter enemy of Israel. But which
faction of the PLO did I secretly belong to? They decided it was the
Popular Front for the Liberation of Palestine, or PFLP, the extreme
political group led by AUB graduate Dr. George Habash. The PLO
thought that the Palestinian struggle against Israel was political
and that human rights work was a distraction inspired by the CIA.
Jordan feared that Al Haq would develop into an alternative bar
association for the striking Palestinian lawyers, who were still part
of the Jordanian bar. The local military government persisted in
summoning my father and giving him ultimatums about my
activities.

But I labored on. The international connections of Al Haq
were increasing. The list of publications exposing Israeli practices
was growing. The organization received high exposure and invita-
tions from around the world to participate in conferences and
present findings on the legal and human rights violations of the
Israeli military occupation. We had received several prestigious
international human rights awards, including one presented by
President Jimmy Carter, and had developed the best law and
human rights library in the Palestinian area. We offered free legal
advice to thousands of applicants, documented violations
throughout the occupied territories, and developed a computerized
database that provided accurate data on all aspects of Palestinian
human rights under Israeli occupation to human rights organizations around the world. The organization was beginning to have
an impact. The image of Israeli occupation was changing. Israeli
apologists had to work much harder to defend the Israeli government's policies. Yet the policies were not changed, and here was the
strength of my father's position. I was only too conscious of my

ineffectiveness against the strong Israeli ideological machine. A confrontation, which took place at this time with the Israeli head of the Supreme Planning Council, comes to mind. He was a slightly stooped young man who spoke with a soft nasal voice, but behind this unassuming facade was the most determined and hard-working ideologue I ever met. His job was to prepare the zoning plans for the expanded Jewish settlements while at the same time restricting Palestinian spatial development, and he did his utmost to promote Israeli settlements in the West Bank.

I had been trying to get planning permission for the new campus of Birzeit University, and he had created all sorts of obstacles. During one of our meetings he retracted a promise he had made during our previous meeting. I reminded him of what he had said. He denied having ever said it. I was furious and called him a liar. I expected this would aggravate him. Perhaps he would react as the woman soldier had done at the airport in 1971 when I was traveling to AUB, but he didn't seem to care. It was this incident that made me realize that in his world order I did not exist, and nothing I could say would make the slightest impression. He was involved in a massive enterprise. He was responsible for the preparation of schemes that would turn all the hills of the West Bank into fields of concrete. Making roads, playgrounds, shopping centers, and whole towns out of wild, empty hills. I was dealing with words. Words meant nothing to him. It was action that mattered. He saw me as my father saw me, a troublesome young man. So what if a Palestinian called him a liar to his face? Who was I anyway? I could say whatever I wanted. My words would not be heard. They were as inaudible as I was invisible and would not affect his program of creating facts on the ground. His arrogant indifference infuriated me more than if he had struck me down with a concrete slab from one of his settlements.

And as though confirming my doubts my father was now asking: "What use is all this hard work you are doing? You are taking time from the law practice, wasting your life and your energy. What for? Do you think that if anything should happen to you or if you should need anything anyone would come to your aid? Do you think you will find reward for your work?"

"I am not doing this for reward" was my response. What I didn't say was that my father's experience had taught me to be extremely cautious and had lowered my expectations to the minimum. I would be delighted if I could be saved from condemnation and not share his fate. And I had reason for optimism. In time, after our work at the organization proved itself, the earlier suspicions that we were a front for various types of political groupings began to dissipate. We could not be a factional organization, because our employees came from many different factions and we helped whoever needed our assistance. We refrained from making political pronouncements and concentrated on doing the work and getting it published. Then it became public information for which we did not claim copyright. The PLO began to find our work useful and often referred to it in its campaigns condemning the occupation. We had finally won legitimacy. And I had succeeded in establishing myself as a public figure whose nationalist credentials and commitment to the cause were not in question. I had finally succeeded in distinguishing myself from my father.

But I was not a success in the eyes of the man I cared most to please. My father was disappointed. He continued to insist that my life made no sense.

CHAPTER EIGHTEEN

BY THE TIME I returned to Ramallah and began to be active in human rights work, my father, with fourteen years of diligent political work behind him since the start of the occupation, started to feel fatigued and desperate. He had come to his own conclusions about the futility of political work in the Palestinian context. In 1948 he had lost his work and property and he could see that the same mistakes were being repeated now. Rhetoric was replacing action. He strongly believed that the threatening talk against the Israeli state by those who couldn't pose a real military threat was most damaging. Israel could continue its harsh measures against the local population using security as justification. He had come to believe that Palestine would not have a good future.

He was afraid, and I felt his fear. It was the fear that comes from living under the rule of a foreign country without any protection. There was danger everywhere, at every point in the day. You could be arrested, stopped in the street, stopped on the roads by a military patrol that could get away with murder on the grounds that you were resisting arrest, or escaping, or refusing an order to stop. The legal system was in disarray. Corruption was rampant. Nothing seemed to work. It took hours just to telephone the court in Nablus. The consequences of bad administration and the absence of development grated on my father, whose every effort at bringing about change was frustrated. There was also the need for permits, which could be withdrawn without appeal. If you were subjected to violence or theft or any kind of domestic crime there was no effective police protection. And then when you were a member of the minority of Anglicans within the minority of Christians, as we were, in a society with a Moslem majority, the sense of being on your own was heightened.

To allay his fear, my father had done what most people in his class and station had done: found people who he could call in case of difficulty who respected him and wished him no harm. He also tried to cultivate functional relations with those with military authority — also the norm for many in the population who understood that without such relations one's life and business interests would be greatly hampered. Like every man in a difficult situation, my father was trying to manage.

And then I came and disrupted all these careful survival tactics. Rather than help or accept what was offered, gratefully and quietly, I had declared war: I spoke out, I asked embarrassing questions.

I had grown up a political virgin in a situation that resembled a political brothel. And I was a hopeless case. My virginity was endemic. It could not be lost. Whatever exposure I got, whatever experience, whatever advice, I held tenaciously to it and would not let go.

My father was particularly worried and did his best to make a man of me according to Arab culture. But I was like the good soldier Schweik coming to a charged battlefield, a highly politicized situation, and refusing to recognize it for what it was. Now I realize how unusual my outlook was. I acted and operated as though there was no reality to this political context. I was incomprehensible to most people, and quite possibly insufferable.

I placed myself in the position of the critic, the divulger of all the ills of those who controlled our life. To my father it was all so idiotic: Where did I think I was living? How could I possibly get away with denouncing those in power as torturers and violators of basic human rights? They would not take it. They would strike back, as was to be expected. And what would it have been for? Who then would protect me?

But father didn't realize that in my own way I was being careful and calculating. Of course I could never be sure, but I

believed that I was slowly building up the credibility of the organization and its friends and supporters in Israel and abroad to the
point that it was possible to speak out as openly as we were doing.

My father was not proud of my activities. What use was criti-
cizing the Israeli occupation for its bad judiciary? It would alienate
the judges and only make them rule against the cases handled by our
office. Had my father not tried to get the lawyers to form a local bar?
And had he not seen how immobilized the lawyers were because of
divided loyalties? Those among the lawyers who paid allegiance to
the different political factions of the PLO and to Jordan would always
make sure that no program of reform succeeded. Under these circumstances should I not stay away from trouble and concentrate on
my own private life and professional work?

I was too much of an enigma, especially to the lawyers and
judges. I was so different as to be worrying. I was not behaving like
other lawyers my age. I did not speak in the same way, didn't behave
in the same manner, didn't smoke, and didn't participate in the same
jokes. And most important of all I was still unmarried at thirty-four.
Why was I showing no interest in marriage? What was wrong?

These questions which I often heard the lawyers ask about me
were, I believe, stimulated by resentment. But the greater jealousy,
the hidden (and sometimes not-so-hidden) aggression was against
my father. Every possible ammunition was used against him. With
my nonconformity I was another weapon in their arsenal. "Why is
your son not getting married?" a paunchy lawyer would ask,
holding a cigarette with one hand, smoothing his scraggly mustache
with a free finger. Or, "Why have you not married off your son
yet?" — thus implying that my father was deficient in the fulfillment of his duties as an Arab parent.

"My son doesn't want to get married," my father would answer,
trying to disguise the anguish in his voice.

"Doesn't want to get married. Why? Is anything wrong?"
Then the joking and laughing would begin along with the sneering
innuendos. My father would listen to all this and burn inside.

He would come home and try and motivate me: "You know what they are saying? That you cannot do it."

I would shrug my shoulders. What do they understand? Why should I care what they think? I had turned my back on their traditional ways. I did not see my life as being fulfilled through marriage and children and if they could not understand this, I would not bother to explain.

It was not that I pretended not to care — I really did not care. I saw my life as much more fulfilling than married life at this point. I was able to do a hundred times more than any married man, and I saw that my life would be fulfilled not through a traditional life, but through writing and building up Al Haq and making a difference in society.

"What is it that you are trying to achieve?" my father would ask.

"Protection of human rights."

"What does this mean?"

"I am developing our legal case."*

"Who for? Who will make use of it?"

"Those who present our case before the world."

"And who will these be?"

"The PLO, I guess."

"But you have nothing to do with them. Why do you think they will listen to an outsider like you?"

"I will deal with this when the time comes. Now my contribution is going to be through Al Haq, not through the national movement."

"But you cannot make a contribution this way. The politicians will decide everything and you will have no influence, all your work will come to nothing."

I can still hear my father's anguished voice telling me: *Don't you understand? I knew what was best for the nation. I knew that in 1967 there was an opportunity not to be missed; a one-time chance. But they*

---

*The legal strategy that I later presented to the PLO negotiating team is published on pages 259-272 of *From Occupation to Interim Accords: Israel and the Palestinian Territories* (The Hague: Kluwer Law International, 1997).

wouldn't let me get on with it. Gaza was still up in arms. They would have been willing to make a compromise then. I had many contacts. I could have negotiated a deal but the political leadership would not allow it. They will not allow you to do anything because they fear your type: people who cannot be bought, who are honest and dedicated. Why do you want to waste your life for nothing? Can you not understand? I care for your interest and well-being. Listen to me.

Yes, I did understand. But I could not suffer in silence. How could I after meeting Khalid at the Tegart jail and hearing about Barzali?

"Do you not understand that political pluralism will never be tolerated? Have you not seen how the organization dealt with me, how they never allowed me to speak my mind?"

"I want to give them advice."

"But they won't take advice. They didn't take it when I offered it."

"But you were a political contender. I am not. Why would they fear me? I am not threatening."

"Because of me. They will never trust you because you are my son. Leave this work, I tell you, and concentrate on your profession."

We would be driving back to the office from court, he would start again: "You will see how it will end. You will remember my words. Jewish settlements will be everywhere. You will have very little left of the land. Nablus will be cut off from Ramallah. You will not even dream of getting back East Jerusalem. It will be lost just like Jaffa. The settlements will grow and expand. I can see it as clearly as I see you. If things continue as now the likelihood of a negotiated settlement will vanish. There will be no land left to establish a Palestinian state. You mark my words. Now you are full of yourself. You are swayed by emotions. When I was your age, I was even more extreme and driven than you. I also refused to listen to those who were more experienced. The time will come when you will be able to see things differently. But it will be too late. Everything will be lost."

"We will never let them get away with it. Never!" I would assure him. By which I meant of course that as long as I was engaged in this fight, I would never let them. I would write and speak and expose their ways. I sincerely believed what I said. My strong convictions prevented me from accepting my father's position. I looked at his generation as the defeated one. In 1948 they had fled, but we had stayed after 1967 and resisted. They were baffled by what happened to them, but we had our eyes wide open. We would not let our land be taken while we remained silent.

"You don't know what you're talking about," my father would say. "You should listen to me. I speak out of experience. If you don't have power you count for nothing. No one will listen to you. How will you be able to help yourself? If something should happen to you who will you turn to? I'm not going to be around forever, you know. What will happen to you when I'm gone? You'll be on your own. No one will come to your defense. This society only responds to power and you have none. Believe me. I know what I'm talking about."

"But why accept the way things are? I don't want to understand and adapt. I want to change things. The reason why everyone suffers the destructive control of the powerful is because they don't have the protection of the law. I want to promote the rule of law. When just laws are made they will apply equally to everyone, strong and weak, rich and poor. This is what I want to dedicate myself to. I don't want to adapt to the crooked ways of society. I want to change them."

"You are a dreamer. An idealist. You will not be able to change this society. You have to accept the way things are. As a lawyer, you are subject at any time to the kind of trouble that you can only get out of through connections with the powerful. Now you have me around to help you. What will happen when I'm gone? How will you manage?"

This was the least of my worries. My father's attitude came partly from concern for my well-being and partly from pride. He could not allow me to do what he had always done: to live my beliefs. Nor could he accept me as a man capable of helping myself. Oddly, we were similar in many ways..I was fighting against the Israeli government officials who violated human rights just as he had fought the Jordanian regime, thirty years earlier. Although the language and the context were different, the motivation was the same. We were both outraged by the behavior of people in power and did what we could to restrain them.

But my father got no praise or support for his efforts. He had endured disillusionment and hardship throughout his life. He did not want me to experience the same fate: expulsion, imprisonment, and betrayal. This was what was on his mind; these were the bitter experiences that infused his lectures to me. He wanted to spare me what he had been forced to endure.

CHAPTER NINETEEN

THE LAST FEW months I spent with my father were the most difficult. Nothing would raise his spirits just as nothing about my life pleased him. One day Ziad Abu Ziad, a political activist with the Fatah faction of the PLO who was training at our office, told him: "I was visiting some Israelis who told me: 'Aziz Shehadeh is the bravest Palestinian in the West Bank.'"

"Tell them that they are wrong. Aziz Shehadeh is a coward," my father answered.

This was not the first time that his spirits were so low that he became self-deprecating. He had often fallen into temporary depressions, but they never lasted. He would pull himself out, but this time nothing seemed to help. I became the target for his frustrations. He continued to nag me about getting married. He found fault in everything I did at the office. He would call me after reviewing a plea that I had written as carefully as I could and say: "This is mediocre work. You know nothing about the law. Your arguments are weak and badly presented. Whenever I review a file that you are handling I can never make head or tail of it. Look how neatly I keep my files. Anyone can follow a case I handle. But of course you have no time to organize your work because you spend all your time on your other work."

I would stand fuming by his desk. From this vantage point I had a good look at his face. Signs of old age were evident: swollen jowls, wrinkles around the corners of his mouth, and pockets underneath his eyes. The thin hair on his balding head still had very little gray. His strong face was beginning to sag, claimed by evidence of deep-rooted anger and despair. Only his eyes retained their strong penetrating gaze.

By now, after six years of practice at my father's side, I had enough confidence in myself to know that he was being unfair. I knew that I was good at what I did and was never sloppy or careless. But this time I determined to hold my tongue. I felt that he wanted me to respond so that we would fight, and I was tired of fighting him.

He would continue: "But of course you cannot concentrate on your work. You are too busy traveling from conference to conference. Writing all these articles and books against the occupation. But then you can afford the time, riding on my back as you do. It is I who is left with all the tedious work. I do all the court work. You just take the easy stuff and think that by doing it you are contributing immensely to the office. Then you use the office to help the extremists. Those who condemned me, my bitter enemies. You want to win their acceptance so that people will say, *He is not like his father*. You are not proud of me. You are a source of worry and trouble. If you go on like this you will destroy all the goodwill I nurtured over the years. And what for? So that those who made my life difficult, who called me a traitor, can remain free to make more trouble. Why aren't you like other men your age? They respect their fathers. They listen and obey. Their fathers need not repeat their words twice. They are grateful for what their fathers gave them when they didn't get a fraction of what I gave you. I gave you the best education, the best home, and how are you paying me back? Men your age are already married with adult children and you refuse to give me a grandson. But then why bother? Why when you have a tolerant father like me? Of course it is much easier this way: no responsibilities, no cares. You are happy with your life the way it is. It is I who have to suffer. You will continue to ride on my back as long as my back can stand it."

Later that evening I felt an emptiness in my stomach as though my insides had been gutted, leaving me with the compromised feeling that only parents are capable of producing in their children. At thirty-four I was too old to continue to be a silent victim.

I kept my peace, but I knew I could not go on like this. My father was making my life intolerable. He was making me unhappy at a time when my life was going well. I was satisfied with my practice. I knew that what I did, I did well, and I was attracting new clients. I was satisfied with my writing. The book I had been working on for the past three years would be published in the States in a few months. Al Haq was successful. I had a good circle of close friends. Why should I allow my father to spoil it all? Why couldn't he leave me alone? Why should I endure his moods and his persistent despondency? At the office he screamed. His work seemed to be perpetual drudgery. If he didn't like working anymore why go on with it? He was not in need of money at this point. At seventy-three he was past retirement age. Why not retire? He said that I could not manage without him, but I could. Of course I could. He flattered himself when he said this. I didn't want to disappoint him and say *I don't need you.* I would spare him the pain of hearing it from me. But in return he should spare me the heavy-handed denunciation of my abilities and character.

My father's attacks did not abate and I decided in the summer of 1985, just a few months before his death, to leave the office. I collected my personal files and put them aside. I was willing to leave everything I had contributed to the practice and begin again on my own. As I was making these arrangements, I was struck by how relieved I felt. No longer would I have to endure my father's debilitating despair. Perhaps this was the only way. I would leave and start my own practice. Perhaps I should have done this a long time ago. I might have difficulties at first but I would work them out without the pressure and agony my father was causing me.

Then emissaries began to come to my house to convince me that I was being cruel to my father.

"Remember," my uncle said, "that your father is seventy-three and you are thirty-four. He is an old man and you are still in your prime. Don't use all your ammunition against him; be kind to his old age."

My mother came too.

"Your father loves you," she told me. "He may be a bit hard on you, but you should not take things so much to heart. Underneath is a very kind man. I know. When he gets angry he does not know what he says, but he really doesn't mean it. I know he only wants the best for you. He is your father. Promise me that you will apologize. Do it for my sake. Please. Please."

I was determined that this fight would not end the way other fights had ended. I did not want to apologize and pretend to accept, without conviction, all the blame, leaving the problems that had given rise to the fight in the first place unresolved. Then in a few months we would be back circling around each other, trying not to get on each other's nerves, until the next outburst, when it would all start again. No, this time I was not going to allow it to end this way. This time I was leaving and not coming back.

But I could not hold my ground. My father was threatening to leave the office. I knew that the office was his whole life. Threatening to leave meant threatening to commit suicide. I could not be held responsible for my father's death. I swallowed my pride and returned.

Then the military authorities waged battle against our office to put pressure on me. One day around lunchtime I was alone in the office with one of the secretaries. Three Israelis in civilian dress burst in. They said they were from the Customs Department. They wanted to check the files. I objected and asked for a search warrant. They pushed me aside and began to rummage through everything. There was a locked drawer in my father's desk. They asked me to open it. I said I did not have the key. Never mind the key, they said, and broke it open. They took everything inside. They took the index of our files. They took any accounts they could find and put everything in a big bag and left. A few days later we received a bill for five million shekels, which they claimed we owed for back payment of value-added tax.

This was a tax the military authorities had imposed on the

West Bank six years before. At Al Haq we had investigated
whether a military occupying power had the right to impose a new
tax and had come to the conclusion that it did not. We were urging
the population not to pay this tax. No one was paying it. The
authorities had not raided any other law office. We were the only
ones. And my father immediately drew the obvious conclusion.
When we met after the raid he looked at me reproachfully, as if to
say: *Now see what you have done to us*.

And as though this was not enough, the Israeli adviser on Arab
affairs to the military commander was calling my father every
other day. Once he had the translation of an interview I had given
to a Swedish journalist, which he said went far beyond what they
could tolerate. Another time it was to say that I was cooperating
with the PFLP and they would take severe measures against me if
this continued.

Then the field-workers of Al Haq were put under administrative detention, which meant imprisonment for periods of six months
or more without charge or trial. During their interrogation, they
were only asked about their association with Al Haq. "So it is *haquq
el insan*," human rights, they were told mockingly. We had conducted a long study on administrative detention and had started an
international campaign to force Israel to stop this practice. Now our
own employees were its victims. I remember attending their administrative hearing carrying with me the galleys for my new book,
Occupier's Law. I knew I would be able to work on it during the long
hours of waiting. When the session started the intelligence officer
was sitting behind me, breathing down my neck. I felt a special kind
of satisfaction to have in my hands the manuscript of the book that
would, more than any other book that had been published, expose
Israeli practices. My frustration at not being able to help my colleagues in a hearing based on secret evidence that not even we, their
defense lawyers, were shown was made more bearable by the fact
that I was getting back at them through my writing.

But if I could get away with my activities against the military officers I was beginning to feel like an imposter before my father. He was afraid. I knew he was afraid. He was trying to monitor my activities because he thought I was close to the point of real danger. But I would not allow him to influence my actions. And I could not help feeling confined by his anxiety and despair. Every day he would ask me what I was doing, what was next. He would plead with me to stop giving interviews to journalists. *I know about these journalists,* he would warn me. *Most of them work for Israeli intelligence. They will only get you in trouble as they once did to me. Listen to me.*

But I was beyond the point of listening. I had not told him about the book that was close to being published, nor about the lecture tour that had already been organized in the United States when I would speak about the Israeli violations and promote my book. These talks were bound to be reported, and the adviser for Arab affairs was sure to have a huge pile of interviews that he would interrogate my father about. And then what? Would he inform my father that I would be arrested upon my return? Would he tell him worse, that he might never see me again? What sort of calls would I receive from my father in the United States? But the book was going to be published, I was going to go through with the lecture tour, and my father could not stop me at this point.

At seventy-three my father's last kingdom was the courthouse. He was unrivaled there. But even in this last arena he was having difficulties. He was like an old gladiator who had been the uncontested hero of his time and depended for his power on his own muscles. But these muscles were now sagging, and gangs were forming to overpower him and pull him from his throne. He was fighting back but he realized for the first time how alone he was and how the power he had always counted on was no longer there.

There was a land case in Ramallah that he had taken through the first court and was now appealing. The defendant's family had been threatening him. They tried to ram his car on the way to Jerusalem. They had come to his office early one morning when he was all alone and threatened him. They had even attacked a client riding in his car, dragging him out and hitting him. My father knew that all these constituted a personal offense but he did not know to whom to turn. And there was another case in Hebron. A brother of the defendant had sent a letter from prison threatening to kill him if he went on with the case. The more my father looked around the more alone he felt. There was no one to stand with him. His opponents had large families and clans to fall back on. He didn't. His small family counted for nothing. A blind half brother and a son who argued his way out, who refused to get engaged, who lived outside all this and pretended to himself that it did not exist. What could he do?

I thought, as did my uncle, that he should leave this risky business. He should stop taking new cases and withdraw from dangerous ones.

"And then what?" my father asked.

"Write your memoirs," I answered.

"Writing is for those who are finished. I am not finished yet."

He went back into the arena with all the force and anger of a man in his last round who refuses to be defeated. I was getting very worried. What would I do if something happened to him? What could I do to stop him?

One of the defendants in the Ramallah case stopped me in the street: "I advise you to convince your father to leave our case. Otherwise you will regret it. Tell him to leave, if you know what is good for you."

I reported this conversation to my father and pleaded with him to leave the case. I didn't want trouble. I wanted to be left to pursue my own fights, which I believed in and knew how to handle. He felt this to be a betrayal. He felt that I wanted to get rid of him, to silence him, to shun him, to push him out, to declare him a useless defeated old man. To see him die.

My dreams were indeed pervaded by the wish for my father's death. In one of them I was lying next to my father on the ground and he rolled over and fell into a hole nearby. I do not remember whether it was I who pushed him.

I began to see contemporaries who had lost their fathers as fortunate. Would my life be much less complicated without my father? Without the constant surprises that he thrust on me, the constant upheavals and moments of danger and threat. The calls to my house, the visits, the gloomy look and anxious face, the admonitions and expressions of disappointment. *Leave me alone,* I begged in my moments of despair. *Leave me alone.*

He never told me straight to my face that I should come to his aid. He was too proud for that. I heard about his troubles indirectly. I saw how he suffered. He was a man whose silences were as expressive and loud as his outbursts. He didn't have to speak any words of blame — his manner expressed it all. We were moving apart, each holding a different set of beliefs and view of reality. For many years I had yearned for his attention but did not get it. Now it was my turn. I was as passionate in my indifference to him now as I had been when I sought to create the unique relationship I always aspired to have with him. I was coming to terms with my loss and was determined to manage without him. He must have been thinking the same of me. He may have secretly hoped I would succeed as an artist and pursue a different life. Instead I came back to become a reluctant lawyer.

My father was handling four cases against people who were extremely dangerous. In two of them he had received direct threats against his life. I was very worried and suspected that he was not telling me everything, but what little I came to know made me extremely concerned. I did not want to deal with this kind of trouble. Why agree to take cases that were potentially so dangerous? He needed neither the money nor the fame. Why not leave these cases? Give them to younger lawyers. To lawyers with stronger connections and bigger families who would know how to handle this kind of danger. I was not the type of man who could help him with this. He could not have thought otherwise. He was always warning me not to act as though I had great support in society when I had none. Why was he not following the advice he had given me? But he could not. It was as though he had a second wind. He acted with the bravado of an adolescent. What was he trying to prove?

"I am not afraid," he would declare. "I will not give up these cases. I will not retreat. I have never been afraid in my life. They cannot intimidate me."

I did not know what to do. The only way I could understand his behavior was to realize that the happiest time in his life was when he left his father and started his own life in Jaffa, away from Jerusalem. He was happiest when he took action against the accepted norm, when he was the rebel, the one who dared to go against everyone else. My attempts to restrain him must have reminded him of the political forces that had prevented him from succeeding in the project in which he had invested so much of his life, or perhaps of his own father.

The military was after us on one side and the thugs of our own society were preparing to do battle with my father on the other. I was swamped with work as I tried to get ready for my monthlong absence. This was a good time in my life, I kept thinking. I have every reason to be happy and pleased with my achievements. But I could not enjoy my success.

Before I left for the States I tried to restore relations with my father. I entered his office in the late afternoon. He was sitting on a brown leather armchair behind the bulky wooden desk that he had had for as long as I could remember. He was wearing a brown suit. The light was dim; the thick drapes of his office were all drawn. I had come because I wanted to talk things over with him before I left. He received me well, but without enthusiasm. He remained seated behind his desk and I sat in front of him like a client. But his voice was soft and conciliatory. It betrayed that he too wanted us to be reconciled. I saw tears in his eyes when I stooped to kiss his cheek. I wanted him to know that when I spoke back to him it was not a sign of disrespect. I wanted us to have a distinguished relationship, not the traditional father–son relationship all around us. It would have been so much easier for me to nod mechanically at everything he said while keeping my own thoughts to myself. Did he hear me? Did he understand? Did he know I loved him? I wonder now whether he did.

In saying good-bye I confessed the purpose of my trip to him but I do not remember him wishing me luck. He did not offer a single word of praise or indicate in any way that I had done well. I did not mind this then, but I did not know that this was to be my last chance to get the approval that I had always sought.

My last conversation with my father took place over the telephone, two weeks before his death. I was in San Francisco on the last leg of my publicity tour. I still had one last speaking engagement in Los Angeles, and then I was to travel to Nairobi to attend the conference of the International Commission of Jurists. I remember standing on the patio of the home where I was staying, looking over the green lawn and the flowering hedges, and thinking: *What sort of life will I go back to in Ramallah?* I dreaded the prospect of return. Even with the fatigue of travel and the concentration required to lecture and to respond to challenges from many hostile audiences, everything was so much easier here. At home I never expected recognition or praise. In fact I hid my successes as if I were afraid of being struck by the evil eye. How different it was here. People were happy that I had succeeded with this book. This was an expansive, vital society so different from the restrictive and oppressive one I had come to think was the norm.

I called my father in Ramallah wanting to tell him the news of the book, but he did not seem interested. He wanted me to do something for the office, which at that point was the last thing on my mind.

"Call Matilda Harb and tell her that the powers of attorney she sent cannot be used. She has to make new ones. Let her read you the text before she signs it at the notary public and check it carefully. Do you hear?"

I carried out his instructions. The last words I would ever hear from him were about Matilda Harb's real estate problems.

Since my return, I have spoken to everyone who spoke to him or saw him during those last hours, so I feel able to reconstruct them in great detail and therefore vicariously to experience those last fateful hours of my father's life. This is the least I could do to propitiate my guilt at not being there for him in his hour of greatest need, for not protecting him from the man who attacked him and took his life. It is as close as I can get to redeeming what has become my most regretted failure with my father.

It happened on a Monday afternoon. A foggy and cold afternoon. The air was soaked with moisture and the fog was low and thick. The orange streetlights lit the fog, making it feel even thicker and decreasing visibility.

That day, as my father was leaving the house after his lunch break, he noticed my young brother look admiringly at his new black cashmere coat.

"Do you fancy it?" he asked him.

My brother, who never wanted to join my father's law office, smiled. My father took his coat off and placed it on my brother's back. It seemed to fit him perfectly. His was the better-built body.

"Keep it," my father said.

My brother smiled proudly as he stood wearing the expensive coat. My father seemed pleased to make him happy. He picked up his old brown coat and was turning to leave the house when his eyes fell on the statute of Buddha. Someone had turned on the lights inside the porcelain belly and had forgotten to turn them off. He went toward it. The light was seeping out of the slightly slit mouth with the mocking yet forgiving smile.

At the office he prepared for the four hearings fixed for the next day's court sessions. He remained at the office from three until five forty-five. Before leaving the office he walked into my uncle's room and asked him if he needed anything. My uncle did not, but my father seemed to linger, going around to the secretaries and asking if they needed anything or needed a lift. No one did. They still had work to do. When he walked out the door he lingered on the landing for a few moments before he went down the stairs.

He was carrying a heavy briefcase loaded with files and books for the next day's cases. He had taken all he needed so that the next day he could go directly to court without having to stop at the office. He walked out to the street. There were only a few people in the street even at this early hour of the evening. He could not have recognized any of them. They were enshrouded in the thick fog that hung over the town as they slid furtively in and out of sight, their bodies emitting orange-lit vapor, reflecting the street-lights, their heads tucked deeply into the collar of their coats. They appeared hardly human.

He walked on the slippery sidewalk to his car. He opened it slowly, threw in the briefcase, and went inside. He drove through the thick fog, using the wipers because it had started to drizzle. Small droplets of rain were falling on his car window, making no sound. He felt the silence of the world, and he felt alone in it. He drove the short distance to his house. The post office road was deserted. He turned the corner, saw a man by our house, and drove up to the garage.

He felt evil approach, perhaps he even saw it, but he did not run. Evil wielded a knife and captured him. It was more evil than he had ever encountered. Evil thrust his knife into his flesh and made a deep cut through his neck and then swept up the knife and dropped him to the ground. He had a last look at this world and then descended in silence.

He continued to bleed and the soft rain continued to pour. He was alone, prostrate on the ground in the fog, fallen, his blood mixing with the rain and flowing down the slope of the driveway toward the gate.

He was alone, dying.

The murderer withdrew his knife, covered his face with a

black-and-white-checkered kaffiyeh, and slid through the night into the dark, empty street. The rain fell on his covered head, wetting his scarf, and when he got to the corner he flung his bloodied knife into the neighbor's garden. But they neither saw nor heard, or if they did they remained inside. When the downstairs neighbor drove his car into the driveway, he saw the prostrate figure and the blood that had formed a pool down by the gate. He went and sounded the alarm.

But what alarm, and who listened? The Israeli police took their time coming. An ambulance was not sent for hours. The area was not cordoned off.

They left him there for the whole town to see. They abandoned him in his death as in his life. They let him bleed. The rain fell over his body; no one even bothered to cover him.

He sacrificed himself to a cause that abandoned him. His death confirmed and demonstrated the absence of all that he had wanted to create: a vital society that could provide for the needs of its citizens and allow for a life of dignity and self-assertion.

Instead there was total dependence on the Israeli police and ambulances and investigators and courts. And when they didn't come he remained prostrate, just as society is prostrate, head down, bleeding its last drops of blood with little chance of regaining lost dignity.

CHAPTER TWENTY

I RECALL THE exact hour of my father's murder because that evening, the second of December 1985, my eyes were drawn to the wall clock a few minutes after six as I sat eating alone in a restaurant in Nairobi. Early the next morning I was scheduled to go on a safari. How often do you find wall clocks in restaurants? But there the clock was, over the swing door leading to the kitchen. And exactly at the fateful hour of my father's death, my eyes were riveted to a restaurant wall in Africa.

I left the restaurant with a feeling of unease and went to my hotel to sleep so I would be ready for my early-morning expedition. I was awakened around midnight by a call from Niall MacDermot, the secretary general of the International Commission of Jurists, who had come to mean more to me at the time than my father. Despite the age difference — I was in my early thirties and he, like my father, in his early seventies — we were friends, and Niall encouraged and guided me in my human rights work. On that fateful night he thrust the awful news at me without palliatives: "Your father has been stabbed. He is dead."

I received the news with a mixture of disbelief — how could Father die — and anger: Why should he die in this way? It was only later that I realized that up to that point in my life I had so identified with my father that I felt the assault against my own person: I was stabbed, but I was the one who survived, who must avenge and expiate not the general violation of a principle this time, or the violence committed against others, but the violation of the right to life of my own father. What made it all the more difficult to take was that the radio announced that the Abu Nidal faction, a renegade Palestinian group, was responsible for my father's murder.

I felt stricken, confused, maimed. The news of my father's murder hit me in a way that I could never have imagined. I had always worried how I would feel when the time came, as it was bound someday to come. *When my father dies, will I be able to feel anything?* I had worried about this failure to respond but now there was no room for such concern. I was swept by deep emotion. At first I felt it in my gut, a blow to my stomach that made me nauseous. My stomach would jump once or twice and then my tears would flow, bitter tears that I could not understand. They were fueled by too many emotions: despair and anger, hurt and pity. Why did it have to happen this way? Why should my father be killed by Palestinians? What injustice and violence had come to explode my world just as I was beginning to enjoy a sense of contentment after years of psychological turmoil?

I had never thought of my father as a victim, never thought that his occasional fears for his life would be justified. I always took these fears as exaggerations, the irrational worries of a sometimes paranoid man. But now the validity of these fears made me question my own beliefs. What if he was also right about the attitudes and positions that I consistently rejected? Would this not make my entire outlook on life suspect? Would this vindicate him against his enemies, including myself?

I heard a knock at the door and got out of bed to open it. It was Niall. Tall, straight, wearing a sympathetic look, his thin lips closed with a pained resolve, he had come to comfort me. But I could not be comforted, nor could I believe that my father was dead.

Bereavement isolates even within the largest of crowds. I was alone with my mourning that next day on the packed plane from Nairobi to Amman, Jordan. I was alone and full of grief, exhausted from crying, from thinking or trying to think, from a lack of sleep. Occasionally I would doze off and dream that I had missed the plane and discovered that what was rumored about my father had turned out to be untrue. My father had not died; it was only hearsay.

When the plane landed, a sober, quiet man sent by Royal

Jordanian Airlines met me on the tarmac. He was kind and atten-
tive, anxious to help. When my luggage did not arrive, I abandoned
it. Outside the airport another man, sent by my brother-in-law in
Amman, was waiting. He was compassionate but not overbearing.
He drove me straight to the Allenby Bridge, the border between
Jordan and the West Bank.

Even as I walked across the shaky bridge, I felt my feet touch
the ground of home, home for the first time without a father. And
in a first moment of clarity, I made my wish, the first of my new
reality: I wished that he would pass his energy to me.

At the time I did not understand why. Only later did I realize
that my father was a source of such tremendous energy and drive
that I often felt deflated and inadequate. Now that this energy was
extinguished, there was bound to be a vacuum, an absence that I
had never even imagined I might have to endure. No matter how
often I had wished that my father were different, I could never con-
ceive of life without him.

After crossing the Jordan River into the West Bank, I found
two friends who hugged me closely, comforting me like a child.
Even the Israeli soldiers at the bridge, usually abrasive, seemed to
keep a respectful distance. I had left home on my speaking tour to
the United States thinking I was the star of a victorious journey,
only to come back the protagonist of a mysterious tragedy.

As we drove to Ramallah, I felt a loud silence permeate my
world. I was conscious that next I would encounter the house
without my father, my mother without my father, Ramallah, my
hometown, without my father. And I felt like a traitor: How could
I, who had disappointed him in so many ways during his lifetime,
now succeed in what I had failed to do when he was alive? I felt that
I had no right to live after his death, no right to be, no right to exercise the freedom I had sought. I felt that life was not going to be
possible, not with a clear conscience. That I should be able to live
without him — would this not mean that I had wanted or somehow
been an accomplice to his murder?

But I also felt as though I was seeing for the first time, hearing for the first time, being born again. Everything seemed calm and quiet, slow. No rush. No goal. No glory. All quaint, dull, ordinary, mediocre. This was the new world without my father. He was the fire, the energy, the anger, the conflict, the explosion, the trouble-maker, the instigator, the energizer. It would all be meaningless without him.

Whose idea was it to take me to the morgue? Did I want it or was it the expected thing to do? No, I wanted to see my father. Not to consecrate the action, not to face the reality, not to establish for myself that it was not just a nightmare, but perhaps because I thought that I ought to, that it was my filial duty toward him, my way of showing respect.

Whatever the reason, I asked to be driven to the morgue immediately. I walked around to the back of the Ramallah hospital where my grandmother had lain for days in pain before slowly dying. I hated everything about the place, its smell, the callousness of its surgeons, the dirt, the hungry cats darting around the corridors, and the memory it brought back to me of my own insensitivity in the face of my grandmother's death in this building.

I walked around underneath the pine trees, and someone went inside to fetch the key. I waited holding my breath, confused before this final encounter, feeling frail and inadequate, unsure whether I could deal with death.

Soon the messenger came back and the door was opened and we entered a dark, dank, and despicable place. Then attendants pulled the stretcher out of the freezer. At first I could only see the familiar shoes, the familiar striped trousers, and then my vision blurred as my eyes filled with tears and I could see nothing else. Why was it shocking that my father lay on the stretcher of death in his familiar gray trousers? Why was it strange that he would wear his same brown shoes? Clothes are indifferent to life and death. I braced myself as I saw the rest of his small suited body. When my eyes reached the head, I saw his round ashen face with the swarthy complexion, weak chin, tight thin lips, and wide mustache. His big black eyes, framed by thick eyebrows with graying hairs, were closed. Long black eyelashes brushed against his cheeks. I was struck by how small his body was. It was as though I saw him for the first time. Then I realized that this was the first look that was not met by his famous intense penetrating gaze, by his eyes that glittered like coal. Now he was cold and still. Death had taken him and death has its own dominion.

I was depleted. My father who was so strong was now silent, cold, captured, and confined to this small hole in the wall. And I was still here, a weak sniffling child who despite his thirty-four years had refused to grow up, refused to accept the violence of society, the high stakes of the powerful and the powerless. I stood before what was a colossal presence, feeling puny and inadequate and bereaved.

CHAPTER TWENTY-ONE

———————

DURING THE WAKE I looked at my father's portrait next to the porcelain statue of the Buddha that he had brought from the old house in Jaffa. My father in the portrait had a big mischievous smile. This, I thought, is the image I would like to be left with: an open face with a wide smile, looking straight at me with his wide black eyes and defying me to live daringly as he did.

I can never know whether his expression in that portrait provoked me to solve the mystery of his death or whether that challenge was something that I assumed on my own. What I do know is that the gap between the despair I was feeling in the wake of his murder and the ease and gregariousness written on his face disturbed me. I found myself addressing him: "You have always done things your way and never took into account how your actions affected us."

But then I checked myself, for I realized that I was blaming my father for his own death.

I knew now, as I had always known, that he could have taken fewer risks in his life. He could have chosen an easier life, but then he would not have been the man he was. The question that remained was whether I would finally be able to come to terms with the man who was my father.

Our final reconciliation would still be some years ahead. Certainly reconciliation could not occur until the investigation into his murder was completed and his assassins brought to justice. Until then I would not feel that I had done my duty as a son.

Two weeks after my father's death, to my great relief and satisfaction, the PLO issued a communiqué distancing itself from the crime.

I brought this to the attention of the police, who seemed neither interested nor surprised. It became apparent that they had discounted from the outset the possibility that the Abu Nidal group was involved as the Agence France Presse broadcast had claimed. Who then was my father's murderer? Only the Israeli police could help me find out.

At the time of the investigation, the country was already in the nineteenth year of Israeli occupation. The government in control was an Israeli military government. The central Israeli police had extended its jurisdiction and responsibilities over the occupied areas and established police stations in the various Palestinian towns in the West Bank that were linked to the police headquarters in Jerusalem. The military and the police cooperated. In theory, whatever was considered threatening to the security of Israel or its citizens, whether in the occupied territories or in Israel, was the responsibility of the military. In practice, the police arrested those accused of security offenses, who would then be tried in military courts staffed by military personnel.

Israel had offered to transfer responsibilities for policing over the Palestinian population to a local Palestinian police. My father had supported this. But as usual his was a singular voice. The political leadership outside rejected this offer and saw it as a measure likely to consolidate and entrench the occupation. Nevertheless, Israel employed Palestinians in these local police stations, trained and incorporated into the system, leaving the higher echelons to be staffed by Israelis.

The Ramallah police station was housed in an old stone building that, as far as I can remember, had always been used as a police station. I used to pass by it on my way to school for many years before 1967, when it housed the Jordanian police. When the Israelis took it over the only change they made was to remove the Arabic sign and put up one written in Hebrew and English, the same sign that appears at every police station in Israel. The corner pine tree on which the violet bougainvillea climbed and bloomed from early summer until the end of autumn remained as glorious and effusive as ever. But during Jordanian rule my father had friends at the station, and all the community knew the policemen who served there. Now it was a different matter. As with other Israeli offices in the West Bank, the place was dominated by Israelis who were involved in their own world, who spoke a language that Palestinians did not understand. Even when they understood Arabic or English, they insisted on speaking Hebrew and pretended not to understand when spoken to in Arabic. You would enter this forbidding place and feel that you had no right to be there. This was not a police force there to help the community, to keep away the criminals, to apprehend the lawbreakers, and to provide security for the local population. This was an Israeli police establishment whose only interest was in Israeli security; its officers would only be interested in a case if they could detect an angle bearing on Israeli security.

The Palestinian community understood this. Everyone did their best to keep away from the military and the police. To the extent it could, the community tried to police itself and deal with delinquents and lawbreakers in its own traditional ways.

But for me, the indifferent and antagonistic police were the only ones who could solve this crime. The other option was to take the law in my own hands, set up my own investigation team, and arrange for the kidnapping of suspects and their interrogation in faraway places, in the fields, somewhere in the hills underneath the olive trees. I knew I was not up to this. As for the local society, it had little to offer me in this investigation. I put my faith, trust, and hope in the Israeli police not because I was under any illusions, but because I did not see that I had an alternative. And yet, despite my clarity on this point, these were confusing times.

I employed two strategies. I would take note of everything I heard and would inform the police. I would dig through my father's files and alert the police to every case that could have involved people who might resort to murder to prevent my father from winning the case against them. He had not been handling criminal cases at the time, only civil cases involving land — and land had become very expensive. The motive therefore was money. The murderer, whoever he was, wanted to remove my father from the case so that he would not lose the case and the money.

My other strategy was to mobilize as many of the Israelis I knew and whom my father knew, all of whom had appeared at our house to pay us condolences and offer their help. I asked them to contact the police periodically and pull whatever strings they could to stress the importance of this case, as well as their own personal interest in its resolution in the best manner and the shortest period of time.

It was a very difficult time for me. All my life I had shared my society's distrust of the police. Now I entreated everyone I knew who had influence to encourage the police. I wanted so much to believe in the Israeli police, to believe that my father's friends shared my interest in achieving justice for him, that I saw only what I wanted to see. A good man who had championed peace between Palestinians and Israelis had been murdered. This was not a political murder; the PLO had denounced it and published an obituary in one of its magazines. This was a criminal action and the murderer could be found among a finite list of possible suspects, from among the four or five contentious cases on which my father had been working before his death. Ours is a small, highly controlled community, and with some small effort the police should have been able to resolve this case. But many people whose help I sought did not share this opinion.

My father was a man with moderate political views in a community perceived by most Israelis as adhering to extremist political positions, where moderates were perceived as traitors. The Agence France Presse report naming the Abu Nidal group as the perpetrator of the murder was aired all over the world. This was how I had received the news in Nairobi. And this was what most Israelis who expressed their sympathy to me thought had happened: the murder of another Palestinian moderate by an extremist Palestinian political group.

Those Israelis who had heard that my father might have been killed because of a civil land case regretted that they were neighbors to a violent society that did not know about the rule of law, that resolved civil disputes not in courts but through threats and murder. They were sure that the man they knew, who on many occasions had spoken at public events in Israel denouncing violence, was different; that he truly did not believe in violence. Yet he was unfortunate enough to live in a violent society and had now become its victim. The heroes who would fight the terrorism and violence inflicted against this peaceful man would be the Israeli police. Although they had to accept, of course, that there were clear limits as to how much the civilizing hand could influence the course of events among people who espoused terror and found violence to be a normal way of life.

The event therefore was received against the background of the prevailing stereotypes, of which only a few people who followed events in this troubled area could free themselves. I was very aware that the hundreds of messages of condolences and sympathy I received from Israel were made within this context. *You and I,* they seemed to imply, *are victims of this evil, Palestinian extremism. We sympathize because we too are the sufferers of the same evil.* The subsequent PLO denial of involvement in the murder did not get coverage in Israel. This enabled the lie about who murdered my father to prevail.

I was of course aware of all this. But I believed that the police would be dealing with hard evidence, not impressions and propaganda. I was prepared to suspend all my earlier beliefs, prejudices, and doubts; to put my faith in the investigation of the enemy that seemed to be the only party able to do the job.

I knew that for many months before my father's death he had received threats from the defendants in several cases, and these I urged the police to investigate. One of these defendants had acted on his threats. Which one was it? Who came or was hired to come on that foggy December evening with a large kitchen knife to kill my father and remove him from the case? The murder weapon was found in the garden of the corner house a few meters away from Father's house. Someone had been seen on several occasions before the murder lurking around the house. Footprints and fingerprints must have been left, and the face of the man loitering could be identified by the neighbors. There was much to go on, and in any case the set of possible suspects was not large.

What I did not appreciate, because I blocked it from my mind, was the absence of motivation on the part of the police. It did not matter that the investigation was monitored by the press, which reported almost daily on every development, or that the victim was a personality known for his moderate views and his advocacy of peaceful coexistence between Arabs and Jews.

The simple truth was that the military and police systems were organized to deal with threats against Israeli security. When a crime took place, all the forces were employed to discover if there were security implications. This meant that there would have been a much higher degree of interest if the PLO had been involved, or if the murder weapon had been a gun, because strict control over firearms was maintained. Much less interest was aroused by the use of a kitchen knife, which anyone could possess. It would be worse still if the crime was committed by a collaborator whom the police had an interest in protecting.

In other words, the abyss between me and those in whom I chose to place my faith was as pronounced as ever. It was the same divide that split the Palestinians and the Israelis. My father's legacy and principles, his friends, my friends, the interest of the world in the case, none of these made the slightest difference, none had the power to make the slightest change in the elements that marked and sustained the division between the two groups. I was only deluding myself when I believed that ours was a special case and would receive special treatment from the Israeli police.

And yet even had I been willing to accept all of this, how could it have changed my strategies? The way I saw it was that I had one of two options: I could either accept that my father was murdered when our occupied society lacked the means to carry out its own investigation, or I could say that, the occupation notwithstanding, the murderer of my father could not remain at large unpunished. Even if the enemy performed the apprehension and punishment, I had to pursue the case to the end. I could not bring myself to choose the first option.

After the murder, the police announced that they had set up a special team to deal with the investigation. This was an encouraging sign. It meant that they were not leaving it to the small and ill-equipped Ramallah police, but had brought in reinforcements from other police departments in the area.

And yet, despite this announcement, we were never introduced to the team, never knew the names of its members. We were expected to help by answering questions. We were not expected to ask questions of our own. At first we submitted to this because we assumed that the police knew what they were doing.

A review of the cases my father was handling at the time of his murder revealed that there were no more than four or at most five dangerous ones. Among these, there were only two cases in which my father had received threats. The first involved land in Ramallah. The defendants in this case were residents of the town who owned a shop right next to my father's office. I told the police about them. I told them that this case had been going on for three years and that there were many meetings held at the office in an attempt to reach a settlement. But these efforts had failed to resolve the dispute and the case continued in court. It had been lost in the lower court and my father had taken it to the appeal court. The family involved had sent many people to advise my father to leave the case. I told the police all this and also about the threats that were made against him.

The police were also told about the case involving land in Hebron that my father was handling on behalf of the Anglican Church. He had taken this case even though he knew the dangers involved and he proceeded to pursue it with his usual zeal. Looking through the file I saw the letter sent to my father from an Israeli jail where one of the two brothers involved in the case was incarcerated. It contained a clear threat to my father's life if he proceeded with the case. I showed this letter to the police. They kept the original. Fortunately I had copied it, and I still have the copy. I was surprised that the prison censor had allowed a letter containing such clear menace to be mailed from prison. I believed that these defendants were prime suspects and expected the police to investigate them.

I also gave the police information about the man my father had seen when he and my mother were leaving the house for Jericho one day in November, just two weeks before the murder. A tall man with ivory skin wearing a white kaffiyeh was standing by the garbage dumpster. I reported how my father had left his car, walked over to him, and asked him what he was doing.

After my father spoke to him he left but came back a few days later and went to the neighbor across the street. An old woman lived alone in that house. She told me that he rang her doorbell. She asked who it was and what he wanted.

"Alms," he answered.

She refused to open the door for him and went around and peeked through the slits of her bedroom window, which over-looked the entrance. She wanted to see whether he would leave. He did not see her. Did he just want to know who was living on the street of the man he was planning to murder?

If this was indeed his mission, he must have left that day feeling assured that this was a quiet, middle-class area. The single old woman across the street was not likely to hear or to come and look should there be a commotion. She posed no threat.

From behind the drawn curtain of the window, the next-door neighbor was able to see the man who had knocked at her door. She described him as a tall man with a straight imposing body, pale, almost white skin, and a sharp nose. He was also wearing a white kaffiyeh. Her description conforms to the description of the man my father had seen next to the dumpster.

We must have gone over all these details with the police scores of times. My mother joked that our statements must have filled files that reached the ceiling. The police's main focus appeared to be taking statements from our family. It was as though the investigation revolved around us. What sort of an investigation was this? Each time a different officer came along he would take the same set of affidavits. The police never spoke to the shop owners near the office or the neighbors near my father's house. They never presented the neighbor with pictures of the Hebron defendants whose names and pictures they must have had. They never made an identikit of this suspect, or a lineup. It was not possible therefore to ascertain whether the man with the ivory skin and white kaffiyeh was indeed one of the brothers in the Hebron case. They seemed to concentrate only on the suspect from Ramallah.

A few weeks passed and still the only visible activity was the statements taken from me and from my mother. Precious time was passing. Every day journalists would call and I would ask them if they had questioned the police. They had, and the police assured them that the investigation was going well. But how could this be when there was no apparent investigation of the murder scene, no questioning to find out if anyone had seen or heard anything?

Journalists were told that the investigation was proceeding at full speed and the police would soon be making an announcement.

But who were the police investigating? Who did they suspect? Why didn't they tell us what was going on?

I asked the neighbors if any of them had been interviewed by the police. They all said no. What was happening? Were the police being neglectful? But why would they not care to carry out a proper investigation in a case as well publicized as this? Surely they must want to prove their effectiveness. I was beginning to express some of these doubts to the journalists who asked about the investigation. Then suddenly, the police made a dramatic announcement. They said that they had detained the two Ramallah suspects. I received this news with a mixture of relief and consternation. Ramallah is a small place. These men had a shop next to my office. I passed them every day on my way to work. Neither had any previous conviction. They were not known criminals. There had never been a killing over a money dispute or court case in Ramallah before. What sort of anger must they have felt that made them want to kill a seventy-three-year-old man? They were rich men and in no financial trouble; why would they kill for money? And yet the police must have had evidence or they would not have detained them — detention without evidence is reserved for the military courts. But what sort of evidence did they have? What if the police were wrong? How would these men feel about us? By accusing them wrongly we would be the cause of their public disgrace. Would the arrest then lead to civil strife between the Christian families in Ramallah, both they and us being Christian? Had the police even considered this? Had we been certain about their guilt, I would not have cared about the consequences. But the police told us nothing. They kept us in the dark.

When the initial period of detention expired, the police got an extension. When the second extension expired, they got a third. The longer the suspects were kept under detention the more strongly we believed that the police must have arrested the real perpetrators. Otherwise why keep known members of the community detained on suspicion of committing murder? Yet when we asked if they had found enough evidence to press charges, they were vague. We assumed that they had to be deliberately vague for the benefit of the investigation. But why could they not trust us? We certainly were not going to harm the investigation. If they would give us information and ask us to keep it to ourselves, we would certainly comply. And yet, I kept thinking, perhaps the police had their own way of carrying out an investigation. They had arrested suspects and this meant progress. I would have to be patient.

We seemed to be the last in our community to hear that the two suspects were getting royal treatment. They were under arrest and yet they were allowed to phone their families. The families were allowed to bring them their own meals. They had even allowed their barber to come in and give them a haircut and shave. They could not be under investigation.

This information increased our suspicions that something was wrong. I began to panic. I had put all my faith in the police and had not pursued any other avenues. If the police failed me, I would have only myself to blame.

I asked the shop owners on our street if the police had ever questioned them about what they might have seen on the night of the murder. They said the police had visited but were most interested in their opinion of the two suspects, not in what they saw that night. This meant that the police had not really investigated all the possible witnesses. And they had still not interviewed any of the neighbors.

One day an acquaintance visited me at the office, saying he wanted to speak to me. He told me that he had seen a van parked in the street one block from my father's office from around six o'clock on the evening of the murder. The van did not have Ramallah license plates. He had heard that soon after the murder it drove away and was then seen in one of the refugee camps. I passed this information on to the police. Again they were not interested in the name of the informant. I noticed that whenever I spoke to them they never had the casefile in front of them. They used odd pieces of papers to jot notes. I doubted whether these ever got filed.

Just as my doubts about the police were at their height, my Uncle Fuad came to my office to express his own doubts.

"I have been a lawyer for more than forty years," he said, "and I know a good investigation when I see one. All the police are doing is taking the same statements over and over. It is not as if anyone is processing the information, or analyzing it and pursuing a clear line of investigation. It does not even appear that they are keeping a file on the case. They continue to ask for the same papers that you give them over and over, as though they keep misplacing them. From the first minute I was not convinced. From the start when they failed to show up at the scene of the murder. They were late and when they came they did not cordon off the area and do what police are supposed to do — check fingerprints and footprints, examine the scene of the crime in search for evidence. They didn't do any of these things."

My uncle had spoken clearly. I could not dispute what he said. But what could we do about it?

"I have little hope," he said, "that the murderer will be found. I fear that my brother's secret is buried with him."

That my father's killer's identity might never be known sent shivers down my spine. How could this be? If two experienced lawyers could not succeed in getting a proper investigation, who could?

I knew all along that whether or not we were satisfied with the work of the police, we had no alternative. Still, after my uncle left and I thought more about what he had said, I was convinced that he was right. I felt a sense of responsibility. It was I who had been arguing that the police were our only hope. Perhaps we should take the matter up with a higher authority. I decided to write to the minister of police and express my apprehensions.

I received a prompt response and an invitation to meet with him to explain in person why I was dissatisfied. With my mother and brother, I went to meet Haim Bar Lev, the Israeli Minister of Police.

We searched for his office in the new government buildings in Shiekh Jarrah in East Jerusalem, passing through many corridors before we finally found it.

The minister had invited the inspector general of police to attend the meeting. Both men were silent and heard us out. My mother poured out her heart as I listened and observed the two men. Bar Lev was a tall man with blue eyes. He came across as kind and sympathetic but he also had a squint that seemed to conceal much. As my mother spoke the minister listened, seemingly moved. But the inspector general was another matter. He had the sharpest eyes I had ever seen. He scrutinized us disapprovingly. Nothing my mother had said and nothing I said afterward seemed to reach him. He was like a hawk observing from a safe distance, disengaged, hovering above, waiting for our energy to wane before scavenging us. For now he would accord us his tolerance of our presence, but he would not offer the privilege of hearing, and certainly not sympathy for the ordeal we were suffering. The meeting did not last long. In the end the minster assured us that he would see to it that the investigation was handled in the best possible manner. We should have no doubt about this and should trust that the police would follow this case with all due diligence to the end.

After our interview with the minster a new head of the investigation team was appointed, a fair-skinned woman in her early forties with long blond hair, a round, attractive face, and brown eyes. She went about her work with apparent intelligence and ease. She seemed to have more time to give to this investigation and competently took charge. She was at least, I felt, a more credible representative to whom we could speak when we had information to give the police. She operated from the Ras el Amoud police headquarters in East Jerusalem, where I felt there was a greater degree of organization than seemed to be the case at the Ramallah police station. I held long meetings with this policewoman, going over all the possibilities once more, repeating everything I had said to the police in Ramallah. Yet I was more than glad to have someone who seemed able to process information and who appeared to keep notes and file information properly and did not ask me questions that I had answered in previous sessions. I was beginning to feel more confident that the police would make real progress.

The appointment of what the police called "a higher-ranking officer to head the team" was duly reported by the press. This was not in the form of an admission of earlier neglect but in recognition of the complexity of the case, which required that it be handled by a more experienced officer.

As the weeks passed I realized that I was once again deluding myself. There may have been an improvement in the rank and competence of the officer handling the file, but it was only a cosmetic change. It was true that this policewoman heard me out, but none of the things left undone before her appointment were carried out now. The neighbors were still not interviewed; the information I had given the police was still not investigated. The two suspects remained under detention but the rumors continued that their arrest was a formality and that they were not interrogated. Then one of the two suspects was released.

I went to the head of the team to find out what was happening. She said that they had absolutely nothing on the man they released. As to the second suspect, they still believed that he knew something that he was refusing to divulge.

I told her what we had heard about the treatment of the suspects. She denied it. She admitted that they were stubborn and not cooperating with the investigation, but she was not giving up. She hoped the man they kept under arrest would break down.

When the new head of the team had taken charge, a Palestinian policeman was also appointed. He was a tall, tense young man who went about his work with great dedication and diligence. We continued to press him to speak to those we felt may have something to say. He was too polite to let us down but his silent, heavy grin implied that he was under pressure and knew more than he could divulge. What, we wondered, did he know, and how could we possibly get him to tell us?

One day I went to visit my mother unexpectedly in midmorning and found her in the living room with this police officer. The moment I opened the door, I felt the involved atmosphere of a conspiratorial silence. The two looked at me as if from behind a thick veil that separated their world from mine. My entry at that inauspicious moment had broken a spell. My mother had been speaking with this officer all morning, and he finally said that he had something important to tell her, something she should keep to herself. He had started to speak when I made my most ill-timed entry. He stopped, and never spoke to her again. Almost three months had passed since the murder, sixty days since the arrest of the two Ramallah suspects.

I was summoned to meet the head of the team at the Ramallah station. She said on the telephone that she had something important to tell me. As I walked in I saw her walking slowly and carefully down the smooth stone stairs holding on to the railing. I remembered she had told me when we first met that she was pregnant, and because she was in her forties she had to be very careful. "I am not young you know," she had said.

She walked past me and told me that she could not see me because she had to leave. "Speak to Mar Sami," she said.

I climbed the worn circular stairs of the old stone building. I was allowed into Mar Sami's room, but he was not ready to speak to me; he was writing something down. As I waited I looked around his office. There was a large aerial photograph of the Ramallah area that showed the Jewish settlement of Psagot perched up on the highest hill; farther west the settlement of Beit El spreading in all directions. The settlements were easy to distinguish because of their architectural style and the rigidity with which everything was organized. On his desk was a calendar with a picture of the Israeli Knesset under strong light. In the foreground was the Dome of the Rock in pastel colors. At the corner of the picture was the coat of arms of Nafet Yehuda, as the police district is known in Hebrew.

When Mar Sami finished writing he looked up at me. He did not remove his spectacles.

"I have bad news," he said. "We are not getting anywhere with the suspect in our custody. We cannot continue to keep him incarcerated indefinitely because we have no evidence against him. He has been released."

I was very angry to hear this. I called the head of the team and left messages until I finally succeeded in getting her on the line. I made an appointment to see her the next day.

At our meeting, which was held at the police station in Ras el Amoud in East Jerusalem, I was in a rage but she was her usual calm self. She spoke as slowly as she moved.

"We will find him in the end, you will see," she said, and then added in a motherly way, "but you have to be patient. We have the best team looking into this. Don't worry. This suspect is very intelligent. He will not speak however long I keep him in. We put him on the lie detector and he passed. But I think he knows something that he is refusing to tell us. I want him to be out. We will keep an eye on him. He is bound to say something to someone about it. Then we will have hard evidence and we will arrest him again. To keep him in like this will get us nowhere. I know his type very well. He will not speak however long we keep him. This is why I decided to release him."

One day I was stopped in the street as I passed the suspects' shop on my way to my office. One of the brothers, who walked with quick, short, nervous steps, rushed to me. He looked me straight in the eyes and said: "We did not do it. We did not kill your father. You must believe me. We had nothing to do with it."

I nodded. But I said nothing.

Later I thought that the man seemed sincere. His eyes, which locked with mine, did not betray any guile. Yet how could I be sure of anything?

───────────

CHAPTER TWENTY-TWO

MY MOTHER WAS the first to give up on the Israeli police. She decided to resort to traditional remedies. She was told about a famous fortune-teller in Tulkarem who was renowned for her clairvoyance. She could look into the future and the past and was rumored to have made great revelations, all of which had come true. She was very popular and it was claimed that she had among her clientele satisfied Palestinians and Israelis in all levels of society. My mother was determined to try her luck. Maybe this fortune-teller would be able to tell her the name. Maybe she would help her at least to remember what my father whispered to her in a dream after his death.

I was unwilling to go with my mother to the fortune-teller. Not even for the sake of my murdered father was I willing to resort to superstition. Instead she took along one of my father's former law interns, Mohammed, just in case this woman should prove to be a dangerous impostor.

She reported that the woman was stout with thick dark hair, oily skin, and a deep, sonorous voice. Before Mother's turn came she saw how this woman treated her other customers: pouring oil, shouting incantations at them, screaming at the devil within them so loudly that she intimidated everyone around. She was obviously very much in demand. The house was filled with all kinds of vegetables and fruits — cucumbers, tomatoes, eggplants, and oranges — that had been brought to this woman, who moved from one corner to another, screaming at one girl, gazing with a penetrating look at another, making her freeze in her place. Despite all this display neither my mother nor her companion were impressed.

When their turn came, the soothsayer took them in to a darkened room where she had a large dish she called the *mandal*. The dish was filled with water over which she poured a few drops of oil. When they settled down she asked my mother's companion to leave. She did not like the look in his eyes, she said. But he refused and insisted on staying with my mother.

"You are not a believer," she told him. "I don't want you here."

After making her preparations she ordered my mother, who was now squatting over the *mandal,* to remove all the gold rings in her fingers and put them behind her. My mother refused and this seemed to infuriate the fortune-teller, who could not tolerate being disobeyed. She promptly ordered my mother and her companion to leave. She was unwilling to read or interpret for them the mysterious patterns that the oil had made in the water of the *mandal* where the assassin's name would appear. My mother was glad to leave at this point. She was not prepared to lose her jewelry for the uncertain prospect of learning the secret, which it seemed was doomed to remain, as my uncle had predicted, buried with my father.

As for me, I could think of only one last thing to do now that I had almost completely given up on the police. I decided to offer a reward for any information that might lead us to the suspect. Whoever committed the murder did it for money, or used a hired hand. If money had been the motivation for the murderer, perhaps money would bring him to justice. We would offer a reward of ten thousand dollars.

But first I consulted with the head of the team. I did not want to be accused of doing anything to harm the investigation. She tried at first to discourage me. Then told me that she needed to consult her superiors and said she would get back to me. She finally phoned and told me that it was our decision — if we wanted to go ahead with this, she did not mind.

On Friday the announcement of a reward of ten thousand u.s. dollars was published in the Arabic daily newspapers and the major Israeli ones. I tried to moderate my comments, careful to criticize the police while still asserting our faith in them. On Saturday I slept

until noon and then went for lunch at my uncle's. He had news.
Someone had phoned about the reward.

"The killer," he had said, "is J. Z." He also said that he would
testify only after we arrested the man. It sounded credible to me.
We discussed the matter during a family gathering. The question
was, should we tell this to the police? We decided not to. Fuad
called Abu Jamal, the owner of one of the popular cafés in East
Jerusalem. He was a Hebronite and known for his strong connections with the underworld.

Abu Jamal said that he knew the man: "He's a drug addict and
a gambler who lives near Terra Sancta, in the Old City of
Jerusalem. His brother had been given a life sentence for the Mahne
Yehuda bombing and was released with the prisoners' exchange.
He is tall and often goes out in the streets begging. I'll come see you
now and tell you more," said Abu Jamal.

As we waited for Abu Jamal's arrival we discussed the matter
further. The description of this man made him seem like a possible
murderer. We were getting excited. But when Abu Jamal arrived it
was clear that he had had second thoughts. Now he tried to convince us that the man whose name we were given by an anonymous
caller could not have committed the crime. "He may be morally
depraved but he could not be the killer," he assured us.

Abu Jamal had arrived in a BMW with two bodyguards, thug-
gish figures from the world of the Old City underground. He had
brought his twenty-two-year-old son. Jamal wore a fitted beige suit
that made him look smart. The son closely resembled his father and
had the same dashing, bold manner, but anxiety had not yet left its
mark on the son's smooth face as it had on his father's weary one.
Whenever Abu Jamal turned to his son his face brightened. He was
obviously very proud of him. The son seemed to derive confidence
from his father and acted like he owned the world. It was a strange
group in Fuad's living room: my uncle; Fuad's ninety-year-old
Aunt Alice; my enfeebled relative Shafiq, who had once been a
famous muscle man but now had a failing heart; my sisters; my anx-

ious mother; Fuad's young children; and the dotty neighbor Almaz, who once during a snowstorm could not find her way back to her house, only a few blocks away from my uncle's house. I winced to think of how the Israeli papers referred to us as "the Shehadeh Family." What a clan!

Later we realized why Abu Jamal must have changed his mind. Why should he get involved in delivering to the police a fellow Hebronite, a Moslem, and a Mafioso like himself? Everything was calculated. It was true that he wanted to have his son get legal training at our office when he graduated from law school. For this he showed enough interest and respect to drive from Jerusalem for a visit at Fuad's home. But he was not going to help us locate this J. Z. and turn him in. He certainly did not want to be involved and the best way to do this was to persuade us that we were after the wrong man. Obviously we should not have let Abu Jamal hear about this important lead. I passed this information about J. Z. to the police, but they did not investigate.

Whenever the press asked us to assess the police we remained restrained. We gave the police the benefit of the doubt every time. But it had gone too far. I called a press conference for March 5, 1986. It was held at the Pasha Room at the American Colony Hotel in Jerusalem, where I had in the past held many other press conferences on the human rights issues of torture and deportations. The room was packed with journalists. On the podium sat my mother, my uncle, and myself. I presented the facts in a written statement that was distributed to the journalists. In it I described the failures of the police investigation. My mother read this impassioned plea:

> A man who worked for fifty years in the field of justice, goodwill, peace, and coexistence between Arabs and Jews, and who in his work as a lawyer always helped others in their own distress and unhappiness, was brutally murdered on the second of December 1985.

My late husband was a brave man. Throughout his life he always spoke his mind, however unpopular his opinions could be. He stood for justice and fought for it. He was at the forefront of those calling for the investigation of corrupt judges who have been tried and made to pay for their crimes. This and other things that my husband did must have made him many enemies. We cannot tell who bore so strong a grudge that they would commit such a brutal crime. But there are many possibilities, some having to do with his professional work, some related to his more public activities. Until each and every one of these possibilities is investigated thoroughly and completely, we remain in suspense. Not only has justice not been done, but we remain afraid, unable to live a normal life, because we do not know who killed Aziz and why. The criminal is now walking freely in the streets and may yet kill another.

I have accompanied my husband throughout his full life of toil and struggle for justice and peace. I have seen him do all that he could for individuals and for the public. I went to many lectures with him in Israel and abroad when he spoke in a way that could have cost him his life many times over. But he never wavered.

Now it is the public who can do something in return. As a wife and as a mother, I call upon the Palestinian public, the Israeli public, and the international public to make my husband's voice heard, to petition, to protest, to urge, to do all you can legally do to impress upon the police authorities my deep concern that the murderer of such a man remains free and at large. The police have proven their efficiency in other cases. The police are our only hope because we would be going against all Aziz stood for should we deal with the matter in any other way. If the police do all that they can, they will solve this crime, and then justice will be done to one who is most deserving.

The press conference was heavily reported. It made something of a stir but brought no concrete results. The public we appealed to did nothing. The police showed neither remorse nor willingness to pursue the investigation in a more serious fashion.

Then my mother and I received a summons, delivered by an Arab policeman at the Ramallah station, to go to the Bethlehem police station to meet a certain Captain Shlomi. We wondered what it could be about. New evidence that had surfaced, perhaps?

We entered an old stone building built by the British during the mandate period in the piazza of the Church of Nativity in Bethlehem. We asked where Shlomi's office was and were directed upstairs. We walked through narrow corridors, climbed the stairs, went down another corridor, and found Shlomi's office. The minute we entered Shlomi began with his tirade.

"You have spoiled this investigation," he said. "You made it not work. It is all your fault. You are to blame."

"What are you saying?" I asked. "What do you mean? What have we done?"

"What have you done? You don't know what you have done? You have spoiled it all. You are responsible for the failure of this investigation."

"You brought us all this way here to scold us?" my mother said. "We thought you had something good to tell us. We thought you were going to tell us that you had made a breakthrough. After all this time, and all what we have been through, now you claim that *we* are the reason the police could not find the murderer? You have called us to come all this way to tell us this? You have no shame."

Two months after this meeting with Shlomi, when we could

not think of what to do next, an Israeli journalist friend suggested that we hire a private investigator to work with the police. He introduced us to one, and we hired the firm. He had a partner who was a former Israeli ambassador in Latin America who had also known my father. They seemed enthusiastic and hopeful. They asked for a large amount of money, which we paid. Then we went through everything all over again. Repeating all the statements we gave to the police, responding to the same questions we had been asked innumerable times, only to be told that the police were refusing to cooperate.

Then at the end of a whole year, they presented us with a small index card on which was typed in Hebrew the name of the presumed murderer whom they said was living in Jordan. But they refused to give us any evidence to support their conclusion. When we spoke to the authorities in Jordan, they asked for evidence. We had none. The index card was just another sort of *mandal*, an Israeli one this time, and just as indecipherable as the first had been.

CHAPTER TWENTY-THREE

Two years later at a reception attended by a number of lawyers my suspicion that the police were protecting the murderer was strengthened. A man turned to me and said: "Congratulations." He was a lawyer from Hebron with big black shiny eyes, a strong mouth with thin expressive lips, and a manner of speaking and moving that made him seem engaged in some urgent secret mission.

"What for?" I asked.

"For the discovery of your father's murderer."

I grew very excited and breathlessly asked: "What do you mean?"

"They have found him. Didn't you hear? They know who did it. Didn't they tell you?"

"No one told me anything. Who did you hear this news from?"

"From a policeman in Hebron who heard the confession."

"Whose confession?" I asked excitedly.

"Then you don't know."

"I know nothing. Tell me quickly everything you know."

The lawyer proceeded to tell me about the murder of an old merchant in Hebron and the arrest of two brothers in connection with this murder. I recognized the names of the brothers. They were the defendants in the land case my father was handling in Hebron at the time of his death.

"And they confessed?" I asked.

"Yes, they confessed to the murder of your father, the lawyer Aziz Shehadeh. This policeman heard the confession with his own ears and he reported it to me."

"Can you take me to see him?"

"Of course."

After two years, we had reached the end of a painful and ago-

nizing ordeal, and I heard about it by accident from a stranger. I
wasted no time and the next day met the lawyer in the center of
Hebron. Together we drove to the headquarters of the Israeli military administration on a hill at the outskirts of the town. It was
another of the British-built Tegart Buildings that dot the Palestinian
countryside. They all have the same dull, bulky gray look with small
slits for windows like the windows of large ships. They also have
panoptical watchtowers that give the sense that eyes are watching
the movement of everyone entering these formidable structures.

We were conscious of being watched as we walked through to
the small angular door, which was most unceremonious for such an
imposing fortress, and went into the dim interior. We went through
long corridors with low ceilings and smooth cement floors and
climbed stairs also made from smooth round stone and walked
through more corridors and climbed more stairs. Then, when we
got to the second floor in the depths of this forbidding labyrinth, we
took more stairs down and walked through a long hall to the police
officer whom my lawyer friend had been advised to see.
Fortunately my friend knew his way around; otherwise it would
have been difficult to navigate. I felt satisfied and relieved when we
knocked on this officer's door, as though I was going to receive a
certificate or a big present that I had been expecting for a long time.
I walked in with a broad smile on my face ready for my gift. We
found a stern Israeli policeman busy with his papers. When the
lawyer introduced me the Israeli officer showed no sign of recognition. My friend told him that I was the son of the lawyer who had
been murdered in Ramallah in 1985 and left me to speak.

"I got the good news that the man you arrested ten days ago has
confessed to my father's murder," I said.

"How did you hear this? Who told you?"

I did not think it was prudent to reveal my source in case the
policeman who had passed the news was not supposed to repeat it
outside this building.

"I heard. Is it not true?"

"Of course it is not true."

"You mean he did not confess?"

"Of course not. I don't know what you are talking about."

"But I heard this from a very good source."

"There are no sources. I am the only person who would know. I'm responsible for the investigation. And I am telling you, there was no such confession."

"Where is the prisoner now?"

"At Thahrieh prison."

"But that's a military prison!" I said.

I felt as though cold water had been suddenly thrown at me. I stuttered: "If you hear anything, will you let me know?"

He was surprised, as if what I was suggesting was presumptuous, an affront. His eyes were fiery. I had heard enough and decided to leave. I turned and walked out into the long corridor with the offices on one side and empty walls on the other, through more dim corridors, and out again through the small door back to the watchful gaze of the guard in the panoptical watchtower.

Now I understood. Only those suspected of offenses against Israeli security and those whom the security apparatus was interested in protecting from trials before Palestinian judges are put in military prisons such as the one in Thahrieh. Our suspect did not fall under the first category. He must then have been of the sort worthy of Israeli protection for services rendered.

This was why when the Intifada began on December 9, 1987, I was ready to embrace the promise it offered of ending the occupation. But at the same time, I could not escape the conclusion that this meant ending the hope that had gotten me through the three years since the murder. The pursuit of individual justice for my father had to be abandoned, and in its place was the hope for a more collective pursuit of justice.

But this switch could not occur without doubt. I could almost hear my father's voice taking issue with my choice. With great dismay he would admonish me: *So you have given up on justice for*

me. You are putting your faith in the public. You are deluding yourself
into believing that something good could come out of this public revolt.
After all I have been through and suffered at the hands of the public, you
put your hope in them to bail me out.

I did not want to hear such traditional misgivings about an
uprising in which I put my faith and hopes for the future. I was sure
that if we all believed in what we were doing, we would win. We
would be able to bring criminals to justice, not selectively but
according to the strict principles of the rule of law. I knew what my
father's opinion of such hope would be, but I refused to allow him
to shake my faith in this popular struggle.

The Intifada was the general rebellion of the sons against their
fathers. Despite the restrictions and hardships imposed on us by the
Israeli military government in the wake of our popular revolt, this
was my time. I embraced the collective struggle and did everything
I could to bring an end to the Israeli occupation and to cause justice
to be meted out not only for my father but also for thousands of
other bereaved and suffering Palestinians. My involvement with
the Intifada was the culmination of a life that had been dominated
by politics. However hard I had tried to steer away from politics, I
was always called back. My pursuit of the investigation in my
father's murder had been an individual one. Despite the prevailing
attitude, I had put my faith in the Israeli police. But this hope was
unfounded. My experience affirmed what was common knowledge: that the Israeli police were there only to serve the occupation.
Whatever crimes the Palestinian agents working for Israel might be
guilty of, they could not be touched. Whatever peaceful politics my
father had pursued, a collaborator was more important to Israel,
and his protection was perceived to be more in the country's interest
than prosecuting a murder.

There was no clearer message than this that individual justice
for a Palestinian was not attainable. The only course left for me was
the collective struggle. I now embraced this collective struggle with
all the energy and commitment that I could muster.

As my involvement with the Intifada deepened I often thought about how my father would have reacted had he lived to see the solidarity now in evidence and the shifting of power from the PLO outside to the United Leadership inside the occupied territories. I believe he would have been supportive.

With the Intifada, my generation found its own way to struggle and to deal with the past. The Intifada liberated me. Until then, I had never believed that I had the right to question the legacy of my father. It also confirmed that the way out for me was not by silencing the ghosts of the past, or by denying my commitment to the struggle. It was futile to deny that for me too politics are fundamental. How could it have been otherwise when everything and everyone in the house where I was born reminded me of my family's past in a city I had never visited, and a way of life that I had never experienced? But now it appeared that the sparkle of false illusion that the Jaffa that loomed on the horizon had offered was to be replaced by a realistic glimmer of a new hope that held the promise of fulfilling Palestinian aspirations.

In October 1991 the Middle East Peace Conference between Israel and the Arabs opened in Madrid. I soon joined the Palestinian negotiating team as legal adviser. Finally I would be able to put the legal case I had worked so long to develop into the hands of the Palestinian forces who were carrying out the negotiations with Israel. My human rights world and the political world had finally dovetailed.

CONCLUSION

THE TRAVELER TO the ancient Nabatean city of Petra, located deep in Wadi Mousa in Jordan, must traverse a mile-long gorge. Two-thirds of the way along, a solid rectangular rock stands with a slightly sloping top beside a surviving stretch of the original Nabatean pavement. It looks as though it has popped out of the ground. A door is carved into the side of this rose-red rock adorned on each side by pilasters topped by capitals, cornices, and a frieze. Whoever carved it did a good job. You are led to believe the door on this massive rock can open and will lead somewhere. But of course it doesn't. Like most of the other monuments in Petra, it is merely a facade.

This image continued to haunt me as I observed the Israeli–Palestinian negotiations from a distance, having left in despair a year after they began. I felt that the Israeli negotiators were trying to recast the occupation into different shapes, providing the Palestinians with mere symbols of liberation. Nor did I change my mind when the first of the Oslo agreements, the Declaration of Principles, was signed on the White House lawn on September 13, 1993. The international fanfare that characterized the signing, and the confidence all sides expressed that a new era of peace and security had been inaugurated, did not change my mind. I could see that the agreement had failed to address the core issues, including the proliferation of Israeli settlements on Palestinian land.

And yet the Oslo agreements did bring about changes on the ground. On December 27, 1995, the Israeli army redeployed and evacuated Ramallah, handing it over to the full control of the Palestinian Authority.

The day of the evacuation, the town was in a carnival mood. Thousands of strollers were in the streets, the long-forbidden Palestinian flag was hoisted everywhere, banners praising the PLO and its leader Yasir Arafat fluttered over the crowded streets, peddlers sold sweets, checkered kaffiyehs and flags of all sizes were everywhere. Untypically, I bought a plastic flag and stuck it in my breast pocket. Shops and coffeehouses, which for the past seven years of the Intifada could open only for a few hours a day, were full to capacity. We all wanted to make up for lost time. Everyone was in a jubilant mood. I stopped the car and walked around to all the forbidden areas: the police station, the prison, the Civil Administration offices, and the army observation posts. The feeling of liberation was intoxicating. To be able to walk anywhere in town without being stopped by Israeli soldiers, always wondering if you would be interrogated, humiliated, beaten, arrested, or made to stand with your legs apart and your hands on the wall. To go in and out of shops without being observed by armed soldiers on top of the taller buildings with guns pointed and ready to shoot. After years of being under the control of the occupier, our town was finally being returned to us.

The carnival mood continued all afternoon. In the evening as I was walking home, I saw in the distant hills to the west, just below the line of the glimmering lights of the coast, a single red light. I wondered what it could be. A new house built on the vacant hills? But it was too remote an area. Was it then some bonfire built by a picnicker having a solo celebration of the liberation of Ramallah? But it was sharper and more focused than the light of a blazing fire. Then I noticed that the light was moving. The red light was the rear light of a car that was driving through our hills. I followed the path of this vehicle as it limned the northwestern circumference of our liberated zone. The carnival stopped for me then and there. I realized that this was a new bypass road being built to serve the settlers of Dolev and Beit El to the northwest of Ramallah and connect them through an alternative route to Jerusalem. This then was the border of what the Oslo agreement called Area A, the self-rule area. The hills where I went for walks and enjoyed the seasonal changes to the land would now be unsafe, with armed settlers and soldiers traveling the new road.

A few weeks later I accompanied one of my clients to see the new Palestinian governor of Ramallah, now housed in the same Tegart building from which the Israeli military had ruled for the past thirty years. It was a bitterly cold and windy morning.

The Tegart is the only cement structure in town. All other buildings are of limestone. It sits on the highest hill with antennae shooting to the sky. It never was, nor will be a mere structure of cement and steel to me. As I walked down the driveway, now without its Israeli guards, and entered the small rectangular door into this oversized fortress unchaperoned, I could still feel the eyes of the former inhabitants peering at me from every corner.

I remembered Estee in the busy office by the courtroom, a hard-working young Israeli woman with delicate features, frizzy hair, and a high-pitched voice, doing her army duty as secretary to the military court. And Eju, a tall and wiry young soldier with nervous energy who always helped me schedule court hearings at convenient times. But our relationship could not advance beyond civility and common decency. They were helping operate a military system of justice in offices only a few meters from the torture chamber where Khalid suffered at the hands of Barzali.

As I walked with my client up the stone stairs, I could still feel the haunting presence of Israeli soldiers following me with their gaze, not leaving me alone. When we reached the top we looked down the empty corridor trying to decide which way to go. I knew we could, if we chose, roam around and explore the vast and intricate secrets of this labyrinthine fortress, but my heart pounded even at the thought.

This place felt different now. The efficient self-assured Israeli men and women soldiers with their mixture of egalitarian and arrogant manners had been replaced by a motley crowd of variously clad Palestinian men, some in blue fatigues, others in khaki, and most in plain civilian clothes, all brandishing pistols or demonstratively holding machine guns. There was an unsettling aura of informality about the place, with its large armed crowds exhibiting the pride of young undisciplined possessors who have all too suddenly come into power.

As I searched for the governor's office, I looked through the small rooms that had served as detention centers and found them crowded with mattresses flung on the floor. Palestinian police now slept here eight to a room. In some of the rooms young men in t-shirts were reclining, and the air was thick with the blue haze of cheap cigarettes.

On the second floor the governor had decorated his office with expensive furniture and artificial blue and red tulips. Civilians with machine guns ushered us into his spacious room.

As I waited for my turn to put my client's case to our new governor, I watched the throngs of people approaching him for favors. I was skeptical about the future of the rule of law under the Palestinian Authority. The PLO had struck a political bargain with the Israeli government: In return for recognition and permission to return to the occupied territories, the Palestinians would police the local population and refrain from insisting that Israel cease its settlement activities. The legal strategy I presented during the negotiations in Washington had been superseded by political expediency and survival.

Now, seven years after the first Oslo agreement was signed, the number of Jewish settlers in the West Bank has almost doubled, to around 380,000 settlers living in more than two hundred settlements. Their new houses are built on our devastated and flattened hills. They drive on straight wide roads that burrow through hills that have been cut in half. The scramble for land is ruining this afflicted landscape.

From the roof of my house I can still see the Mediterranean coast. On clear evenings I go up and look, as my father used to in

the 1950s, at the view that is not a facade: the growing lights now
extend along the entire horizon and below, a dazzling display of
small waltzing spots of light glittering with life. While Israel pros-
pers, our towns and villages continue to be squeezed by ever-
expanding Israeli settlements planned to further disrupt the
territorial contiguity of our land. The prospects of a negotiated final
settlement appear more distant than ever.

I walk in the streets of Ramallah on a bright winter morning during
the second Palestinian Intifada. Last night a middle-aged woman
was killed by bullets shot from the nearby settlement of Psagot
perched on the eastern hill overlooking the town. She was shopping
for the Moslem feast of Al Adha. As I walk past the spot where the
woman fell, I am stopped by the barber. He leaves a client waiting
and comes out carrying his familiar scissors and mother-of-pearl
comb. He digs the comb in his thick unruly hair as we stand
together on the sidewalk. His black eyes are buried in his puffy
cheeks. He looks beyond me in the direction of the settlement as he
invokes in his own mind the memory of my father who was his
client from the days when they both lived and worked in Jaffa.

"Every day I think of your father. He is constantly on my mind.
I remember so clearly when he used to sit right there on this chair
and as I cut his hair he would tell me how the time was slipping: 'If
we don't make peace now with Israel, it will be too late. There will
be more and more settlements. Now is our chance.' I swear to God
these were the words he spoke to me twenty-five years ago. The
man had vision. He saw much farther than all of us. He had a head
on his shoulders. But no one listened to him. No one. What's the
use? Where would we be now if only we had listened?"

He searches for the comb anchored in his bushy hair, pulls it up
with his nimble fingers, and without saying another word hobbles
back to his shop.

Sometimes when I shave before the mirror in the morning, I
see my father standing by the sink next to the kitchen in the cold

damp house downstairs from my grandmother's where we lived when I was a child. He is shaving. I bring him my school report card and tell him I was the first in class. He does not turn. Still concentrating on the mirror, he glances at me with a sideways look. He says nothing, but his smiling eyes fill me with joy. I watch as he brings his head closer to the mirror and purses his lips. I can hear the blade scratch against his thick hair. He shaves carefully around his mustache.

I briefly stare at my face in the mirror and finish shaving in preparation for a new day.

Ramallah
February 9, 2001

AFTERWORD

A PALESTINIAN SON'S SEARCH FOR JUSTICE

It was the summer of 1994 when I received a call from the Director of the Ramallah Hospital. "A man believed to be your father's murderer has just been admitted. He was brought here from Hebron with severe gunshot wounds to his stomach. Do you want to come and see him?"

Six years had already passed since the policeman at the Hebron military headquarters had denied that this same man had confessed to my father's murder.

The patient had sustained his injuries in a drive-by shooting near his home in Hebron. The Hebron Hospital would not accept him; he was known to be a murderer and a collaborator. So he was sent to Ramallah where he was accepted.

In the ensuing days, I mulled over whether to go to the hospital to see the man I had been searching for over the past eight years. I followed reports of his condition. I learned that he was in a bad state, that he smelled abominably and then that his leg was amputated. I was told that he had a visitor whose identity was not known and that he lay in his bed all day and moaned. Then his brother came to visit him. He was described as gloomy and fierce, "like a wild animal." He brought a watermelon with him. It was prohibited to bring food into the rooms but who was to stop him. The two brothers stabbed open the red melon and proceeded to eat it with their fingers, sucking the juice which dripped everywhere. It wasn't long before the other patients in the room asked to be moved out. Permission was granted. Everyone at the hospital could understand their need to keep away. A few days later the patient's situation deteriorated and his moaning grew louder. He died. I did not visit.

That was the week of my forty-third birthday. My father appeared to me in a dream. Together we were organizing some shelves in the house. He came over to me and hugged me, his head on my shoulder and chest. It was warm and loving and we were very close and happy. I felt then that perhaps after his murderer had died father's spirit became peaceful. Perhaps it was more likely that I could finally welcome my father with open arms, now that I was relieved of the burden and guilt of the search for his murderer. This was the first dream that I'd had for a long time when my father appeared accepting, loving and peaceful.

It took another twelve years before confirmation finally came that this collaborator who died at the Ramallah hospital was indeed the murderer of my father. It came via a friend, a British historian, who had heard it from a former Israeli cabinet minister who had access to the secret files of the security service. Now that I had confirmation of what I had long suspected, the painful memories of my father's murder investigation — the two most difficult years of my life — began to return. Not only had those conducting the sham investigation in whom I put my trust known the identity of the murderer all along, they also exploited my vulnerable state and misguided me.

The criminal investigators had claimed that the murderer came from a Christian family living in Ramallah whose shop was next to our law office. They proceeded to put the accused behind bars and then, without indicating that he was innocent of the murder, released him leaving me to understand that he was their prime suspect but that they lacked evidence to indict him. They must have hoped that I would take the law in my own hands. In this way they would be able to show the world how primitive were the ways of Palestinians including those like myself who claimed a commitment to the rule of law. Like every colonizer throughout history Israel has always sought to pit Palestinians against each other and drive them to desperate action.

Those were the most difficult years of my life. It was writing that saved me from debilitating despair. Seven years later, when the signing of the Oslo Accords dashed the hopes I had placed in the Israeli-Palestinian negotiations, I experienced another crippling bout of despair. I could have suffered a spiritual death similar to that which father endured in the early eighties when he already felt that the situation was getting desperate and the chances of peace were diminishing. Had he the talent and inclination to write his life might have taken a different turn. Instead he warned me that it was only power that counted. He was unwilling to accept that writing was also an exercise of power, capable of moving people, changing perception and mobilizing forces in new directions. It was the writing of *Strangers in the House* that saved me.

Now that the truth has been revealed, the questions I asked then have returned with greater urgency: what was it that this murderer had offered the Israeli state that he could count on murdering a man like my father with impunity? Was he instrumental in land deals that they needed for their Jewish settlements? Was it the recruitment of other collaborators? Or was he just a petty henchman doing the dirty work of terrorizing for hire? I knew that every colonial regime works through recruitment of collaborators from the colonized population. Yet what hurt me most was the thought that as I made my rounds through the strata of Israeli bureaucracy and society appealing to the various officials and friends of my father, whether the Minister of Police, the Head of the Investigation or the Justices of the High Court or other well connected friends of my father who duly came to pay their condolences, they all must have known that the murderer could not be brought to justice because he enjoyed a special status in Israel for the services he rendered to the Jewish state.

It appears that in Israel it is the Security Service more than any other agency that controls the state. It determines what is crucial for Israel's survival and security. Between justice for a man who sought peace and a despicable collaborator, the security services — and the state behind them — chose the later. The hegemony of "security" and its monopoly over policy has not declined over time. If anything it has gained in strength and dominance. In this sense the case of the investigation of my father's murder continues to be representative of the larger picture of the relations between the two societies. Tens of thousands of Arab civilians inside Palestine and Lebanon, Israel's northern neighbor, have been indiscriminately murdered in incursions and wars by the powerful Israeli air, sea and ground forces in the misguided belief that this was necessary to secure the Jewish state. The preference for collaborators over those seeking peace follows the same logic.

With the opening of the Israeli records of the 1967 war, historians were able to read the files kept on the meetings held with my father and the other Palestinians from the West Bank who approached the Israeli government with a peace plan for ending the conflict soon after the war ended. The Israeli historian, Tom Segev,* describing these Palestinians as "collaborators," writes: "The Israelis' notes reveal an ambivalent value system in their attitude towards the collaborators: they needed them, they encouraged them and they scorned them."

Over the years, Israel's preference for dealing with collaborators rather than patriots amongst the Palestinians has not changed as the investigation into my father's murder so painfully revealed to me. As I was to learn from my personal experience of the negotiations that followed the Madrid International Peace Conference in 1991, the same attitude continued to prevail. Twenty-four-years after my father had submitted his proposals for peace, Israel still shunned those Palestinians seeking to negotiate a genuine peace

---

*Segev, Tom, *1967, Israel, the War, and the Year That Transformed the Middle East*, Metropolitan Books, Henry Holt and Company, New York 2007, p. 515

treaty. Instead they sought collaborators with whom they could sign a surrender document. Rather than counting on peace as the best guarantee for its security, Israel continues to count exclusively on its military might refusing to recognize its Palestinian foe as a national group entitled, like all national groups, to self determination.

Last summer I was approached by a producer from a local Palestinian television station who was preparing a documentary film about my work. In the course of the preparation the researcher sent to interview me asked whether I wanted to discuss my father's murder. It was then that I realized that if I were to do so I would have to refer to my father as a *shaheed* [martyr] otherwise it would sound odd to local Palestinian viewers who would only use the verb 'murder' to describe the killing of a collaborator. But I could not do so. In my eyes the crime perpetrated against my father could not be ameliorated by referring to him as a *shaheed*.

My father was murdered in cold blood by a despicable collaborator working for the Israeli state. This was why the Israeli investigators covered up for his heinous crime and never brought him to justice. My search for secular justice, whether for my father or more broadly my people, would not be compromised by elevating the consequence of its absence with references to godly matters. I was brought up to leave matters of religion and the affairs of the afterlife to other authorities.

This experience made me realize how distant my sense of justice has moved from many in my own society and what a new reality Israel has helped create. It now has to contend with this amongst the new generation of Palestinian Arabs and Muslims in the countries surrounding it. It saddened me that I did not even consider using the opportunity of the local television program to argue for my belief in secular justice. But then how could I hope to present a strong and convincing case? My own long and painful ordeal in the course of the sham investigation into my father's murder offered only a testimony of the absence of such justice.

But it goes beyond the individual case of my father. In the twenty-first century the case of Palestine remains one of the last surviving examples of a country usurped by a colonial project exploiting religion to deprive Palestinians of their land. I am convinced that only when these weird contortions of history, religion and international law are challenged will Arabs and Jews come to accept each other, as my father and I were able to do. No strangers will then remain in our house.

Ramallah
May 2009